Introduction to Driverless Self-Driving Cars

The Best of the AI Insider

Dr. Lance B. Eliot, MBA, PhD

Disclaimer: This book is presented solely for educational and entertainment purposes. The author and publisher are not offering it as legal, accounting, or other professional services advice. The author and publisher make no representations or warranties of any kind and assume no liabilities of any kind with respect to the accuracy or completeness of the contents and specifically disclaim any implied warranties of merchantability or fitness of use for a particular purpose. Neither the author nor the publisher shall be held liable or responsible to any person or entity with respect to any loss or incidental or consequential damages caused, or alleged to have been caused, directly or indirectly, by the information or programs contained herein. Every company is different and the advice and strategies contained herein may not be suitable for your situation.

DEDICATION

To my incredible son, Michael and my incredible daughter, Lauren.

Forest fortuna adiuvat (from the Latin; good fortune favors the brave).

CONTENTS

Dr. Lance B. Eliot

ACKNOWLEDGMENTS

I have been the beneficiary of advice and counsel by many friends, colleagues, family, investors, and many others. I want to thank everyone that has aided me throughout my career. I write from the heart and the head, having experienced first-hand what it means to have others around you that support you during the good times and the tough times.

To Warren Bennis, one of my doctoral advisors and ultimately a colleague, I offer my deepest thanks and appreciation, especially for his calm and insightful wisdom and support.

To Mark Stevens and his generous efforts toward funding and supporting the USC Stevens Center for Innovation.

To Lloyd Greif and the USC Lloyd Greif Center for Entrepreneurial Studies for their ongoing encouragement of founders and entrepreneurs.

To Peter Drucker, William Wang, Aaron Levie, Peter Kim, Jon Kraft, Cindy Crawford, Jenny Ming, Steve Milligan, Chis Underwood, Frank Gehry, Buzz Aldrin, Steve Forbes, Bill Thompson, Dave Dillon, Alan Fuerstman, Larry Ellison, Jim Sinegal, John Sperling, Mark Stevenson, Anand Nallathambi, Thomas Barrack, Jr., and many other innovators and leaders that I have met and gained mightily from doing so.

Thanks to Ed Trainor, Kevin Anderson, James Hickey, Wendell Jones, Ken Harris, DuWayne Peterson, Mike Brown, Jim Thornton, Abhi Beniwal, Al Biland, John Nomura, Eliot Weinman, John Desmond, and many others for their unwavering support during my career.

And most of all thanks as always to Lauren and Michael, for their ongoing support and for having seen me writing and heard much of this material during the many months involved in writing it. To their patience and willingness to listen.

Dr. Lance B. Eliot

INTRODUCTION

This is a book that provides a readable introduction to the foundational aspects of driverless self-driving cars.

Advances in being able to someday achieve true self-driving cars have been fostered by innovations in Artificial Intelligence (AI) and Machine Learning (ML). We are nearing the day when vehicles can control themselves and will not require and nor rely upon human intervention to perform their driving tasks (or, that <u>allow</u> for human intervention, but only *require* human intervention in very limited ways).

There are important technological aspects that serve as the cornerstone for self-driving cars. I cover many of these crucial technological elements, and point out both their strengths and weaknesses. It is vital that we all have our eyes wide open about what technology can and cannot do. Other books and many of the pundits about self-driving cars seem to either ignore, underplay, or want to pretend they aren't concerned about the drawbacks associated with the technologies we are going to be having at the core of life-and-death actions involving driving cars on our roadways. I want you to know it all, the good, the bad, and the ugly.

We must all be cognizant of what self-driving cars mean to our society, our economy, our way of living, etc. Thus, this book covers not just the technology, but also delves into the socioeconomics of self-driving cars, and blends together discussions of high-tech, business, economics, social, and political dynamics and other factors underlying where we are going with these autonomous vehicles. As a versed technologist, I am eager to see what we can produce in terms of AI and having cars that can drive in whatever manner a human could drive a car. At the same time, as a *responsible* technologist, I believe it is imperative that the future of these marvelous machines be properly formed by considerations beyond mere technology.

1

I've written several books on the topic of self-driving cars. These books are a compendium of thought pieces that I've crafted and posted in various channels. For many years, I've been known as the *AI Insider* for my insights on where AI is headed. Based on these writings, and upon feedback from my readers and listeners to my podcasts, I have selected the pieces herein that seemed to garner the most interest and that have received accolades for especially being informative and engaging about self-driving cars.

If you become intrigued by the topic of self-driving cars (which I hope that you do!), I urge you to consider delving further into the topic beyond the material that I've presented in this book. As such, you might be interested in my companion books that I have written that cover additional key innovations and fundamentals about self-driving cars. Those books are entitled **Advances in AI and Autonomous Vehicles: Cybernetic Self-Driving Cars**, **Self-Driving Cars: The Mother of All AI Projects**, **Innovation and Thought Leadership on Self-Driving Driverless Cars**, **New Advances in AI Autonomous Driverless Self-Driving Cars**, and **Autonomous Vehicle Driverless Self-Driving Cars and Artificial Intelligence** (they are all available via Amazon and via other major booksellers). See Appendix A of this herein book to see a listing of the chapters covered in those books.

WHAT THIS BOOK PROVIDES

What does this book provide to you? It introduces many of the key elements about self-driving cars and does so with an AI based perspective. I weave together technical and non-technical aspects, readily going from being concerned about the cognitive capabilities of the driving task and how the technology is embodying this into self-driving cars, and in the next breath I discuss the societal and economic aspects.

They are all intertwined because that's the way reality is. You cannot separate out the technology per se, and instead must consider it within the milieu of what is being invented and innovated, and do so with a mindset towards the contemporary mores and culture that shape what we are doing and what we hope to do.

Each of the chapters addresses a key aspect about self-driving cars. For those of you that might have already seen some of these chapters in my other books, I've updated the material and/or modified some of it since it first appeared. Nonetheless, the same overall points are raised and my stand on the topics still follows what I had earlier stated.

I often get asked questions about self-driving cars during my various presentations at conferences and university speaking engagements, and those questions are typically the focus for my written pieces. I will provide next the key question that I am addressing in each chapter, along with a succinct answer, so that you'll have a contextual sense of what the chapter indicates.

Chapter 1: Self-Driving Car Moonshot: Mother of All AI Projects

Q: Is the development of a true self-driving car going to be easy to achieve or is it going to be hard to achieve?

A: It is going to be really hard to create a true self-driving car. This might seem surprising since everyday we are being bombarded in the media about how imminent self-driving cars are. Don't be fooled. This is a moonshot. As the CEO of Apple has famously said, it is the mother of all AI projects.

Chapter 2: Grand Convergence Leads to Self-Driving Cars

Q: What had led to self-driving cars suddenly seemingly becoming possible and generating so much media attention?

A: There is a grand convergence of several technologies and innovations that have brought about the possibility of self-driving cars. The topic is stoked by the incremental advances that are now found in modern day cars and by the various roadway experiments that the auto makers and tech companies have been undertaking.

Chapter 3 Why They Should Be Called Self-Driving Cars

Q: Are they called driveless cars, or self-driving cars, or autonomous cars, or robot cars, or what is the best way to refer to these new cars?

A: I argue that saying "self-driving cars" is the simplest, fairest, and most reasonable moniker. That's what I tend to call them.

Chapter 4: Richter Scale for Self-Driving Car Levels

Q: *Are all self-driving cars the same in terms of what they can do?*

A: There are several levels of self-driving cars. The highest level is known as Level 5 and would be what we all might really consider a true self-driving car. I explain the various levels.

Chapter 5: LIDAR for Self-Driving Cars

Q: *Is there any particular hardware technology that has prompted the ability to develop self-driving cars?*

A: Yes, I assert that LIDAR is an essential hardware technology for self-driving cars and that continued advances in LIDAR will further make progress toward self-driving cars. That being said, there is some debate on this point and I provide the counter-arguments about why LIDAR is perhaps not so crucial.

Chapter 6: Overall Framework for Self-Driving Cars

Q: *What's the big picture for all of the elements needed for self-driving cars?*

A: I provide a framework that provides a handy overview of the elements underlying self-driving cars.

Chapter 7: Sensor Fusion is Key for Self-Driving Cars

Q: *There are a bunch of sensors on self-driving cars, and so how does all that sensory data get put together?*

A: One of the key capabilities of a self-driving car is sensor fusion, which stitches together the sensory data to provide a real-time indication of what the driving status of the self-driving car is.

Chapter 8: Humans Not Fast Enough for Self-Driving Cars

Q: *When a self-driving car has problems, will a human be able to take over the driving?*

A: Many of the self-driving car makers are pretending that humans can take over when needed from a self-driving car, but the ability for humans to be quick enough to respond (and be given sufficient warning) is a concern and we are heading for trouble.

Chapter 9: Solving Edge Problems of Self-Driving Cars

Q: *It seems like all of the problems with being able to achieve a self-driving car are already all solved, so what's left to do?*

A: Only the more obvious and straightforward aspects are being solved today – there's a large set of so-called crucial "edge" problems that have yet to be solved.

Chapter 10: Graceful Degradation for Faltering Self-Driving Cars

Q: *What happens when a self-driving car falters?*

A: We need to have graceful system degradation when a self-driving car falters. The approaches being used today are limited and questionable, and need to be improved.

Chapter 11: Genetic Algorithms for Self-Driving Cars

Q: *I've heard there is something called "genetic algorithms" and it will help with self-driving cars, what is it?*

A: I explain what genetic algorithms do and how they will be aiding the further advancement of self-driving cars.

Chapter 12: Blockchain for Self-Driving Cars

Q: *Does bitcoin and blockchain have anything to do with self-driving cars?*

A: Yes, especially blockchain, which is the underpinning for bitcoins. I explain what blockchain and bitcoin will do for self-driving cars.

Chapter 13: Machine Learning and Data for Self-Driving Cars

Q: *What is Machine Learning and how does it help self-driving cars?*

A: I explain what Machine Learning is, and also how the data about self-driving cars is vital for further advances in self-driving cars.

Chapter 14: Cyber-Hacking of Self-Driving Cars

Q: *Should we be worried about the cyber security of self-driving cars.*

A: We all need to be concerned about the cyber security of self-driving cars. I provide ways in which cyber-hackers will attack self-driving cars and what needs to be done about it.

Chapter 15: Sensor Failures in Self-Driving Cars

Q: *Will the sensors on self-driving cars always work correctly?*

A: Sensors on self-driving cars will break and fail just like any other piece of hardware. I describe how this can happen and what self-driving cars need to be ready to do.

Chapter 16: When Accidents Happen to Self-Driving Cars

Q: *Will self-driving cars ever get into accidents?*

A: Yes, self-driving cars will definitely get into accidents. I explain how this will happen and what we need to be prepared for.

Chapter 17: Backdoor Security Holes in Self-Driving Cars

Q: *Could someone sneak a backdoor security hole into a self-driving car?*

A: Yes, it is possible for someone to put a backdoor security hole into a self-driving car. I explain how this can happen and what needs to be done about it.

Chapter 18: Future Brainjacking for Self-Driving Cars

Q: *Can we potentially communicate with our self-driving car via telepathy?*

A: Though not telepathy, there are advances in the Brain Machine Interface (BMI) that some call brainjacking, and we might someday use this to communicate with self-driving cars.

Chapter 19: Internationalizing Self-Driving Cars

Q: *Will a self-driving car that is made in the USA be able to drive in another country?*

A: Self-driving cars will need to be programmed to be able to work properly in whatever country they are driving in.

Chapter 20: Are Airline Autopilots Same as Self-Driving Cars

Q: *If airplanes already have autopilots, why can't we just make a self-driving car that uses an autopilot capability?*

A: There are misnomers about what an airplane autopilot actually does. So, I clear that up, and explain that we are not going to see much carryover from existing autopilot capabilities into self-driving car capabilities.

Chapter 21: Marketing of Self-Driving Cars

Q: *Will the way in which cars are marketed today be the same once we have self-driving cars?*

A: We'll see changes in how cars are marketed once we have true self-driving cars. I explain what those changes will be.

Chapter 22: Fake News about Self-Driving Cars

Q: *Is what I read in the media true about what self-driving cars are and can do?*

A: Sadly, much of the media is reporting "fake news" about self-driving cars. I explain what that means and how to detect it.

Chapter 23: Product Liability for Self-Driving Cars

Q: *If a self-driving car goes crazy, who is liable?*

A: This will be new ground for the auto makers and tech companies, and I cover some of the potential product liability exposures they will have with their self-driving cars on the market.

Chapter 24: Zero Fatalities Zero Chance for Self-Driving Cars

Q: *I keep reading about "zero fatalities" once we have self-driving cars, is this true?*

A: We won't have zero fatalities with self-driving cars. It's a myth. I explain why. Let's all aim for zero, but realize it doesn't make much sense.

Chapter 25: Road Trip Trickery for Self-Driving Cars

Q: *I have seen videos touting self-driving cars and the short clips seem to show that they are able to drive just like humans, is this true?*

A: Much of the self-driving car videos are tricked-up to make you assume that the self-driving car can drive like humans. I explain what the tricks are and how to be wary.

Chapter 26: Ethical Issues of Self-Driving Cars

Q: *How will a self-driving car be able to make tough life-or-death driving related decisions?*

A: The advent of a self-driving car opens up a can-of-worms of ethical issues and we need to figure out what we want our self-driving cars to be able to decide upon.

Chapter 27: Ranking of Self-Driving Cars

Q: *Who is making self-driving cars and how do they compare?*

A: I provide a popular ranking of self-driving cars and their makers, and critique which ones are doing it right and which ones are maybe a bit afield.

Chapter 28: Induced Demand Driven by Self-Driving Cars

Q: *Once we have self-driving cars, will we be free of any traffic congestion?*

A: There will be "induced demand" that accompanies the advent of true self-driving cars, which means that we might not see the oft promised dream of no traffic congestion due to self-driving cars.

WHY THIS BOOK

I wrote this book to try and bring to the public view many aspects about self-driving cars that nobody seems to be discussing.

For business leaders that are either involved in making self-driving cars or that are going to leverage self-driving cars, I hope that this book will enlighten you as to the risks involved and ways in which you should be strategizing about how to deal with those risks.

For entrepreneurs, startups and other businesses that want to enter into the self-driving car market that is emerging, I hope this book sparks your interest in doing so, and provides some sense of what might be prudent to pursue.

For researchers that study self-driving cars, I hope this book spurs your interest in the risks and safety issues of self-driving cars, and also nudges you toward conducting research on those aspects.

For students in computer science or related disciplines, I hope this book will provide you with interesting and new ideas and material, for which you might conduct research or provide some career direction insights for you.

For AI companies and high-tech companies pursuing self-driving cars, this book will hopefully broaden your view beyond just the mere coding and development needed to make self-driving cars.

For all readers, I hope that you will find the material in this book to be stimulating. Some of it will be repetitive of things you already know. But I am pretty sure that you'll also find various eureka moments whereby you'll discover a new technique or approach that you had not earlier thought of. I am also betting that there will be material that forces you to rethink some of your current practices.

I am not saying you will suddenly have an epiphany and change what you are doing. I do think though that you will reconsider or perhaps revisit what you are doing.

For anyone choosing to use this book for teaching purposes, please take a look at my suggestions for doing so, as described in the Appendix. I have found the material handy in courses that I have taught, and likewise other faculty have told me that they have found the material handy, in some cases as extended readings and in other instances as a core part of their course (depending on the nature of the class).

In my writing for this book, I have tried carefully to blend both the practitioner and the academic styles of writing. It is not as dense as is typical academic journal writing, but at the same time offers depth by going into the nuances and trade-offs of various practices.

The word "deep" is in vogue today, meaning getting deeply into a subject or topic, and so is the word "unpack" which means to tease out the underlying aspects of a subject or topic. I have sought to offer material that addresses an issue or topic by going relatively deeply into it and make sure that it is well unpacked.

Finally, in any book about AI, it is difficult to use our everyday words without having some of them be misinterpreted. Specifically, it is easy to anthropomorphize AI. When I say that an AI system "knows" something, I do not want you to construe that the AI system has sentience and "knows" in the same way that humans do. They aren't that way, as yet. I have tried to use quotes around such words from time-to-time to emphasize that the words I am using should not be misinterpreted to ascribe true human intelligence to the AI systems that we know of today. If I used quotes around all such words, the book would be very difficult to read, and so I am doing so judiciously. Please keep that in mind as you read the material, thanks.

INTRODUCTION TO DRIVERLESS SELF-DRIVING CARS

COMPANION BOOKS

If you find this material of interest, you might want to also see my other books on self-driving cars, entitled:

"Advances in AI and Autonomous Vehicles: Cybernetic Self-Driving Cars"
  by Dr. Lance B. Eliot
  ISBN: 0692915176
  https://www.amazon.com/dp/0692915176

"Innovation and Thought Leadership on Self-Driving Driverless Cars"
  by Dr. Lance B. Eliot
  ISBN: 0692926429
  https://www.amazon.com/dp/0692926429

"Self-Driving Cars: The Mother of All AI Projects"
  by Dr. Lance B. Eliot
  ISBN: 0692914544
  https://www.amazon.com/dp/0692914544

"New Advances in AI Autonomous Driverless Self-Driving Cars"
  by Dr. Lance B. Eliot
  ISBN: 0692048359
  https://www.amazon.com/dp/0692048359

"Autonomous Vehicle Driverless Self-Driving Cars and Artificial Intelligence"
  by Dr. Lance Eliot and Michael B. Eliot
  ISBN: 0692051023
  https://www.amazon.com/dp/0692051023

CHAPTER 1

SELF-DRIVING CAR MOONSHOT: MOTHER OF ALL AI PROJECTS

CHAPTER 1

SELF-DRIVING CAR MOONSHOT: MOTHER OF ALL AI PROJECTS

Apple's CEO Tim Cook recently stated that the development of a self-driving car is the "mother of all AI projects." I agree with him wholeheartedly. He couldn't have said it any better. This is a succinct statement that says it all.

Some of you might question the boldness of the statement. On the surface, it seems like making a self-driving car is cut and dry. You hear every day about how we are on the verge of the self-driving car. If you believe that crock, I urge you to read about AI fake news on self-driving cars. We are a long ways away from having a true self-driving car. When I say a true one, I mean a Level 5 self-driving car. We are years and years away from achieving a Level 5 self-driving car, which essentially is a self-driving car that can drive in whatever manner that a human could drive a car.

This is a really, really, really hard thing to do.

Can you get a car that will drive along an open highway and pretty much act as a souped-up cruise control? Absolutely. We've got that right now in the Tesla and other upcoming "self-driving" cars. Can any of those cars take evasive action on their own initiative to avoid a car accident by realizing that there is a motorcyclist up ahead that is about to fall off his bike and land into traffic and therefore the self-driving car is wise enough to switch out its lane, doing so fully aware of the other traffic around it, and quickly go onto the shoulder? No.

This involves many aspects of human intelligence. This requires using judgment on-the-fly. It requires predicting the future. It requires preparing a plan of what to do. It requires carrying out the plan. It means adjusting the plan as the event evolves. It includes maneuvering the car suddenly and with care. It requires being aware of what the car is doing and trying to achieve. You could aim to program something for this particular scenario, but if you then vary the scenario the system would be unlikely to adjust to the new situation.

We need many more advances ahead of us to do this. We need advances in sensory devices. We need advances in the AI capabilities. Some of these advances we don't even know right now where they will arise from. Besides saying it is the mother of all AI projects, some liken this to being like a moonshot. Whenever someone refers to an innovation as a moonshot, they usually mean that it is something we can't do today, and for which we hope to do in the future, but how to get there is an open question that will require various miracle like breakthroughs to achieve.

That being said, let's do a step-by-step comparison to what a moonshot really was. In other words, let's retrace how we got to the moon, and see how those aspects are relevant to the creation of a true self-driving car and also how various factors differ from what we are doing for getting to a true self-driving car.

1. Big Stretch Goal

When it was proposed to go to the moon, no one really knew how we would get there. It was a big stretch goal. As Kennedy said, "We choose to go to the moon in this decade and do the other things, not because they are easy, but because they are hard."

Achieving a self-driving car is a big stretch goal, we don't yet know how to get there, and I would say: "We choose to develop a self-driving car and do other AI things, not because they are easy, but because they are hard."

2. Money Maker or Because-its-there

Going to the moon was not especially a money maker kind of engagement. It wasn't like we were going to cultivate the moon and start selling moon rocks and moon fruit to make money from the expedition. We wanted to go there to prove we could. It was bragging rights. It was pride.

Self-driving cars equals big bucks. It is the pot of gold at the end of this rainbow. I agree with the futurists that say it will transform society. This is big business. Now, I do agree that there are many other more altruistic reasons for having self-driving cars. But, really, for those firms putting in the time and effort right now, it's the money.

3. National Goal versus Private Goal

For the United States, getting to the moon was a national goal. It unified us. It gave us something to rally around. It allowed us to show that we were better than certain other countries.

There isn't a unified national goal around achieving a self-driving car. It's a mainly a private oriented goal. Car makers want to go there. Tech companies want to go there. The government is generally supportive of others that want to get there, but it is not fitting the whole bill and not taking an active role other than primarily as regulator.

4. It's a Race to Be First

The moonshot was a race. Who would get to the moon first? Turns out, it was pretty much a one-person race, in the end. A deadline had been established, get there by the end of the decade. We had a race and a finish line, along with a clear cut deadline.

For a self-driving car, there's a race by private firms to get there. Lots of participants in this race. It is assumed that whichever firm gets there first will grab up all the market share. Or at least be perceived as sterling and get lots of attention and boosted prices in their shares. There is not a known or stated deadline. No one knows how long it will really take. Some might tire of the race and drop out. Other new entrants might jump in. The finish line is somewhat nebulous in that though we could say it is whomever can achieve a Level 5 has reached the end, but we don't have a test per se to say what is really a Level 5 car and so the ending point is a bit murky.

5. Funding

The moonshot was mainly funded by the government. Which is funding from taxpayers.

Self-driving cars are funded by commercial ventures, by investors. Sure, there is some research done by universities and government funded, and government agencies doing research, but we're not going to see self-driving cars being produced by those entities. It's going to be commercial companies.

6. Public Excitement or Public Trepidation

So, the public was pretty excited about getting to the moon. It was a national rallying cry. Children in school knew to cheer for the astronauts and for every flight into space.

For self-driving cars, the public is keenly interested, but somewhat unsure and nervous. Will the self-driving cars be safe? Will they go berserk? Will they cost too much? Will the government try to control us by taking over our self-driving cars?

7. Technology Innovations

Getting to the moon required advances and innovations in technology. It helped spur the computer era that we know today and which benefited from immensely.

Some believe that for self-driving cars we already have the hardware we need. Elon Musk famously has claimed that the hardware on the latest Tesla's is sufficient for self-driving cars. This remains to be seen. The software side is a big question and so most would agree we don't have the AI part of this figured out. Elon thinks that once the AI part is figured out, he can just over-the-air pump the AI into the car and it will be a true self-driving car. We'll see. Anyway, I believe we need a lot of added technology innovations to get to a true self-driving car.

8. One-Time Achievement Versus Ongoing

Getting to the moon ended-up being a kind of one-time achievement. We got there. We walked around. We came back a few times.

A self-driving car is not the same in that we'll likely get a true self-driving car of capability X, and then want to evolve it to capability Y, and then to capability Z, etc. This is going to be an ongoing achievement.

9. Societal Impact Direct or Indirect

The moonshot had indirect impacts on society. It did not change the day-to-day lives of people. Some offshoots of the moonshot did ultimately change our lives, but the actual arriving at the moon did not. It might have created great spirit, which then led to other interests and later advances in technology. But the everyday person was not directly impacted by landing on the moon.

A self-driving car is going to change it all. All people will be directly impacted. Some say for example that it will change how the elderly live and what they can do. Some say it will change how we interact with each other. This is profound and transformative innovation.

10. Series of Steps Versus One Giant Leap

Getting to the moon took a series of painstaking steps. We first figured out how to get a rocket into outer space. We then took up monkeys. We then took up humans. We orbited the earth. We went to the moon but did not land. We finally then went to the moon and landed. It was not one giant leap overnight that got us there.

Self-driving cars are the same. We are going to get there one step at a time. That being said, some believe that we don't need to do this a step at a time. Rather than getting to Level 3, and then to Level 4, and then to Level 5, some say that the way to get there is to go from now to Level 5. Google's earlier plans were that way. They wanted to skip the intervening levels and get us to a Level 5. Doubtful about this. It is going to be more incremental than one giant leap.

11. Known by an Event Versus By Emergence

People remember where they were when we landed on the moon. It was a huge event. A life remembering event.

For a true self-driving car, I am doubtful that it will be that one day have some car maker that announces they have a Level 5 car and here it is. Voila. Take away the cape and there's a true self-driving car. Instead, it will emerge over time. There goes the Level 5 self-driving car, being tested again and again.

12. Things Will Go Wrong

You might know about Apollo 13, the mission that had to abort the moon mission and come back home. It was a success in that it proved that we could handle such an emergency. It was an example too of things that can go wrong. There were other notable setbacks too during the moon aiming years.

We have not yet had much go wrong per se on the path to self-driving cars. I am predicting that we will have lots go wrong (read my other books that cover product liability for self-driving cars). Nobody is speaking about it, but we are going to have accidents involving self-driving cars. We are going to have lawsuits. Just hope that it is doesn't curtail our enthusiasm and drive toward self-driving cars.

13. The New Norm

We had hoped that going to the moon would become a regular activity. People would live on the moon. Shuttles would go back-and-forth. Being there would be no different than living on Earth, other than the obvious precautions and living conditions differences. You would ride on a space rocket driven bus to get there and back. Hasn't happened yet.

For self-driving cars, it is intended to become the new norm. Once they are proven, eventually all cars will likely be self-driving cars. The only exceptions will be collector type of cars. The new norm will be self-driving cars.

14. Systems Intelligence

Getting to the moon required great skills in advancing computer hardware and software, but it was not AI. We didn't need systems that could act and "think" as humans can.

For a true self-driving car, we need intelligence on par with human intelligence. We need to get systems to behave as humans do. We can try to do this with black box approaches such as deep learning, or via white box approaches of programming the system, or a combination of the two. In any case, AI is a requirement. No AI, no self-driving cars.

The above covers some of the similarities and differences between a true moonshot and a true self-driving car in terms of being able to advance ourselves to achieve those aspects. The moonshot was the mother of all projects at the time.

Today, solving cancer is the mother of all medical projects (I realize some might argue that and claim it is some other medical malady). For AI, there are other AI achievements we are aiming to get to, but a self-driving car is definitely worthy of being consider the mother of them all.

In fact, I've stated many times that if we can do a self-driving car, it also means we can do AI at an incredible level that we can use that same AI for solving lots of other hard problems. Getting there is half the fun, and actually having a self-driving car that is truly a Level 5 will be a marvel of AI and mankind.

CHAPTER 2

GRAND CONVERGENCE LEADS TO SELF-DRIVING CARS

Dr. Lance B. Eliot

CHAPTER 2

GRAND CONVERGENCE LEADS TO SELF-DRIVING CARS

Why now?

As head of the Cybernetics Self-Driving Car Institute and a frequent speaker about self-driving cars and autonomous vehicles, I often get asked the question of why are we now seeing such a widespread interest and advancement in self-driving cars. Some inquirers feel that this is like suddenly discovering a new movie star and wonder what sparked that person to vault into stardom. Tagging onto that analogy, I explain that just like the proverbial small-time actor that starved and took on any off off-Broadway acting roles they could find, it has taken many years of toiling in research labs and universities that has preceded the now more visible appearance of self-driving cars.

Since the invention of the horseless carriage, there have been dreams of someday having a car that can drive itself. During the pre-computers era, attempts to develop a self-driving car were pretty much DOA (Dead on Arrival), since the kind of technological capability to achieve self-driving cars did not yet exist. During the early days of the introduction of computers, researchers realized that the potential for a self-driving car reasonably now existed, doing so by harnessing computers to act on behalf of a human driver. If you take a look at the body of literature on autonomous vehicles, you'll see that there have been hundreds of academic and research institutions and thousands of professors and researchers that have been pursuing the dream of a self-driving car for years and years. One of the most famous instigators

27

towards self-driving cars has been the Department of Defense (DoD), for obvious reasons of battlefield purposes, along with the DARPA sponsored competitions that have helped to push innovations in robotics forward immensely and that are directly pertinent to self-driving cars.

So, my first point is that it is not as though we all woke-up in the last year or two and suddenly decided to invent self-driving cars. The desire for a self-driving car has been around for a long time, and the advances toward it have been incrementally advancing. That being said, it has been a slow and snails paced progress toward a self-driving car. No overnight successes here. Inch by inch, we continue to make our way toward the self-driving car. I say this because some think that maybe there was a "silver bullet" that finally opened the door for a self-driving car to emerge. I know that some will claim that perhaps neural networks should be the winner for anointing self-driving cars as viable, while others would say that it is instead LIDAR (see Chapter 4 on LIDAR for self-driving cars), and some would offer other singular aspects of technology to assert that is the "it" that triggered the self-driving car craze.

Though it is often easiest to try and simplify the world and make the claim that one particular innovation led to a new world order, in this case I argue that anyone laying the credit at the feet of just one advancement is either ignorant about the field of self-driving cars, or miscomprehending things, or pushing a particular love-fest piece of high-tech, or has not taken a contemplative moment to reflect on what has taken place and continues to take place in the self-driving car arena. If you really step back and take a macroscopic look at the self-driving industry, you would come upon the notion that where we are today can be described in two words.

Grand convergence.

There, that says it all. It is a grand convergence. There have been a slew of key high-tech advances, combined with societal and business aspects, all of which have come together to create a circumstance and ecosystem that allows for the emergence of self-driving cars. Each of the members of this grand convergence have contributed mightily. No one in particular reins more supreme. At the same time, if some of the members were not present, it is questioned whether we would now be as far along as we are. Self-driving cars would still be toward infancy rather than maturing toward practical reality. Like links in a chain, each member of the grand convergence has made a contribution. Any contribution that had been missing would have left a missing link and we might not be at this pivotal juncture of nearing the realization of self-driving cars.

Allow me to also clarify that when I refer to self-driving cars, you need to know that there are an array of differences of meaning about what constitutes a self-driving car. According to the Richter scale of self-driving cars (SAE's scale), we are only in the mid-way range of the levels of self-driving cars. Right now, self-driving cars are around levels 2 and just poking into level 3 (per the official SAE scale). We still have a fight on our hands to get to level 4. And, getting to level 5 is like a moonshot. Don't let anyone trick you into thinking otherwise. Even though each day there seems to be wild claims about a level 5 self-driving car coming upon us any day, it will be many more years before we see a true level 5 self-driving car. Mark my words!

What then are the members of the club of grand convergence? The membership includes various technologies. Technologies though must be understood within a context of existence. If I invent a better mousetrap, but the mousetrap is so expensive that no one can afford it, the technology will be waylaid until it somehow reaches a point of being more affordable. Thus, the technology must also be understood within a context of the social and business factors that allow for the technology to be deployed.

Here's my list of the members of the grand convergence that is leading us toward self-driving cars:

- **Size of sensors**

The sensors that go onto and into a self-driving car have been getting smaller and smaller. This is significant because they are easier to place onto and into a car, they add less weight, and they don't cause a car to become the size of a truck just to have the sensory capabilities needed to be a self-driving car. If you look at the self-driving cars of a few years ago, you can see how bulky those sensors once were. These sensors continue to be miniaturized and more readily used for self-driving cars.

- **Price of sensors**

The sensors for self-driving cars used to be immensely expensive, meaning that if you wanted to have a self-driving car that the cost of the sensors alone would make the price of the car be astronomical. In some cases, the sensors come to a million dollars in cost. Now that sensors are getting less expensive, it becomes more realistically viable to have an affordable self-driving car.

- **Speed of sensors**

The sensors for self-driving cars are getting faster and faster. The speed of capturing data is crucial since a car might be zooming along at 80 miles per hour and the self-driving car has to in real-time collect and process the data. We'll continue to see the sensors speed-up.

- **Size of processors**

If you wanted to put a vacuum tube based computer onto a car, you wouldn't even know there was a car underneath it. In that sense, the size of computers during the last 30-50 years has made a big difference in everything that is computer-based, including for example our cell phones. Likewise, the number of processors needed for a self-driving car is quite high, and so the miniaturization of processors is helping to make them available within self-driving cars.

- **Price of processors**

The cost of computer processing continues to drop dramatically. That's why we see them in the Internet of Things (IoT) too. Self-driving cars need gobs of processors, and so the decreasing price of processors is making this possible.

- ## Speed of processors

I feel the need, the need for speed. Processors inside a self-driving car are doing a lot. They need to analyze the sensory data. They need to run the AI software that allows the car to drive. All of this requires very fast processors if the self-driving car is going to contend with driving in real-world environments. Processors are getting faster and faster, fortunately.

- ## Internet connectivity

Some self-driving cars are independent of the Internet and don't need such interconnectivity to do what they do. On the other hand, it is more than likely that true self-driving cars will need to have some kind of interconnectivity, presumably via the Internet, but could be via some other means. Perhaps the most notable aspect of this would be the vast amount of data that a self-driving car is collecting and its ability to then share that with a centralized system, which can analyze it, and provide not only insights to the contributing self-driving car but also do likewise for a vast network of interconnected self-driving cars.

- ## Machine learning/AI

Within the field of AI, machine learning continues to provide capabilities to aid self-driving cars. The notion is that rather than trying to program explicitly whatever a self-driving car needs to know, we can have a self-driving car become "capable" by learning from data about driving. There are various techniques of machine learning which are now competing with each other to see which techniques provide the greatest benefit for advancing self-driving cars.

- ## Neural networks

Neural networks are one kind of machine learning type of technique and are perhaps the most known or discussed approach. This is an effort to try and mimic somewhat how the human brain works, by simulating neurons in a network like way. It used to be that simulating neural networks was hard to do in-the-large because of the

31

computational processing needed, but with advances in processors we've been able to make this more possible. This is why for "deep learning" we can have much larger neural networks, of which the results are more impressive than were the earlier smaller or more shallow ones.

- ## Algorithms

You probably have heard that we are in the era of algorithms. Much of what runs our society on a computer based aspect is based on algorithms, ascertaining what actions should be taken by systems. Likewise, for self-driving cars, the advancement of algorithms and the ready availability has made them usable for self-driving cars.

- ## Big Data

To allow machine learning and also neural networks to do their thing you need data, lots of data. Advances in being able to collect, transform, process, and analyze Big Data has made self-driving cars "smarter" and more capable. A future key aspect involves data and machine learning for self-driving cars.

- ## Open Source

I know this member of the grand convergence, open source, might seem strange to those that are at the periphery of self-driving cars. What does open source have to do with self-driving cars, they ask. The open source world has brought into the fold many software developers that otherwise would never have known about or been able to contribute to the software of self-driving cars. To-date, much of the software was locked away in academic research libraries, or was held close to the vest by private self-driving car makers. This opening up of such software has led to more contributors and more advances in self-driving car than otherwise would have likely occurred. A burgeoning field is open source and self-driving cars.

- ## Automated Driver Assist Systems (ADAS)

We have grown-up with the ability to engage our cars into cruise control. Now, we have cars that can do parallel parking and other kinds of one-trick-pony car driving aspects. The advancement of ADAS is helping humans to get accustomed to having their car take-on self-driving car tasks. Those that develop ADAS see that they can get toward a self-driving car by expanding ADAS and making it more wholistic.

- ## Belief in Possibility

I would assert that a belief in being able to achieve self-driving cars is a crucial aspect underlying the advances in technology. If no researchers or developers thought it was a possibility, they would focus their energies elsewhere. By having a belief that it is possible, and that it is possible within a reasonable time frame, they are willing to devote their attention to this realm.

- ## Consumer Interest

Though you can invent technologies without caring whether consumers will have any interest in it, when you have a potential for widespread consumer interest, it helps to raise the stakes and get the attention of a myriad of inventors and developers. Consumers are primed to accept self-driving cars. They've seen the ADAS advances, and they want more.

- ## Investors

Money makes the world go around. Academic researchers that have toiled in self-driving cars have been scrapping together NSF grants and DoD grants for years have finally seen the spigot start to flow. Now, venture capitalists and other investors are agog about self-driving cars. The money is flowing. This drives the technologies and the technologists, since they can get the money needed to explore and experiment, plus they are certainly attracted to the potential for personal wealth.

- ### **Herd Mentality**

Self-driving cars cannot be invented by one person alone. The number of aspects of a self-driving car means that you need lots and lots of inventors and developers to each be contributing this or that piece of the larger puzzle. Fortunately, with a herd mentality that has taken place toward the advent of self-driving cars, you have enough of a widespread army of inventors and developers that each of the pieces is coming together.

- ### **Applied Research**

Foundational or basic research about self-driving cars has been augmented by applied research. Besides universities and colleges, we've seen a cottage industry of entrepreneurs that have now staked out space in the applied research toward self-driving cars.

- ### **Google**

You've got to give credit to Google for wanting to take-on the moonshot of self-driving cars, now via their Waymo entity, having been the first highly visible tech company to really take this seriously. That being said, they weren't being altruistic, since their efforts have obviously gotten them a tremendous amount of publicity over the years, and likely attracted other top high-tech talent to them, regardless whether that talent was immersed into any of the self-driving cars aspects. For Google, it was a good bet toward high-tech that might someday pay-off and that at the same time paid-off handsomely in publicity and attracting talent. They have now also spawned many former Googlers into helping to push along self-driving cars by having made the leap to other firms or going forth with their own new ventures.

- ### **Tesla**

Elon Musk is quite the character and his charm and publicity-getting attention has made the self-driving car craze what it is today. Tesla is a pioneer that has pushed forward on ADAS in a manner that we would likely not have had any of the conventional car makers try to do. Musk is a visionary that has taken a chance at spending on something earlier than most thought would make sense to do. The jury is still out whether Tesla will make the leap toward a true self-driving car, and some think maybe they'll get eclipsed. In any case, the Tesla remains a formidable challenger and something that has opened the eyes of the public, the investors, and the inventers about the strong possibilities of self-driving cars. Go, Elon, go.

- ## Media Frenzy

Self-driving car developers and inventors have pretty much been working in the shadows for many years. Not much interest by the media. A little bit of an advance here or there sometimes caught the attention of the media, for a moment. Without media coverage, it is hard to get a large preponderance of interest toward these advances and the technologies and technologies that make them happen. The media now seems to be in a frenzy to cover any and all advances of self-driving cars. I've though criticized some of that media coverage as being fake news, see Chapter 10 on that topic.

- ## Ride Sharing

What does ride sharing have to do with self-driving cars? You bet it has a lot do with self-driving cars. Ride sharing has brought to the forefront of our attention that we depend upon our cars and that there is a need for convenience of car access. With the billions of dollars that have flowed to ride sharing, it has coincided with the realization that if we had self-driving cars it would profoundly impact ride sharing. Ride sharing is helping to drive attention toward self-driving cars. See my article on the topic of blockchain and self-driving cars.

I have now laid out my list of the members of the grand convergence. Do you have other members you'd like to add to it? Be my guest. Do you believe that some of the member don't belong on the list? I think I've made a pretty strong case for each one, and keep in mind that I am not saying one is the most significant, I am saying they all had and have a contributory role toward the "sudden" appearance of self-driving cars.

Welcome to the bandwagon for self-driving cars. You can contribute too. No need to be a propeller head, since as you can see from my list, there are lots of ways in which the self-driving car realm is being formulated and grown. I hope that mainly I have dispelled the prevailing myth that there has been one factor alone that has led to the advent and now popularity of the self-driving car topic.

There isn't a magic appearance of say penicillin or the breakthrough of the invention of fire that has been the silver bullet to make self-driving cars either possible or of interest. Furthermore, the grand convergence is so strong now that I doubt we'll see a fading of interest or advances. The appetite by everyone involved, inventors, investors, developers, media, consumers, regulators, and so on, has become so pronounced that we are now on our way to the moon, whether we want to get there or not, and we'll continue to see advances in self-driving cars, even if it takes longer than some of the pundits have been predicting.

This train is underway and it isn't going to stop.

CHAPTER 3

WHY THEY SHOULD BE

CALLED

SELF-DRIVING CARS

CHAPTER 3

WHY THEY SHOULD BE CALLED SELF-DRIVING CARS

Stop for a moment and ponder this simple question. How do you refer to the newly emerging cars that are able to be driven by automation? Some call this automotive next-generation of cars by using the moniker of "self-driving cars" (it's what I prefer too, which I'll explain in a moment). Some refer to them as driverless cars. Others call them autonomous vehicles. A few people are calling them by the catchy acronym HAV's, which stands for Highly Automated Vehicles. I've also heard people utter exceedingly "science fiction" sounding phrases such as auto-piloted vehicles, and even the downright scary sounding robot-cars or the cooler version, robo-cars.

I realize that you might be thinking, does it really matter what we call them? Isn't a rose, a rose, by any other name? I emphatically argue that it does greatly matter what we call them. The names we use for things do matter. Many stakeholders are going to care about these mobile, AI-driven machines with wheels that cruise along our streets and highways. At first, it was mainly technologists that cared about them. Then, business persons cared about it, since the research labs where these futuristic cars were born have begun to see actual practical progress. Now, we've got politicians involved, regulators wanting to have a say, reporters weighing in about them, and the general public itself is queasy, excited, unsure and at times outright concerned about where these magical beasts are going to end-up being and doing on our roads.

Let's parse each one of these alternative ways to refer to self-driving cars. First, consider the phrase of "driverless cars" – I would assert that by using the word "driverless" you are making an important semantic mistake. You are suggesting that there is no one and even nothing that drives the car. Apparently, the car is just able to drive without any kind of intervention or control. Now, I know that those of you that are advocates for the phrase "driverless cars" will say, Lance, come on, the driverless part of things refers to the notion that there isn't a human driver involved. Further, those advocates would say it is "obvious" that a driverless car means that it is a car driven by a computer and it is implied that by saying driverless there is no human driver and thus who or what else could be driving the car other than a computer. To me, this is incredibly tortured logic. It requires us to make a mental leap that because it says "driverless" that it is really trying to say "human driverless car." I assure you that many people don't and aren't able to make that leap.

Furthermore, I think there is an even more sinister aspect to the driverless car naming. I believe it allows for a ready-made excuse for the automation that is driving the car. In other words, suppose a "driverless car" rams into a wall unexpectedly and not purposely. Well, some would say that's what you get if a car is driverless, i.e., there is nothing at all driving the car. It takes attention away from the real fact that there is something driving the car. There is automation driving the car. And it should be held responsible, which I mean to suggest that whomever wrote the system and put the system in place is responsible. By using the phrase "driverless cars" we are going along a slippery slope of forgetting and even hiding the fact that there is automation driving the car, and it, and those behind it, need to be accountable for what it does.

That's why I prefer to say self-driving cars. It immediately suggests that the car is able to drive itself. The car is doing the driving. There is a "self" driving the car, and it is generally obvious that it is not a human. Most instantly get the idea that self-driving means that the car has some kind of AI-based capability that allows it to do the driving of the car. This phrasing of self-driving car is a compact way to say it, using words that are easy to understand, and pretty much rolls off the tongue.

I promised that I would examine all the variants, and so now let's take a look at the other phrases. Calling these cars the phrase of "autonomous vehicles" has historically what they have been called in research labs. There is a tradition there. The reason why this isn't quite as useful as self-driving cars is that the word "autonomous" is one of those primped ten dollar words. I've seen non-technical people that have their eyes glaze over when they hear the word "autonomous" — it just sounds like a really big-time weighty word. I am not suggesting that the general public could not handle it, but just that it is the kind of word more naturally spoken by techies and less likely to catch-on in everyday use.

This brings up another facet, namely the aspect that the word "vehicle" is being used in the phase of autonomous vehicles. Again, this uses a rather formal word. Sure, people refer to their Department of Motor Vehicles (DMV), and so I realize that the word "vehicle" is accepted in general use, but I think that most people tend to say the word "car" rather than using the word "vehicle" when thinking about cars. Of course, autonomous vehicles is actually a broader terminology than saying self-driving cars, since the word "vehicle" could mean any kind of vehicle, whether a car, a motorcycle, and so on. I know that you might be worried that if we go with "self-driving car" as a phrase we will get stuck trying to come up with a name for motorcycles (self-driving motorcycle, autonomous motorcycles, headless motorcycles, or what?). We can cross that bridge when that day comes.

You can probably guess what I think of the Highly Automated Vehicles phrasing. Surprisingly, I do kind of like having a nifty acronym, in this case HAV, but I doubt it would catch-on. We already have HOV in common use, which refers to High-Occupancy Vehicle lanes, and I would wager a bet that if we also try to use HAV it will become confusing to everyone, i.e., did you mean to say HAV or HOV? I once again think the word "cars" is better for now, versus using the word "vehicles" and so I suppose we might aim for HAC (Highly Automated Cars).

But, this is lacking too. By saying "highly automated" it is kind of a slippery way of being noncommittal about the automation. It is "highly" automated and so does that mean it can actually drive the car, or is it really just a cruise control kind of thing? Self-driving car beats out the HAV because you right away know what the automation can do, namely a self-driving car is able to self-drive that car!

The phrasing of robot-cars or robo-cars can be rejected outright. The use of the "robot" part of the phrasing makes us think of movies that have transformer-like robots, which we don't really have. If you were making a car that had a robot that actually walked and got into the car and drove it, then I suppose you might start saying robot-car or robo-car. Admittedly, there are robots that can indeed do that right now, in a limited way.

Overall, though, that's not what we're going to see in self-driving cars. There will not be a robot in the front seat. All of the AI and computers will be hidden from view, stashed away in the engine compartment and other areas of the body of the car.

For the above reasons, I am an advocate of calling these new-fangled cars by the phrase of self-driving cars. It is the simplest, most elegant, catchy, and meaningful way to do so. The last phrase that I wanted to tackle is the "auto-pilot vehicle" phrase. What is wrong with saying auto-pilot? I think it perhaps overly anthropomorphizes the car.

When you hear the word "pilot" you tend to think of an airplane pilot. Auto-pilot is already used widely for referring to airplanes. Most people don't really know what an auto-pilot system can and cannot do. Trying to reuse the word "auto-pilot" for cars is going to be confusing and also have people get muddled in what the vehicle automation is able to do.

The next time that you hear someone refer to self-driving cars, and if they use one of these other buzzwords, I hope you'll raise up your hand and offer to politely "correct" them about how they are referring to these new cars.

At research labs, I realize many would not get caught dead using the phrase self-driving cars because it seems superficial and almost gutter-like. For them, I expect that the HAV or similar will continue to persist, which is fine. For most of the rest of the world, I anticipate that the self-driving car moniker will gain popularly and in a Darwinian fashion win out over other competing phrases. Either way, we should not call a rose by the name of sunflower, which would be confusing and I think that a rose should be called a rose. Just as a "self-driving car" should be referred to as a self-driving car.

Dr. Lance B. Eliot

CHAPTER 4

RICHTER SCALE FOR
SELF-DRIVING CAR LEVELS

CHAPTER 3

RICHTER SCALE FOR
SELF-DRIVING CAR LEVELS

In the Los Angeles area, we get about 10,000 earthquakes each year. Ten thousand earthquakes! Yes, at first glance it seems like a tremendous number of earthquakes, and you would assume that we are continually having to grab hold of desks and chairs to be able to withstand the shaking. Not so. It turns out that very few of the earthquakes are of such a severity that we even are aware that an earthquake has occurred.

Charles Francis Richter provided in the 1930's a handy scale that assigns a magnitude number to quantify how much power an earthquake has. His now popular Richter-scale is logarithmic and starts essentially at zero (no earthquake), and then indicates that a 1.0 to 1.9 would be a micro-earthquake that is not felt or rarely felt, while a 2.0 to 2.9 measured quake would be one that is slightly felt by humans but that causes no damage to buildings and other structures, a 3.0 to 3.9 is often felt but rarely causes damage, a 4.0 to 4.9 is felt by most people via noticeable shaking and causes none to some minimal damage, a 5.0 to 5.9 is felt widely and has slight damage, etc.

The Richter-scale has at the top of the magnitude scale a value of 9.0 or greater, and any such earthquake would tend to cause near total destruction in the area that it hits.

For Southern California, we get several hundred quakes that are around a 3.0 each year, and just a few larger ones annually such as about a dozen that are in the 4.0 range. When we get the "big" ones in a heavily populated area, perhaps in the high 4's, that's when you tend to hear about it on the news. The scale is not a linear scale and so keep in mind that a 4.0 is actually significantly higher in power than a 3.0. A linear scale is one that you could say that for each increase in the quake magnitude that the amount of impact would be relatively proportional for the increase.

In contrast, the Richter-scale, since it is logarithmic, you should think of the increase as taking many jumps upward for each time that you boost the number, i.e., a 4.0 is many jumps upward from a 3.0, and a 5.0 is even more jumps upward from a 4.0. Another way to think of this is to imagine that say a 4.0 is to a 3.0 is like the number 40 is to the number 3 (more than ten times it), while a 5.0 to the number 3 would be like the number 500 to the number 3 (more than one hundred times it).

Why would you care about the Richter scale?

I want to tell you about the ways in which we can measure the capabilities of a self-driving car, of which there is a popular scale used to do so, and in some ways it is analogous to the Richter scale.

The self-driving car capabilities scale was developed by the Society for Automotive Engineers (SAE) and has been variously adopted by other entities and international and national governmental bodies including the U.S. Department of Transportation (DOT) and its National Highway Traffic Safety Administration (NHTSA). The latest SAE standard is known as the "J3016" which was originally released in October 2014 and then had an update in September 2016. The formal title for the standard is: "Taxonomy and Definitions for Terms Related to On-Road Motor Vehicle Automated Driving Systems."

Let's consider the nature of this SAE-provided self-driving car scale and its significance.

The scale ranges from 0 to 5, and is typically characterized as this:

Level 0: No automation

Level 1: Driver assistance

Level 2: Partial automation

Level 3: Conditional automation

Level 4: High automation

Level 5: Full automation

We don't assign intervening units within a level, and so it is always referred to as for example a Level 2 but not as a Level 2.1 or Level 2.6, instead it is just a level 2. This is therefore unlike how the Richter scale works.

With this SAE self-driving car scale, the levels are simple integers of 0, 1, 2, 3, 4, 5. The lowest value, the 0, means no automation, and the highest value, the 5, means the fullest automation. The values in-between, namely the 1, 2, 3, 4, are used to indicate increasingly added capabilities of automation. In that sense, the Richter scale is alike since as the numbers go up, the impact or significance goes up too. The SAE scale caps out at the value of 5, the topmost value.

The Richter scale is pretty much easily measured in that we can use seismographs to measure the ground shaking and then be able to state what the quake was in terms of magnitude. Unfortunately, similarly differentiating a self-driving car is not so readily determined. The criteria offered by the SAE allows us to somewhat decide whether a self-driving car is at a particular level, but there is not enough specificity and too much ambiguity that it is not as sure a thing that we can tag a particular self-driving car as absolutely being at a particular level. SAE emphasizes that their definitions are descriptive and not intended to be prescriptive. Also, they are aimed to be technical rather than legal (we will ultimately have lawsuits about whether a self-driving car is a particular level, mark my words!).

We cannot say for sure that a given self-driving car is exactly a specific level per se. Judgment comes to play. It depends upon what capabilities the self-driving car seems to have. We would need to closely inspect the self-driving car to ascertain whether it has the features needed to be classified as to a certain level. The features might be full-on and we could all generally agree that the self-driving car has the capability, or we might disagree about whether the features are entirely there or not, and if partially there then we might debate whether the self-driving car merits being classified as to the particular level.

Here's a bit more detail at each level:

Level 0: No automation, human driver required to operate at all times, human driver in full control.

Level 1: Driver assistance, automation adds layer of safety and comfort in very function-specific manner, human driver required for all critical functions, human driver in control.

Level 2: Partial automation, automation does some autonomous functions of two or more tasks, such as adaptive cruise control and automated lane changing, human driver in control.

Level 3: Conditional automation, automation undertakes various safety-critical driving functions in particular roadway conditions, human driver in partial control.

Level 4: High automation, automation performs all aspects of the dynamic driving task but only in defined use cases and under certain circumstances such as say snow or foul weather gives control back to human, human driver in partial control.

Level 5: Full automation, automation performs all aspects of the dynamic driving task in all roadway and environmental conditions, no human driver required or needed.

There is slipperiness in the levels 1, 2, 3, and 4, and so we will see self-driving car makers that will claim their self-driving car is at one of those levels and we'll need to collectively debate whether they are accurately depicting the capabilities of the self-driving car. A level 0 is relatively apparent and does not require much debate since it is a car that has no self-driving capabilities whatsoever. A level 5 is also relatively apparent (well, somewhat, as I discuss later on herein), since it is a self-driving car that can do anything a human driven car can do.

Whenever I hear anyone talking about self-driving cars, they often get muddled because they fail to differentiate what level of a self-driving car they are referring to. This is akin to referring to earthquakes but not also mentioning the magnitude. If I say to you that I endured an earthquake last week, what do you think that I mean? Did I experience a 9.0 that is utter destruction? Did I experience a 4.0 that is a somewhat hard shake with usually minimal damage? Or was it a 1.0 that I likely did not even feel and I am exaggerating about what happened? You don't know what I am referring to until I tell you the magnitude of the quake as per using the Richter scale. The same is the case about self-driving cars. If I tell you that I was taken around town by a self-driving car, you would be wise to ask me what level of self-driving car it was.

I was at an Autonomous Vehicle event, and there were some fellow speakers arguing vehemently about the present and future of self-driving cars. One was saying that we have self-driving cars today, while the other one was saying that we are years away from having self-driving cars. Who was right and who was wrong? Well, it depends upon what you mean by the phrase "self-driving cars." If you are allowing that a self-driving car is anything measured in the SAE levels of 0 to 5, then you could say that we do already have self-driving cars because we certainly have cars that are at the levels 0, 1, and 2. On the other hand, if you consider the only true self-driving car to be a level 5, then you would be correct in saying that we don't have any self-driving cars today since we don't yet have a level 5 self-driving car.

When talking with people that aren't involved in the self-driving car industry, I have found they are apt to refer to a self-driving car and be ambiguous about what they mean. Even most regulators and legislators are the same way. I usually try to make them aware that there is a scale, the SAE scale, and then inform them about it. Otherwise, without using some kind of scale like SAE's, you can have enormous confusion and nearly religious debates about belief in self-driving cars and doubt about self-driving cars, all because you aren't referring to the same things. A level 5 is completely different than a level 2, and so arguing blindly about "self-driving cars" is unproductive and exasperating until you state what level of self-driving car you mean.

One aspect that is sometimes used to make it easier to understand the levels of self-driving cars involves mentioning these three factors:

- **Eyes on the road**

- **Hands on the wheel**

- **Foot on the pedals**

At the higher levels of self-driving cars, you presumably can temporarily take your eyes off the road, you can temporarily take your hands off the wheel, and you can temporarily take your foot off the accelerator and brake pedals. Up until level 5, the human driver though is still considered the true driver of the car. Thus, even if you opt to temporarily take your eyes, hands, and feet off of the control of the car, in the end it is you the human that is still responsible for driving the car.

I have exhorted in many venues that this is really a dangerous situation since the automation that suddenly hands control back to the human can catch the human unawares, and the ability for the human to react in time to save themselves from a deadly crash is measured often in split seconds and not sufficient for the human to properly take back control of the car. Also, humans get lazy and do not consider this temporary aspect of putting their eyes, hands, and feet afield of the controls as something that is "temporary" and will often start to read a book or otherwise become wholly disengaged from the driving of the car (leading to great danger).

A level 5 self-driving car is presumably one of the crispest of definitions since it indicates that a car must be able to be driven by the automation in all situations without the use of a human driver. Unlike level 4, which says that if the roadway or environmental conditions are especially harsh that the automation can give up and hand control over to the human, the level 5 requires that no human driver be needed at any time for any reason whatsoever. This is the ultimate in self-driving cars. We aren't there yet. We aren't even close, in my opinion. Achieving a level 5 self-driving car is the nirvana and something that is very, very, very, very hard to do.

This aspect of the level 5 being so hard to achieve is part of my basis for making a comparison to the Richter scale. Going from level 0 to level 1 is a significant jump, and so you might liken it to a logarithmic step up. Going from a 1 to 2, or a 2 to 3, or 3 to 4, those are sizable steps too, though it might be argued they are not logarithmic in scale. Going from a 4 to 5, it can be argued is logarithmic. This is due to the aspect that completely eliminating the need for any human driver is a really big step. A level 4 car might be pretty darned good, and you might say that well it just cannot do driving in snow or in a severe storm, but to me, until you have gotten a car to be driven fully by automation in all circumstances, it isn't a true self-driving car.

Google has been aiming at the level 5 and knows that it is one of those moonshot kind of initiatives. They eliminated any controls within the car, in order to make a bold statement that the human driver is not only not needed to drive the car, but that the human driver cannot drive the car even if they want to drive the car (since there aren't any controls to use). Many of the self-driving car makers are hopeful of eventually getting to a level 5 car, but for now, they are developing self-driving cars that are within the levels 2 to 4 range. Meanwhile, they have futuristic concept cars that show what the look-and-feel of a level 5 car might be in the future, but these concept cars are hollow and just something used to showcase design aspects.

Keep in mind that a self-driving car maker can skip levels if they want to do so. Some self-driving car makers are progressing from one level to the next, trying to achieve a level 2 before they get to a level 3, and achieve a level 3 before they get to a level 4, etc. There is no requirement they do it this way. You can skip a level if you like. Furthermore, your self-driving car might have some features of a lower level and other features of a higher level, and so it is a mixture and not readily categorized into just a particular level. As mentioned earlier, there is judgment involved in deciding whether a self-driving car has earned its claimed level. Ford has announced they are skipping level 3 and going straight to level 4, aiming to do so by the year 2021.

Some self-driving car makers are predicting they will have a level 4/5 by the year 2019, but I am dubious whenever I see someone saying that they will be a dual level consisting of specifically levels 4 and 5, because as stated herein that a level 5 is a different beast and you either can do a level 5 or you cannot.

Indeed, we are likely to have "false" claims about a self-driving car in terms of the level it has achieved. I put the word false into quotes because a self-driving car maker might genuinely believe or want to believe that they have achieved a level, even though others might argue that the self-driving car has not achieved that level. The word false might suggest someone trying to be sneaky or nefarious, which could certainly happen, but it could also be done due to ambiguity of the definitions. Today, for example, most would agree that the Tesla self-driving cars are at a level 2. But, some claim that Tesla's self-driving cars are at 3. We can pretty much argue about this until the cows come home, and it is for me not much of an argument worth undertaking. We know and all agree that today's Tesla is not a 4 and not a 5, which therefore means it is quite a bit below what we envision a true self-driving car to be.

I don't want to seem like I am denigrating anything less than a 4. I do believe that we are pretty much going to be evolving self-driving cars from one level to the next. It makes sense to do things that way. If you are trying to bring self-driving cars to the market, you would typically bring any evolved features to the market as soon as you think you can. On the other hand, if you are doing as Google has been doing, which is more of a moonshot research project, you might not feel the need and nor the pressure to get the self-driving car into the market and thus will just keep pushing until you can get a level 5. We have though seen Google changing its posture on this, and perhaps realizing that getting into the market with their self-driving cars sooner rather than once they later on get to a level 5 might be a prudent thing to do.

For a level 5 self-driving car, some argue that the level 5 must not have any controls inside the car that would allow a human to drive a car. In other words, there isn't a steering wheel and there aren't pedals. There is no apparent physical means to allow a human to drive. The concept cars show that the humans are partying it up as passengers and there is no driver. The interior might have swiveling seats and the passengers can face each other, with no need to be looking forward and peering out the front windshield. The self-driving car is doing all the driving and so the interior compartment is just like a limo with no need for the passengers to care about the driving of the car.

This argument about the controls is open to ongoing debate. Suppose we did put controls inside the car, does it imply that the human driver is needed? Some say that no such implication is inferred. They say that humans might want to drive the car, and so they should be given the option to do so, if they wish to do so. By providing the normal steering wheel and pedals, it gives the human that option. The automation could still be one that is able to always drive the car, and there is never a need for a human to use those controls. Perhaps for nostalgia sake, a human might want to drive the car, or maybe they are a car buff and just enjoy driving.

The counter-argument is that if you put controls into a level 5 self-driving car then you are asking for trouble. The human driver might opt to take over the controls from the automation, but maybe the human is drunk, or maybe the human hasn't driven in years and is rusty in terms of driving, or maybe they take the controls over at the wrong moment just as the automation is doing a delicate maneuver. For those reasons, some say that a level 5 should never have any controls for a human driver.

There are also some that assert that maybe we go ahead and allow a human driver to drive if they choose to do so (not because they must), but they won't use conventional physical steering wheel and pedals to do so, and instead the human might use their voice to drive the car or use their smart phone or a touch screen to drive the car. Meanwhile, the self-driving car "utopia" people suggest that if you allow humans to drive in a level 5 car that you are going to mess-up the future when all cars are being self-driven by automation. Via automation, all cars will be able to communicate via automation and synchronize with each other in this utopian vision, while if you allow even one human to be a driver in a level 5 car then you will mess-up that utopia.

One of the current falsehoods, I assert, involves the claims that the self-driving cars are "safer" as you make your way up the levels. In other words, it is suggested that a level 4 self-driving car is safer than a level 3 self-driving car, and a level 3 is safer than a level 2. I think this is debatable. You need to keep in mind that all of the levels other than 5 will still have the human driver involved. Even if the automation is more sophisticated, you still have the human driver in the equation. Maybe you might claim that if the human driver is doing less as the levels get higher, the portion of the driving they aren't doing is getting safer, and so overall the stats will show that the safety has been increased. This is an argument that we'll need to see if it bears out. Also, even a level 5 cannot be seen has utterly safe per se, which I have covered in many of these essays the importance of self-driving cars and safety.

One technological aspect that is of fascination today is whether we know what kind of technology is needed to achieve a level 5 self-driving car. There are some that believe you must have LIDAR to get to level 5, while others believe you won't need LIDAR to get there. Tesla claims that the hardware they have on their latest cars, consisting of 8 cameras and 12 ultrasonic sensors, and some other sensory devices and processors, will be sufficient for getting to a level 5. Don't know if this will be the case.

With the rapid advances in sensors and in processors, it could be that the hardware Tesla has today either will be insufficient to get to level 5, or might hold them back from getting to level 5. Given that they seem to be somewhat anchored to their hardware (entrenched due to investment), they might also see other more nimble self-driving car makers that adopt more modernized hardware as time evolves, and Tesla might be "stuck" with the older hardware that at one time seemed extremely state-of-the-art. We've seen companies do this many times in other industries, wherein they put a stake in the ground about the hardware, they get jammed up because of this, and others swoosh past them by adopting new hardware instead.

Another factor to consider about self-driving cars and their levels is whether you are referring to a pilot or prototype car, versus a self-driving car that actually is working on the public roadways. If I have a laboratory with an acre sized obstacle course and I have my self-driving car drive it, and I claim it is a level 5 self-driving car, does that really constitute a level 5? I would argue that it does not. To me, a level 5 is a self-driving car that can handle any situation that a human driver can drive, meaning driving in the suburbs, in the inner city, in the open road, and so on. A prototype that is able to make its way around an artificial driving course is not much proof in my book.

I would also suggest that we need the equivalent of a Turing test for self-driving cars at the level 5. Those of you into AI know that the Turing test consists of ascertaining whether you can differentiate the behavior of a system between what the AI does and what a human can do. In essence, if the system can do whatever a human can do, and if you can't ferret out that it is AI, you could then indicate that the AI is exhibiting artificial intelligence of the equivalence of human intelligence. This also means that you need to have a sophisticated human for comparison, because if you use a human that is not sophisticated you are then making a false comparison.

Likewise, for a self-driving car at the level 5, we are indicating that the automation must be able to drive in any situation that a human can. How far do we stretch this? A normal human driver is unlikely to be able to drive a car in extreme circumstances, such as on a race track at high speeds. Does the level 5 car need to be able to do that, or is it only required to do normal driving. There are human drivers that are inept at driving on ice. Does this exempt the level 5 car from being forced to show that it can drive on ice, since "humans" cannot do it either (or, at least some humans cannot). The nature and definition of human driver is itself ambiguous and so it leaves more room for interpretation about level 5 self-driving cars. I am prepared to propose a Turing test equivalent, and if anyone wants to then call it the Eliot test for self-driving cars, I'd be honored.

In any case, now you have an appreciation for what it means to be referring to a car as a self-driving car, and let's all be working toward the vaunted level 5. Take a look at the diagram depicting at a high-level the levels of a self-driving car (you can find more details in the official SAE guide from which the diagram was sourced).

Summary of Levels of Driving Automation for On-Road Vehicles

This table summarizes SAE International's levels of *driving* automation for on-road vehicles. Information Report J3016 provides full definitions for these levels and for the italicized terms used therein. The levels are descriptive rather than normative and technical rather than legal. Elements indicate minimum rather than maximum capabilities for each level. "System" refers to the driver assistance system, combination of driver assistance systems, or *automated driving system*, as appropriate.

The table also shows how SAE's levels definitively correspond to those developed by the Germany Federal Highway Research Institute (BASt) and approximately correspond to those described by the US National Highway Traffic Safety Administration (NHTSA) in its "Preliminary Statement of Policy Concerning Automated Vehicles" of May 30, 2013.

Level	Name	Narrative definition	Execution of steering and acceleration/ deceleration	Monitoring of driving environment	Fallback performance of dynamic driving task	System capability (driving modes)	BASt level	NHTSA level
Human driver monitors the driving environment								
0	No Automation	the full-time performance by the *human driver* of all aspects of the *dynamic driving task*, even when enhanced by warning or intervention systems	Human driver	Human driver	Human driver	n/a	Driver only	0
1	Driver Assistance	the *driving mode*-specific execution by a driver assistance system of either steering or acceleration/deceleration using information about the driving environment and with the expectation that the *human driver* perform all remaining aspects of the *dynamic driving task*	Human driver and system	Human driver	Human driver	Some driving modes	Assisted	1
2	Partial Automation	the *driving mode*-specific execution by one or more driver assistance systems of both steering and acceleration/deceleration using information about the driving environment and with the expectation that the *human driver* perform all remaining aspects of the *dynamic driving task*	System	Human driver	Human driver	Some driving modes	Partially automated	2
Automated driving system ("system") monitors the driving environment								
3	Conditional Automation	the *driving mode*-specific performance by an *automated driving system* of all aspects of the *dynamic driving task* with the expectation that the *human driver* will respond appropriately to a *request to intervene*	System	System	Human driver	Some driving modes	Highly automated	3
4	High Automation	the *driving mode*-specific performance by an *automated driving system* of all aspects of the *dynamic driving task*, even if a *human driver* does not respond appropriately to a *request to intervene*	System	System	System	Some driving modes	Fully automated	3/4
5	Full Automation	the full-time performance by an *automated driving system* of all aspects of the *dynamic driving task* under all roadway and environmental conditions that can be managed by a *human driver*	System	System	System	All driving modes	-	

CHAPTER 5

LIDAR FOR

SELF-DRIVING CARS

CHAPTER 5

LIDAR FOR
SELF-DRIVING CARS

Is LIDAR the secret sauce for self-driving cars?

I'll explain what LIDAR is, and also offer insights about the two different camps that fervently believe either that LIDAR is an absolute must for the advent of self-driving cars or believe that LIDAR is optional and likely overly expensive so as to not be needed for self-driving cars. Besides the technology underlying LIDAR and what it does, I'll also bring you into the world of mystery spying and intrigue that has recently been emerging around LIDAR as evidenced by the lawsuit between Google's Waymo and Uber, along with the recent ranking of self-driving car makers that put Tesla at 12th position, a much lower ranking than what most would assume and rated low due to Elon Musk's posturing that LIDAR is not needed. Get ready for a wild and engaging ride on the story of LIDAR.

Have you ever seen a picture of a Google self-driving car?

If so, you'll notice that there is a kind of "hat" on the top of the car that looks like a flashing beacon or siren light, akin to what you might see on top of a fire truck or maybe an ambulance. Most people assume that this beacon or cylinder is there to warn other drivers that a self-driving car is in their midst. It seems almost like the kind of warning signs you see on a car being driven by a teenager that is learning to drive. Watch out, get out of the way, neophyte driver is here on the roads! Well, in the case of the Google self-driving car, you'd be wrong that the beacon is there for you. It is there to provide a crucial sensory capability to the self-driving AI, namely it is a device that emits a laser light beam and then receives a return that helps the system identify nearby objects that are out and around the car.

Called LIDAR, the beacon is an essential sensory device for most self-driving cars. It sits purposely on the top or roof of the car so as to have an unobstructed view. Originally called LIDAR as a mishmash of the words Light and Radar, it eventually became also known as Light Detection And Ranging, but some also refer to it as Light Imaging Detection And Ranging. You will also see it spelled in different ways, such as some people use LIDAR, while others use Lidar, LiDAR, LADAR, and other variations. Whatever way you want to spell it or say it, the end result is that it is a sensory device that emits a laser light beam which then gets back a reflection and can try to ascertain the distance between itself and whatever objects the light bounces off.

It is a range detector.

This range detector can be used to create a 3-dimensional mapping of what surrounds a self-driving car. The laser beam can be rotated in a circle, 360 degrees, and as it does so it is detecting the distances to nearby objects. The system then can reconstruct each of these range detections to try and create a kind of mental map of the surrounding area. There's a large standing object over to the right, and a squat object over to the left of the car. Piecing together a jigsaw of these puzzles pieces, the system figures out that the large standing object on the right is a telephone pole, and the squat object to the left is a fire hydrant. Once the system figures this out, it can then use higher-level logic to determine that it should avoid hitting the telephone pole and avoid hitting the fire hydrant, but it "knows" those objects are there and in case the self-driving car needs to take a sudden evasive maneuver and wants to go off-the-road to avoid a head-to-head car collision.

Rather than the laser beam rotating, modern versions use mirrors that rotate instead. This can speed-up the range detection and also allow for gathering more data at once. There are single-lens LIDAR and there are multi-lens LIDAR, of which the former is less expensive and easier to data process while the latter is more expensive and takes greater data processing to handle. The amount of algorithmic processing of the data being collected is tremendous. You need to get the data and reduce the noise and distortions, you need to do feature extraction to identify the skeletons of objects, you need to deal with the geometric facets and cope with the reflections from the objects, etc.

LIDAR has been around since the 1960s. This is a surprise to many in the self-driving car field since they seem to think that LIDAR was invented just for self-driving cars. Nope. It has been used for all kinds of purposes, and a great deal of the time was used in airborne applications. There are lots of terrestrial applications too, including for example in archaeology and for farming. This is pretty much tried and true technology. That being said, there are continual advances taking place. Let's discuss the impact of those advances.

One advancing aspect of LIDAR is that it is getting less expensive as a sensory device. The early versions on self-driving cars like Google's car were typically around $100K in cost (they were using a now older LIDAR model of Velodyne, a vendor that makes LIDAR's, and it was the HDL-64E LIDAR sensor at the time). As you can imagine, we are not going to have self-driving cars for the masses if the cost of one sensor alone on a self-driving car costs $100K. This would cause the cost of a self-driving car to go into the hundreds of thousands of dollars, after adding up all the other sensory devices and specialized software involved. Only the very wealthy could afford such a car. Furthermore, from the perspective of the car makers, they would only have a tiny market size to sell the self-driving car into. The Holy Grail of self-driving cars is to sell into the masses. There are currently around 250 million cars in the United States and about 1 billion cars worldwide. Car makers are eyeing that they could ultimately replace all those cars with self-driving cars and so that's a huge market. Game on!

Another advancing aspect of LIDAR is that it is getting better and faster. If you are dependent upon LIDAR as a means to guide a self-driving car, you need the LIDAR to work very quickly. Realizing that a car is moving along at say 80 mph, you need to have a sensory device that can grab the range detections in real-time, and accurately, so that the AI of the self-driving car can figure out what is going on. With each second that passes, your car has moved forward about 120 feet.

Think about that for a moment. In one second, your car has moved forward over one hundred feet in distance. As your car moves along, it needs to rapidly ascertain what is ahead of it, what is the right, what is the left, and what is behind it.

Keep in mind too that the other objects around the self-driving car are not necessarily stationary, and thus you need to have the LIDAR detecting that another car is coming at you or veering toward you. The speed of the LIDAR detecting objects is crucial, since otherwise your self-driving car is "blind" as to what is happening. Suppose the LIDAR hiccups for even a brief second of time, it would be like you are driving your car and suddenly closing your eyes or look away from the road. This split-second diversion could cause a life-or-death aspect of your car hitting someone else or going into a ditch.

LIDAR is notorious for not being able to reliably detect close-in objects very well and so Google even mounted conventional radar black-boxes to the front and rear of their self-driving car. The LIDAR also can be obscured by other areas of the roof of the self-driving car, and so if you were to mount ski racks or something else on your self-driving car, you need to make sure that LIDAR still has an unobstructed view. Moisture in the air has often been troubling for LIDAR too. If there is rain, snow, or fog, it can cause the laser light to bounce oddly and so you won't get back clear and usable reflections from objects. This is gradually being dealt with in newer versions of LIDAR.

The speed of processing is also being enhanced. Some believe that conventional silicon-based chips can't handle in a speedy manner the huge volume of the range detections. Researchers and startup high-tech firms are exploring the use of Gallium nitride (GaN) transistors, which can potentially process at faster speeds than silicon. Price is a factor again, and so if you get faster in one tech but the cost goes up, you need to balance against slower tech that is less expensive. Indeed, there are LIDAR's that are down into the mere hundreds of dollars cost range, but those are slower and tend to be such low-resolution that few believe they are tenable for use in a true self-driving car scenario.

Now that I've covered the fundamentals about LIDAR and its use for self-driving cars, we can shift into the intrigue part of the story.

You might assume that everyone believes that LIDAR is necessary for self-driving cars. It is usually used in combination with cameras and other sensory devices such as conventional radar. You might think of this as a human that combines a multitude of their sensory capabilities for driving a car, such as your eyes, your ears, etc. The self-driving car fuses together the data from a multitude of sensors and then tries to map the world around the car and the AI then figures out what the car should be doing. Get ready to be shocked when I tell you who isn't using LIDAR.

Are you sitting down? Tesla is not using LIDAR.

Furthermore, Tesla appears to have no interest in using LIDAR. According to Elon Musk, he doesn't believe that LIDAR is a capability needed for self-driving cars. His comments about LIDAR have drawn both criticism and praise. Those that praise his views believe that LIDAR is a misleading path and that we don't need it for self-driving cars. We can do what is needed with the other sensory devices, they say, and using LIDAR is unnecessary. Why bother with something that you don't need and will only increase the cost of the self-driving car? On the other hand, the camp that says LIDAR is essential is just about all the other self-driving car makers. Yes, Tesla is pretty much alone in their view that LIDAR is unnecessary.

Notice that Elon Musk has not said that LIDAR is bad or wrong. He believes that LIDAR is applicable for other kinds of applications, such as for his spaceships. He just doesn't think it is worthy for self-driving cars. Cynics say that he wants to avoid having to retrofit all of the existing Tesla's to have LIDAR, which would be quite costly. He will supposedly claim that LIDAR is not needed due to not having used it at the start, and now that he's far along on his self-driving cars that it would be costly and also look like he was "wrong" that he didn't earlier adopt LIDAR.

A recent ranking of self-driving car makers even put Tesla into the lowly position of 12th place, primarily because Tesla is not using

LIDAR. The camp that believes in the importance of LIDAR has cheered this ranking and kind of thumbed their nose at Elon Musk. The camp that believes LIDAR is not needed has suggested that the ranking was biased by techies that favor LIDAR and so it is an unfair ranking. If you were ranking baseball batters and believed that the use of an aluminum bat was better than a wood bat, and your ranking was based on the type of bat used, you can imagine the rancor that would come out after the ranking was published. Does it really make a difference as to which bat you use? Shouldn't the batter be judged based on the outcome of their batting? Some believe that a ranking that assumes the use or non-use of LIDAR is a crucial factor ought to be tossed out, for the same logic as the use of the bat when ranking baseball batters seems questionable.

How important is LIDAR? You might have read in the mainstream media the lawsuit of Google's Waymo against Uber (it produced some headlines). In that lawsuit, a Google contends that self-driving car executive had left Google and founded a self-driving truck company, Otto, which was then bought up by Uber, and furthermore Google alleges that the former executive downloaded a bunch of documents before he left Google. Those documents were purportedly about LIDAR. Google is doing their own proprietary research into LIDAR and trying to advance LIDAR technology, which as I've mentioned here is an especially crucial element of the Google self-driving car strategy.

Recently, Uber went into court and denied that they have used anything that might have been taken from Google. Uber seems to be claiming that they could only find one document that might have been taken from Google, out of the alleged 14,000 that were supposedly taken. Uber also indicates that the Google research was about single-lens LIDAR, while Uber is forging ahead with multi-lens LIDAR, and so it is the case that Uber has not tried to leverage the Google propriety LIDAR, even if they had it, so Uber says. Uber has also tried the classic "their lawsuit is baseless" tactic by throwing other aspects into the mix. So far, the judge doesn't seem to be buying into Uber's positions and it appears that Uber is going to have a lot more explaining to do.

Beyond the intrigue, the point is that LIDAR is a secret sauce for some self-driving car makers. In fact, pretty much for nearly all of the self-driving car makers. The potential for LIDAR is gigantic in that if the preponderance of self-driving cars are built to require LIDAR, it will mean that you'll be needing LIDAR devices on ultimately say 250 million cars in the United States and maybe 1 billion cars worldwide. For those that see big dollars ahead, many are investing in LIDAR makers right now.

This is a bit of a bet that you are taking, though, because if Tesla is right that we really don't need LIDAR for self-driving cars, ultimately the market will likely want to keep the cost of self-driving cars as low as possible, and so maybe chuck out the LIDAR due to its added cost. This is reminiscent of the 1980s when there was a war between Beta and VHS formats. For those that bet on VHS, they won, while those that betted on Beta took a hit. Should you load-up your stock portfolio with LIDAR makers? You decide, and about five to ten years from now, we'll know if you were right in your decision.

CHAPTER 6

OVERALL FRAMEWORK FOR SELF-DRIVING CARS

CHAPTER 6

OVERALL FRAMEWORK FOR SELF-DRIVING CARS

When I give presentations about self-driving cars and teach classes on the topic, I have found it helpful to provide a framework around which the various key elements of self-driving cars can be understood and organized (see diagram at the end of this chapter). The framework needs to be simple enough to convey the overarching elements, but at the same time not so simple that it belies the true complexity of self-driving cars. As such, I am going to describe the framework here and try to offer in a thousand words (or more!) what the framework diagram itself intends to portray.

The core elements on the diagram are numbered for ease of reference. The numbering does not suggest any kind of prioritization of the elements. Each element is crucial. Each element has a purpose, and otherwise would not be included in the framework. For some self-driving cars, a particular element might be more important or somehow distinguished in comparison to other self-driving cars. You could even use the framework to rate a particular self-driving car, doing so by gauging how well it performs in each of the elements of the framework.

I will describe each of the elements, one at a time. After doing so, I'll discuss aspects that illustrate how the elements interact and perform during the overall effort of a self-driving car.

———

At the Cybernetic Self-Driving Car Institute, we use the framework to keep track of what we are working on, and how we are developing software that fills in what is needed to achieve Level 5 self-driving cars.

D-01: Sensor Capture

Let's start with the one element that often gets the most attention in the press about self-driving cars, namely, the sensory devices for a self-driving car.

On the framework, the box labeled as D-01 indicates "Sensor Capture" and refers to the processes of the self-driving car that involve collecting data from the myriad of sensors that are used for a self-driving car. The types of devices typically involved are listed, such as the use of mono cameras, stereo cameras, LIDAR devices, radar systems, ultrasonic devices, GPS, IMU, and so on.

These devices are tasked with obtaining data about the status of the self-driving car and the world around it. Some of the devices are continually providing updates, while others of the devices await an indication by the self-driving car that the device is supposed to collect data. The data might be first transformed in some fashion by the device itself, or it might instead be fed directly into the sensor capture as raw data. At that point, it might be up to the sensor capture processes to do transformations on the data. This all varies depending upon the nature of the devices being used and how the devices were designed and developed.

D-02: Sensor Fusion

Imagine that your eyeballs receive visual images, your nose receives odors, your ears receive sounds, and in essence each of your distinct sensory devices is getting some form of input. The input befits the nature of the device. Likewise, for a self-driving car, the cameras provide visual images, the radar returns radar reflections, and so on. Each device provides the data as befits what the device does.

At some point, using the analogy to humans, you need to merge together what your eyes see, what your nose smells, what your ears hear, and piece it all together into a larger sense of what the world is all about and what is happening around you. Sensor fusion is the action of taking the singular aspects from each of the devices and putting them together into a larger puzzle.

Sensor fusion is a tough task. There are some devices that might not be working at the time of the sensor capture. Or, there might some devices that are unable to report well what they have detected. Again, using a human analogy, suppose you are in a dark room and so your eyes cannot see much. At that point, you might need to rely more so on your ears and what you hear. The same is true for a self-driving car. If the cameras are obscured due to snow and sleet, it might be that the radar can provide a greater indication of what the external conditions consist of.

In the case of a self-driving car, there can be a plethora of such sensory devices. Each is reporting what it can. Each might have its difficulties. Each might have its limitations, such as how far ahead it can detect an object. All of these limitations need to be considered during the sensor fusion task.

D-03: Virtual World Model

For humans, we presumably keep in our minds a model of the world around us when we are driving a car. In your mind, you know that the car is going at say 60 miles per hour and that you are on a freeway. You have a model in your mind that your car is surrounded by other cars, and that there are lanes to the freeway. Your model is not only based on what you can see, hear, etc., but also what you know about the nature of the world. You know that at any moment that car ahead of you can smash on its brakes, or the car behind you can ram into your car, or that the truck in the next lane might swerve into your lane.

The AI of the self-driving car needs to have a virtual world model, which it then keeps updated with whatever it is receiving from the sensor fusion, which received its input from the sensor capture and the sensory devices.

D-04: System Action Plan

By having a virtual world model, the AI of the self-driving car is able to keep track of where the car is and what is happening around the car. In addition, the AI needs to determine what to do next. Should the self-driving car hit its brakes? Should the self-driving car stay in its lane or swerve into the lane to the left? Should the self-driving car accelerate or slow down?

A system action plan needs to be prepared by the AI of the self-driving car. The action plan specifies what actions should be taken. The actions need to pertain to the status of the virtual world model. Plus, the actions need to be realizable.

This realizability means that the AI cannot just assert that the self-driving car should suddenly sprout wings and fly. Instead, the AI must be bound by whatever the self-driving car can actually do, such as coming to a halt in a distance of X feet at a speed of Y miles per hour, rather than perhaps asserting that the self-driving car come to a halt in 0 feet as though it could instantaneously come to a stop while it is in motion.

D-05: Controls Activation

The system action plan is implemented by activating the controls of the car to act according to what the plan stipulates. This might mean that the accelerator control is commanded to increase the speed of the car. Or, the steering control is commanded to turn the steering wheel 30 degrees to the left or right.

One question arises as to whether or not the controls respond as they are commanded to do. In other words, suppose the AI has commanded the accelerator to increase, but for some reason it does not do so. Or, maybe it tries to do so, but the speed of the car does not increase. The controls activation feeds back into the virtual world model, and simultaneously the virtual world model is getting updated from the sensors, the sensor capture, and the sensor fusion. This allows the AI to ascertain what has taken place as a result of the controls being commanded to take some kind of action.

By the way, please keep in mind that though the diagram seems to have a linear progression to it, the reality is that these are all aspects of the self-driving car that are happening in parallel and simultaneously. The sensors are capturing data, meanwhile the sensor fusion is taking place, meanwhile the virtual model is being updated, meanwhile the system action plan is being formulated and reformulated, meanwhile the controls are being activated.

This is the same as a human being that is driving a car. They are eyeballing the road, meanwhile they are fusing in their mind the sights, sounds, etc., meanwhile their mind is updating their model of the world around them, meanwhile they are formulating an action plan of what to do, and meanwhile they are pushing their foot onto the pedals and steering the car. In the normal course of driving a car, you are doing all of these at once. I mention this so that when you look at the diagram, you will think of the boxes as processes that are all happening at the same time, and not as though only one happens and then the next.

They are shown diagrammatically in a simplistic manner to help comprehend what is taking place. You though should also realize that they are working in parallel and simultaneous with each other. This is a tough aspect in that the inter-element communications involve latency and other aspects that must be taken into account. There can be delays in one element updating and then sharing its latest status with other elements.

D-06: Automobile & CAN

Contemporary cars use various automotive electronics and a Controller Area Network (CAN) to serve as the components that underlie the driving aspects of a car. There are Electronic Control Units (ECU's) which control subsystems of the car, such as the engine, the brakes, the doors, the windows, and so on.

The elements D-01, D-02, D-03, D-04, D-05 are layered on top of the D-06, and must be aware of the nature of what the D-06 is able to do and not do.

D-07: In-Car Commands

Humans are going to be occupants in self-driving cars. In a Level 5 self-driving car, there must be some form of communication that takes place between the humans and the self-driving car. For example, I go into a self-driving car and tell it that I want to be driven over to Disneyland, and along the way I want to stop at In-and-Out Burger. The self-driving car now parses what I've said and tries to then establish a means to carry out my wishes.

In-car commands can happen at any time during a driving journey. Though my example was about an in-car command when I first got into my self-driving car, it could be that while the self-driving car is carrying out the journey that I change my mind. Perhaps after getting stuck in traffic, I tell the self-driving car to forget about getting the burgers and just head straight over to the theme park. The self-driving car needs to be alert to in-car commands throughout the journey.

D-08: VX2 Communications

We will ultimately have self-driving cars communicating with each other, doing so via V2V (Vehicle-to-Vehicle) communications. We will also have self-driving cars that communicate with the roadways and other aspects of the transportation infrastructure, doing so via V2I (Vehicle-to-Infrastructure).

The variety of ways in which a self-driving car will be communicating with other cars and infrastructure is being called V2X, whereby the letter X means whatever else we identify as something that a car should or would want to communicate with. The V2X communications will be taking place simultaneous with everything else on the diagram, and those other elements will need to incorporate whatever it gleans from those V2X communications.

D-09: Deep Learning

The use of Deep Learning permeates all other aspects of the self-driving car. The AI of the self-driving car will be using deep learning to do a better job at the systems action plan, and at the controls activation, and at the sensor fusion, and so on.

Currently, the use of artificial neural networks is the most prevalent form of deep learning. Based on large swaths of data, the neural networks attempt to "learn" from the data and therefore direct the efforts of the self-driving car accordingly.

D-10: Tactical AI

Tactical AI is the element of dealing with the moment-to-moment driving of the self-driving car. Is the self-driving car staying in its lane of the freeway? Is the car responding appropriately to the controls commands? Are the sensory devices working?

For human drivers, the tactical equivalent can be seen when you watch a novice driver such as a teenager that is first driving. They are focused on the mechanics of the driving task, keeping their eye on the road while also trying to properly control the car.

D-11: Strategic AI

The Strategic AI aspects of a self-driving car are dealing with the larger picture of what the self-driving car is trying to do. If I had asked that the self-driving car take me to Disneyland, there is an overall journey map that needs to be kept and maintained.

There is an interaction between the Strategic AI and the Tactical AI. The Strategic AI is wanting to keep on the mission of the driving, while the Tactical AI is focused on the particulars underway in the driving effort. If the Tactical AI seems to wander away from the overarching mission, the Strategic AI wants to see why and get things back on track. If the Tactical AI realizes that there is something amiss on the self-driving car, it needs to alert the Strategic AI accordingly and have an adjustment to the overarching mission that is underway.

D-12: Self-Aware AI

Very few of the self-driving cars being developed are including a

Self-Aware AI element, which we at the Cybernetic Self-Driving Car Institute believe is crucial to Level 5 self-driving cars.

The Self-Aware AI element is intended to watch over itself, in the sense that the AI is making sure that the AI is working as intended. Suppose you had a human driving a car, and they were starting to drive erratically. Hopefully, their own self-awareness would make them realize they themselves are driving poorly, such as perhaps starting to fall asleep after having been driving for hours on end. If you had a passenger in the car, they might be able to alert the driver if the driver is starting to do something amiss. This is exactly what the Self-Aware AI element tries to do, it becomes the overseer of the AI, and tries to detect when the AI has become faulty or confused, and then find ways to overcome the issue.

D-13: Economic

The economic aspects of a self-driving car are not per se a technology aspect of a self-driving car, but the economics do indeed impact the nature of a self-driving car. For example, the cost of outfitting a self-driving car with every kind of possible sensory device is prohibitive, and so choices need to be made about which devices are used. And, for those sensory devices chosen, whether they would have a full set of features or a more limited set of features.

We are going to have self-driving cars that are at the low-end of a consumer cost point, and others at the high-end of a consumer cost point. You cannot expect that the self-driving car at the low-end is going to be as robust as the one at the high-end. I realize that many of the self-driving car pundits are acting as though all self-driving cars will be the same, but they won't be. Just like anything else, we are going to have self-driving cars that have a range of capabilities. Some will be better than others. Some will be safer than others. This is the way of the real-world, and so we need to be thinking about the economics aspects when considering the nature of self-driving cars.

D-14: Societal

The societal aspects also impact the technology of self-driving car. For example, the famous Trolley Problem involves what choices should a self-driving car make when faced with life-and-death matters. If the self-driving car is about to either hit a child standing in the roadway, or instead ram into a tree at the side of the road and possibly kill the humans in the self-driving car, which choice should be made?

We need to keep in mind the societal aspects will underlie the AI of the self-driving car. Whether we are aware of it explicitly or not, the AI will have embedded into it various societal assumptions.

D-15: Innovation

I included the notion of innovation into the framework because we can anticipate that whatever a self-driving car consists of, it will continue to be innovated over time. The self-driving cars coming out in the next several years will undoubtedly be different and less innovative than the versions that come out in ten years hence, and so on.

Framework Overall

For those of you that want to learn about self-driving cars, you can potentially pick a particular element and become specialized in that aspect. Some engineers are focusing on the sensory devices. Some engineers focus on the controls activation. And so on. There are specialties in each of the elements.

Researchers are likewise specializing in various aspects. For example, there are researchers that are using Deep Learning to see how best it can be used for sensor fusion. There are other researchers that are using Deep Learning to derive good System Action Plans. Some are studying how to develop AI for the Strategic aspects of the driving task, while others are focused on the Tactical aspects.

A well-prepared all-around software developer that is involved in self-driving cars should be familiar with all of the elements, at least to the degree that they know what each element does. This is important since whatever piece of the pie that the software developer works on, they need to be knowledgeable about what the other elements are doing.

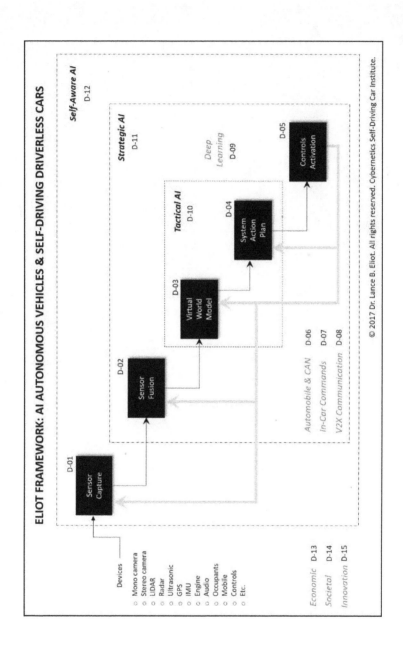

CHAPTER 7

SENSOR FUSION IS KEY FOR SELF-DRIVING CARS

Dr. Lance B. Eliot

CHAPTER 7

SENSOR FUSION IS KEY FOR SELF-DRIVING CARS

There are essentially three main system functions of self-driving cars: (1) car sensor-related system functions, (2) car processing related functions that we tend to consider the AI of the self-driving car, and (3) car control related functions that operate the accelerator, the brakes, the steering wheel, etc.

I am going to discuss today mainly the sensors and an important aspect of sensory data usage that is called sensor fusion. That being said, it is crucial to realize that all three of these main systems must work in coordination with each other. If you have the best sensors, but the AI and the control systems are wimpy then you won't have a good self-driving car. If you have lousy sensors and yet have strong AI and controls capabilities, you will once again have likely problems because without good sensors the car won't know what exists in the outside world as it drives and could ram into things.

As the Executive Director of the Cybernetic Self-Driving Car Institute, I am particularly interested in sensor fusion, and so I thought it might be handy to offer some insights on that particular topic. But, as noted above, keep in mind that the other systems and their functions are equally important to having a viable self-driving car.

A self-driving car needs to have sensors that detect the world, and there needs to be subsystems focused on dealing with the sensors and sensory data being collected. These can be sensors such as cameras that collect visual images, radar that makes use of radio waves to detect objects, LIDAR, that makes use of laser light waves, ultrasonic sensors that use sound waves, and so on. There are passive sensors, such as the camera that merely accepts light into it and therefore receives images, and there are active sensors such as radar that sends out an electromagnetic radio wave and then receives back the bounce to then figure out whether an object was detected.

The sensory data needs to be put together in some fashion, referred to as sensor fusion, in order to make sense of the sensory data. Usually, the overarching AI processing system is maintaining a virtual model of the world within which the car is driving, and the model is updated by new data arriving from the sensors. As a result of the sensor fusion, the AI then needs to decide what actions should be undertaken, and then emits appropriate commands to the controls of the car to carry out those actions.

An apt analogy would be to the way that the human body works. Your eyes are receiving visual images. Those images are conveyed to your brain. Your brain has a mental model of the world around you. Based on the images, the brain updates the model. Using the model, the brain ascertains what your body should do next. Let's suppose you are in Barcelona and at the running of the bulls. You are standing on a street corner waiting for the madcap bulls to arrive. Your brain has a mental model of the streets and the people around you. Your eyes suddenly see the bulls charging toward you. The images of the charging bulls stream into your brain. Your brain updates the mental model of the situation, and determines that you ought to start running like mad. The brain then commands your legs to engage and start running. It directs them to run away from the bulls and down the street to try and escape them.

In this analogy, we had a sensor, your eyes. It was collecting visual images. The eyes themselves don't do much with the images per se. They are predominantly dealing with getting the images. There is some fault tolerance capabilities of your eyeballs, in that even if your eye is partially covered up you can still use it to capture images. Furthermore, if you eye gets occluded, let's say that you get something in your eye like a piece of lint, the eye is able to continue functioning but also realizes that something is amiss. This is transmitted to the brain. There isn't much image processing per se in the eyeball itself in terms of making sense of the image. The eyeball is not (at least as we know) figuring out that the creature running toward you is a bull. It is up the brain to take the raw images fed by the eyeballs and try to figure out what the image consists of and its significance.

Your brain keeps a context of the existing situation around you. Standing there in Barcelona, your brain knows that your body is at the running of the bulls. It has a mental model that then can make good sense of the image of the charging bull, because your brain realizes that a charging bull is a likely scenario in this present world situation you find yourself in. Suppose that instead you were standing in New York Times Square. Your mental model would not likely include the chances of a charging bull coming at you. Your brain could still nonetheless process the aspect that a charging bull was coming at you, but it would not tend to fit into the mental model of the moment. You might be expecting a taxi to run at you, or maybe a nut wearing a spider-man outfit, but not probably a wild charging bull.

Humans have multiple senses. You take the sense of sight and your brain uses it to inform the mental model and make decisions. You also have the sense of touch, and ability to detect odors, the sense of taste, and the sense of hearing. There are various sensory devices on your body that pertain to these aspects. Your ears are your sensory devices for hearing of sounds. Those sounds are fed into the brain. The brain tries to figure out what those sounds mean. In the case of being in Barcelona, you might have heard the pounding hoofs of the bulls, prior to actually seeing the bulls coming around the corner. Your brain would have updated the mental model that the bulls are nearby. It might have then commanded your legs to start running. Or, it might opt to wait and determine whether your eyes can confirm that the bulls are charging at you. It might want to have a secondary set of sensory devices to reaffirm what the other sensory device reported.

On self-driving cars, there can be just one type of sensory device, let's say radar. This though would mean that the self-driving car has only one type of way of sensing the world. It would be akin to your having only your eyes and not having other senses like your ears. Thus, there can be multiple types of sensory devices on a self-driving cars, such as radar, LIDAR, and ultrasonic.

There are individual sensors and potentially multiples of those by type. For example, a Tesla might come equipped with one radar unit, hidden under the front grill, and then six ultrasonic units, dispersed around the car and mounted either on the outside of the skin of the car or just inside of it. Each of these types of sensors has a somewhat different purpose. Just as your eyes differ from your ears, so do these sensor types.

Radar for example is used for distance detection and speed of objects, typically at a range of around 500 feet or so. Ultrasonic sensors are usually used for very near distance detection, often within about 3 to 6 feet of the car. The radar would tend to be used for normal driving functions and trying to detect if there is a car ahead of the self-driving car. The ultrasonic sensors tend to be used when the self-driving car is parking, since it needs to know what is very nearby to the car, or can also be used when changing lanes while driving since it can try to detect other cars in your blind spot.

Recall that I mentioned that your eyes can do some amount of fault detection and have a range of fault tolerance. Likewise with the sensors on the self-driving car. A radar unit might realize that its electromagnetic waves are not being sent out and returned in a reliable manner. This could mean that the radar itself has a problem. Or, it could be that it is trying to detect an object beyond its normal functional range, let's say the stated range is 500 feet and there is an object at 600 feet. The radar wave returns from the object might be very weak. As such, the radar is not sure whether the object is really there or not. There can also be ghosting which involves situations whereby a sensor believes something is there when it is not. Think about how you sometimes are in a very dark room and believe that maybe you see an image floating in the air. Is it there or does your eyeball just get somewhat confused and falsely believe an image is there? The eyeball can play tricks on us and offer stimulation to the brain that is based on spurious aspects.

For self-driving cars, there have been some researchers who have purposely shown that it is possible to spoof the sensors on the self-driving car. They created images to trick the self-driving car camera into believing that the self-driving car was in a context that it was not (imagine if you were standing in Barcelona but I held up a picture of New York Times Square, your eyeballs would convey the image of New York Times Square and your brain needs to figure out what is going on, is it a picture or have you been transported Star Trek style into New York). Researchers have spoofed the radar. You might already know that for years there have been outlawed devices that some had in their cars to fool the radar guns used by police. The device would trick the radar gun into showing a speed that was much less than the speed of the actual driving car. Sorry, those were outlawed.

A sensor can produce what is considered a false positive. This is a circumstance involving a sensor that says something is present, but it is not. Suppose the radar reports that there is a car directly ahead of you and it is stopped in the road. The AI of the self-driving car might suddenly jam on the brakes. If the camera of the self-driving car is not showing an image of a car ahead of you, this conflicts with what the radar has said. The AI needs to ascertain which is correct, the radar reporting the object, or the images that don't show the object. Maybe the object is invisible to the camera, but visible to the radar. Or, maybe the radar is reporting a ghost and the radar should be ignored because the camera shows there is no object there. If the radar is correct and the object is there, but the camera doesn't show it to be there, the camera would be said to be reporting a false negative. A false negative consists of a sensor saying that something is not present when it actually is there.

Any of the sensors can at any time be reporting a false positive or a false negative. It is up to the AI of the self-driving car to try and figure out which is which. This can be hard to do. The AI will typically canvas all its sensors to try and determine whether any one sense is doing false reporting. Some AI systems will judge which sensor is right by pre-determining that some of the sensors are better than the others, or it might do a voting protocol wherein if X sensors vote that something is there and Y do not then if X > Y by some majority that it will decide it is there. Another popular method is known as the Random Sample Consensus (RANSAC) approach. Risk is also used as a factor in that it might be safer to falsely come to a halt than it would be to risk ramming into an object that you weren't sure was there but it turns out is there.

This is where sensor fusion comes to play. Sensor fusion consists of collecting together sensory data and trying to make sense of it. In some cars, like certain models of the Tesla, there is a sensor fusion between the camera and the radar, and then this is fed into the AI of the car. The AI of the car then receives a combined sensor fusion from those two units, and must combine it with other sensory data such as the ultrasonic sensors. I mention this because there is not necessarily one central place of sensor fusion in a self-driving car. There can be multiple places of sensor fusion. This can be important to note. Imagine if your brain was receiving not the raw images of the eyes and the ears, but instead some pre-processed version of what your eyes and ears had detected. The sensor fusion in-the-middle is going to be making assumptions and transformations that then the brain becomes reliant upon.

Within the self-driving car, there is a network that allows for communication among the devices in the self-driving car. The Society for Automotive Engineers (SAE) has defined a handy standard known as C.A.N. (Controller Area Network). It is a network that does not need a host computer, and instead the devices on the network can freely send messages across the network. Devices on the network are supposed to be listening for messages, meaning they are watching to see if a message has come along intended for that device. The devices are usually called Electronic Control Units (ECU) and are considered nodes in this network. This CAN is similar to the TCP-IP protocol and allows for asynchronous communications among the devices, and each message is encompassed in an envelope that indicates an ID for the message along with error correcting codes and the message itself.

The sensor fusion is often referred to as Multi-Sensor Data Fusion (MSDF). By taking the data from multiple sensors, there is a low-level analysis done to ascertain which sensors are Ok and which might be having problems. The MSDF will have a paradigm or methodology that it is using to decide which sensors are perhaps faulty and which are not. It will ultimately then send along a transformed indication of the raw sensor data and also then some kind of conclusions about the sensory data, and push that along to the brains of the self-driving car, the AI. The AI system or processing system then updates the model of the environment and must decide what to do about it at a higher-level of abstraction. The outcome is typically a command to the controls of the car, such as to speed-up, slow down, turn left, turn right, etc.

The Field-of-View (FOV) of the self-driving car is vital to what it knows about the outside world. For example, a radar unit at the front grille of the car is typically going to have a fan-like wave of radar detection, but it is only with respect to what is directly in front of the car. Objects that are at off-angles of the car might not be detected by the radar. The radar is for sure not detecting what is behind the car and nor to the side of the car in this instance. The AI system needs to realize that the info coming from the radar is only providing a FOV directly ahead of the car. It is otherwise blind to what is behind the car and to the sides of the car.

LIDAR is often used in today's self-driving cars to create a 360-degree model of the surrounding environment. The LIDAR uses laser light pulses and often is made to rotate continuously in a 360-degree circle. By doing so, the LIDAR can provide object detection of objects completely around the car. When combined with the front-facing radar, and a front-facing camera, and ultrasonic sensors on the sides of the car, a more full-bodied world model can be constructed and maintained. You might wonder why not have a zillion such sensors on the self-driving car, which would presumably allow for an even more robust indication of the outside world. You could certainly do so, though it causes the cost of the car to rise, and the weight and size of the car to rise.

Self-driving car makers are all jockeying to figure out how many sensors, which sensors, and which combination of sensors makes sense for a self-driving car. More sensors, more data, more to process, more cost of hardware. Less sensors, less data, less to process, lower cost of hardware. As I have previously mentioned, Elon Musk of Tesla says he does not believe LIDAR is needed for self-driving cars, and so there is not LIDAR being used on Tesla's. Is he right or is he wrong? We don't yet know. Time will tell.

There is some point at which a self-driving car is safe or not safe, or safer versus not safer than another one. This is why I have been predicting that we are going to see a shake-up eventually in self-driving cars. Those that had chosen some combination of sensors that turns out to not be as safe are going to lose out. We don't know what the right equation is as yet. In theory, the testing of self-driving cars on public roadways is going to reveal this, though hopefully not at the cost of the loss of human lives.

Based on the sensor data, there is usually Multi-Target Tracking (MTT) that needs to be undertaken. The raw data needs to be examined to identify features and do what is known as feature extraction. From a camera image, the sensor fusion might determine that a pedestrian is standing a few feet away from the car. If there is concern that the pedestrian might walk into the path of the car, the AI might decide to track that pedestrian. Thus, as subsequent images are captured from the camera, the pedestrian becomes a "target" object that has been deemed to be worthy of tracking. If the pedestrian seems to be about to get run over, the AI might then task the brakes to do a hard-braking action.

There is a need for the AI system to consider the sensory data in both a spatial manner and a temporal manner. Spatially, the sensor data is indicating what is presumably physically around the car. There is a car ahead, a pedestrian to the right, and a wall to the left of the car. For temporal purposes, the AI needs to realize that things are changing over time. The pedestrian has now moved from the right of the car to the left of the car. The car ahead is no longer ahead since it has pulled to the side of the road and stopped. The AI is reviewing the sensory data in real-time, as it streams into the AI system, and besides having a spatial model of the objects it must also have a temporal model. Object in position A is moving toward position B, and if so, what should the self-driving car do once the object gets to position B.

Notice that the AI therefore needs to be aware of the present situation and also predicting the future. We do this as human drivers. I see a pedestrian, let's say a teenager on his skateboard. He's on the sidewalk and moving fast. I anticipate that he is going to jump off the curb and possibly intersect with the path of my car. I therefore decide to swerve in-advance to my left and avoid hitting him once he makes the jump. The AI of the self-driving car would have been receiving sensor data about the teenager and would have had to make the same kinds of predictions in the model of the world that it has.

For those of you that are aware of the speed of microprocessors, you might be right now wondering how can all of this massive amount of sensory data that is pouring in each split second be getting processed in real-time and quickly enough for the self-driving car to make the timely decisions that are needed.

You are absolutely right that this needs tremendously fast processors and a lot of them too, working in parallel. Let's trace things. There is a radar image captured, and the ECU for the radar unit does some pre-processing, which takes a split-second to do. It then sends that along the CAN to the sensor fusion. This takes time to travel on the network and be received. The sensor fusion is getting likewise data from the camera, from the ultrasonic, from the LIDAR. The sensor fusion processes all of this, which takes another split-second. The result is sent along to the AI. The AI needs to process it and update the world model. This takes time. The AI then sends a command to the controls of the car, which goes across the CAN network and takes time to happen. The controls then receive the command, determine what it says to do, and physically take action. This all takes time too.

If the processors are not fast enough, and if the lag time between the sensor data collection and the final act of telling the controls to engage is overly long, you could have a self-driving car that gets into an accident, killing someone.

Not only is it about the raw speed of the processors, but it is also what the processing itself is doing. If the AI, for example, deliberates overly long, it might have reached a correct decision but no longer have time to implement it. You've probably been in a car with a human driver that hesitated to try and make the change of light at an intersection. Their hesitation put them into a bind wherein they either try to rocket through the now red light or come to a screeching halt at the edge of the intersection. Either way, they have increased the risk to themselves and those around them, due to the hesitation. Self-driving cars can get themselves into exactly the same predicament.

Here's then some of the factors about sensors and sensor fusion that need to be considered:

- Cost
- Size
- Weight
- Scalability
- Reliability
- Cooling
- Mounting Space
- Self-Diagnosis
- Error Reporting
- Fault Tolerance
- Flexibility
- Redundancy
- Spoofness
- Etc.

Sensor fusion is a vital aspect of self-driving cars. For those of you who are software engineers or computer scientists, there are ample opportunities to provide new approaches and innovative methods to improving sensor fusion.

Self-driving car makers know that good sensor fusion is essential to a well operating self-driving car. Most consumers have no clue that sensor fusion is taking place and nor how it is occurring. All they want to know is that the self-driving car is magical and able to safely take them from point Y to point Z. The better sensor fusion gets, the less obvious it will be, and yet the safer our self-driving cars will be.

CHAPTER 8

HUMANS NOT FAST ENOUGH FOR SELF-DRIVING CARS

CHAPTER 8

HUMANS NOT FAST ENOUGH FOR SELF-DRIVING CARS

You are driving your car and suddenly a child darts into the street from the sidewalk. You see the child in the corner of your eye, your mental processes calculate that the car could hit the child, and you then realize you should make an evasive move. Your mind races as you try to decide whether you should slam on the brakes, or swerve away, or both, or maybe instead try to speed-up and get past the child before your car intersects with him.

As your mind weighs each option, your hands seemingly grab the steering wheel with a death-like grip and your foot hoovers above the accelerator and brake pedal, awaiting a command from your mind. Finally, after what seems like an eternity, you push mightily on the brakes and come to halt within inches of the child. Everyone is Okay, but it was scary for driver and child.

How long did the above scenario take to play out? Though it took several sentences to describe and thus might seem like it took forever, the reality is that the whole situation took just a few seconds of time. Terrifying time. Crucial time. If you had been distracted, perhaps holding your cellphone in your hand and trying to text a message to order a pizza for dinner, you would have had even less time to react. Driving a car involves lots of relatively boring time, such as cruising on the freeway when there is no other traffic, but it also involves moments of sheer terror and second-by-second split-second decision making and hand-foot coordination.

This ability to react to a driving situation is an essential element of AI-based self-driving cars, specifically self-driving cars that are relying on human drivers to help out (there are some self-driving cars that intend to remove human drivers entirely out-of-the-loop, but most are not, at least right now). For self-driving cars that expect the human driver to be ready to take over the controls, the developers of such self-driving cars had better be thinking clearly about the Human Computer Interaction (HCI) factors involved in the boundary between human drivers and AI-automation driving the car.

Suppose that an AI-automation was driving the car in the above child-darts-into-street scenario. Perhaps the AI-automation is "smart" enough to make a decision and avoid hitting the child. But, suppose the AI-automation determines that it is unable to find a solution that avoids hitting the child, and so it then opts to hand over the controls to the human driver. Depending upon how much time the AI-automation has already consumed, the time leftover for the human driver to comprehend the situation and then react might be below, maybe even far below, the amount of time needed for the human mental calculations and hand-foot processes to be performed.

A recent study by Alexander Eriksson and Neville Stanton at the University of Southampton tries to shed light on what kinds of reaction times we're talking about (their study was published in the *Human Factors: The Journal of the Human Factors and Ergonomics Society* on January 26, 2017). They undertook a study using a car simulator, and had 26 participants (10 female, 16 male; ranging in ages from 20 to 52, with an average record of 10.57 years of normal driving experience) try to serve as a human driver for a self-driving car. In this capacity, the experiment's subjects sat awaiting the self-driving car to hand over control to them, and they then had to react accordingly. The simulation pretended that the car was going 70 miles per hour, meaning that for every second of reaction time that the car would move ahead by about 102 feet.

They setup the scenario with two situations, one wherein the human driver was focused on the self-driving car and the roadway, and in the second situation they asked the human driver to read passages from the *National Geographic* (now that's rather dry reading!). In the case of the non-distracted situation, the humans had a median reaction time of 4.56 seconds, while in the distracted situation it was 6.06 seconds.

Though it is expected that the reaction time for the distracted situation would be longer, it is also somewhat misleading to focus solely on the reaction times. I say this because the reaction time was how long it took for them to take back control of the car. Meanwhile, the time it took for them to take some kind of action ranged from 1.9 seconds to 25.7 seconds.

Let me repeat that last important point. Taking back control of a self-driving car might be relatively quick, but taking the right action might take a lot longer. Regardless though about the right action, notice that it took about 5-6 seconds to even take over manual control of the car. That's precious seconds that could spell life-or-death (and a distance of roughly 500-600 feet at the 70 mph speed), since either a collision or incident might happen in that time frame (or distance), or it might mean that the time now leftover prior to a collision or incident is beyond your ability to avert the danger.

We should also keep in mind that this was only in a simulated car. The participants were likely much more attentive than they would be in a real car. They knew they were there for a driving test of some kind, and so they were also on-alert in a manner that the everyday driver is likely not. All in all, the odds are that any similar study of driving on real roads would discover a much longer reaction time, I'd be willing to bet.

Let's consider some of the salient aspects of the Human Factors Interaction involved with a self-driving car and a human driver:

No Viable Solution

If the AI-based system of the self-driving car cannot arrive at a solution to the driving problem, it could mean that there just isn't any viable solution at all. Thus, handing the car driving over to the human is like saying, here, have at it, good luck pal. This is a no-win circumstance. The human driver is not really being given an option and instead simply being passed the buck.

Hidden Problem

The AI-based system might "know" that a child is darting from the sidewalk, but when it hands control over to the human the question arises as to how the human will know this. Yes, the human driver is supposed to be paying attention, but it could be that the human driver cannot see the child at all (suppose the AI-based system used a radar capability, but that visually the child is unseen by the human). In essence, these self-driving cars are not giving any hints or clues to the human driver about what has caused the urgency, and it is up to the human driver to be omniscient and figure it out.

Cognition Dissonance

This is similar to the Hidden Problem, in that the context of the problem is not known by the human, but suppose the human makes an assumption that the reason the self-driving car is handing over the control is because there is a trash truck up ahead that needs to be avoided, and meanwhile it is actually because the car is about to hit the child. There is a gap, or dissonance, between what the human is aware of and what the AI-based system is aware of.

Reaction Time

We've covered this one already, namely, the amount of time needed for the human to regain control of the car, plus the amount of time needed for the human to then take proper action. The AI-based system has to hand-over control with some semblance of realizing how much time a human might take to figure out what is going on and also have time to still be able to take needed action.

Controls Access

A human driver might have put their feet aside of the brake and accelerator, or might have their hands reaching behind the passenger seat to grab a candy bar. Thus, even if they are mentally aware that the self-driving car is telling them to take the controls, their physical appendages are not able to readily do so. This is a controls access issue and one that should be considered for the design of self-driving cars in terms of the steering wheel and the pedals.

False Reaction

This is one aspect that not many researchers have considered and certainly none or seemingly none of the self-driving car makers seem to have been contemplating. Here's the case. You are a human driver, you get comfortable with a self-driving car, but you also know that at some random moment, often when you least expect it, the AI-based system is going to shove the controls back to you. As such, for some drivers, they will potentially be on the edge of their seat and anxious for that moment to arise.

This could also then cause eager-beaver drivers to take back control when the AI-based system has not alerted them, and the human might make a sudden maneuver because they think the car is headed towards danger. The human is falsely reacting to an unannounced and non-issue. The human could dangerously swerve off the road or flip the car, doing so because they thought it was time to take sudden action.

CONCLUSION

Overall, the rush toward self-driving cars is more so focused on getting the self-driving car to drive, rather than also focusing on the balance between the human driver and the AI-based system. There needs to be a carefully thought through and choreographed interplay between the two. When a takeover request is lobbed to the human (these are called TOR's in self-driving parlance), there needs to be a proper allocation of TORLT (TOR Lead Time).

Without getting the whole human-computer equation appropriately developed, we're going to have self-driving cars that slam into people and the accusatory finger will be pointed at a human driver, which, might be unfair in that the human might have actually been attentive and willing to help, but for whom the self-driving car provided no reasonable way to immerse the human in helping out. We can't let the robots toss a live hand grenade to a human. Humans and their alignment with the AI-based computer factors will be vital for our joint success. Think about this the next time you are the human driver in a self-driving car.

CHAPTER 9

SOLVING EDGE PROBLEMS OF SELF-DRIVING CARS

CHAPTER 9

SOLVING EDGE PROBLEMS
OF SELF-DRIVING CARS

Whenever there is a final piece to a puzzle that is very hard to solve, it often referred to as achieving the "last mile." This colloquial phrase arose from the telecommunications industry and has been based on the notion that the final leg of reaching a customer is often the most costly and arduous to undertake. We might layout fiber optical cable underground along a neighborhood street, but then the real difficulty comes to extending it to reach each household on that block. Physically connecting to the customer premises becomes a logistically enormous problem and one that is not readily solved under reasonable cost and time constraints.

This same phenomenon is found throughout our daily lives. We can often get something 80% or 90% or even 99% done, and then get stuck at that final 20% or 10% or 1% at the end. Now, sometimes, that last piece is not necessarily overly essential and so whether you can get that final oomph or not might not be crucial. In other cases, the final aspect determines whether the entire effort was successful. Imagine flying troops to a foreign land, they rope down from a helicopter hovering over a bad guys domicile, they break down the door of the property, they rush into the place, but then the evil doer manages to escape out a hidden passageway. After all of that effort, after all that likely preparation, and yet in the "last mile" things went awry and so the entire mission is for not.

The word "mile" in this context is not to be taken literally as a distance indicator. Instead, it is to be considered a metaphor for whatever is the last bit of something that needs to be done. You are at work, you are putting together an important presentation for the head of the company. You slave away for days to put together the presentation. On the day of the presentation, you get dressed-up in your finest work clothes, and you rehearse the presentation over and over. Finally, the meeting time arrives, you go to the conference room to make your presentation. The company head is there, waiting impatiently to see and hear your presentation. You load-up your presentation and connect to the screen. But, it turns out, the screen won't work. You are stuck. You try to wave your hands in the air and pretend that the presentation is being shown, but that "last mile" undermined you. Hope this story didn't give you a nightmare.

Anyway, there is a "last mile" that we are facing in the self-driving cars realm. If not figured out, this last piece of the puzzle will prevent self-driving cars from achieving true self-driving car capabilities. Right now, self-driving cars are not true self-driving cars in the sense that we don't yet have a Level 5 self-driving car. We aren't going to ultimately have Level 5 self-driving cars if we don't solve the "last mile" aspects.

At the Cybernetics Self-Driving Car Institute, we are specifically focusing on the "last mile" of software needed to ultimately arrive at true self-driving cars. We are doing this by concentrating on the "edge problems" that few others are currently thinking about.

What is an "edge problem" you might ask? In computer science, we often carve up a problem into its core and then identify other portions that we claim to be at the edge of the problem. This is a classic divide-and-conquer approach to solving problems. You tackle what you believe to be the most essential aspect of the problem and delay dealing with the other parts. Often, this is done because the so-called edges of the problem are vexing. They are extremely difficult to solve and you don't want to postpone making progress by inadvertently trying to tackle the hardest part of the overall problem.

Indeed, today's self-driving car makers are primarily dealing with what most would perceive as the core of the driving task. This entails having a car be able to drive along a road. You can use relatively straightforward and at times simplistic methods to have a car drive down a road. For a highway, you have the sensors detect the lane markings of the highway. By finding those, you now have identified a lane into which you can have the car drive. There's a striped line the right of the car, and another striped line to the left of the car, both of which provide a kind of virtual rails like for a train into which you just need to keep the car confined. You next use the sensors to detect a car ahead of you. You then have your car follow that car that's ahead, and play a kind of pied piper game. As that car ahead speeds-up, you speed-up. If it slows down, you slow down.

Many novice human drivers such as teenagers who are learning to drive will use this same approach to driving. They watch what other cars do, and even if the teenager doesn't comprehend all the other aspects surrounding the driving task (road signs are overwhelming, watching for pedestrians is distracting, etc.), they can at least do the simplistic follow-the-leader tactic. You've probably noticed that most of the existing self-driving cars act in the same way. You as the human must first navigate the car into a situation that allows for this simplistic approach to be used. For example, you drive your car from your house onto the local freeway, and once you are safely on the freeway, you then engage the self-driving car capability. It is about the same as using cruise control, which we've had for many years. You as the human do the "hard" work of getting the car into a circumstance whereby the myopic piece of AI automation can then perform its task.

The amount of intelligence embodied in today's self-driving cars is quite shallow. Shallow is a way we use to describe whether an AI system is robust or whether it is brittle. A shallow AI system is only able to do a particular task, and once you start to go outside a rather confining scope, the AI system is no longer able to cope with the situation. Today's self-driving cars demand that a human driver be instantly ready to intervene for the AI of the self-driving car, once it gets itself at the bounds of what it can do. These bounds aren't impressive and so the human must be ready at all times to intervene. Only if you have a pristine driving situation is the AI able to proceed without human intervention.

Thus, if you are on a freeway or highway, and if it is a nice sunny day, and if the traffic is clearly apparent around you, and if the surface of the road is normal, and if there aren't any other kinds of nuances or extraordinary aspects, the self-driving car can kind of drive the car. Toss even the slightest exception into the mix, and the self-driving car is going to ask you as the human driver to intervene. This ability of the AI is good enough perhaps for a Level 2 or maybe a Level 3 self-driving car, but we aren't going to get readily to a safe Level 4 and certainly not at all to a true Level 5 if we continue down this path of assuming a straightforward driving environment.

I am not saying that we shouldn't be proud of what self-driving cars are now able to undertake. Pushing forward on self-driving car technology is essential toward making progress, even if done incrementally. As I have stated throughout this book, Google's approach of aiming for the Level 5 self-driving car has been laudable, and while we've seen Tesla aim at the lower levels of self-driving cars, we need someone coming along at the lower levels to gain acceptance for self-driving cars and spur momentum toward the Level 5. Google has concentrated on experiments, while Tesla has concentrated on day-to-day driving. Both approaches are crucial. We need the practical, everyday experience that the Tesla and other existing self-driving cars are providing, but we also need the moonshot approaches such as that of Google (though, as I've mentioned, Google too has now shifted toward the let's-get-something onto today's roads too).

I've been pressing continually about the various edge problems that confront the self-driving car marketplace. These edge problems are the "last mile" that will determine our ability to reach Level 4 and Level 5. Solving these edge problems also aids the Level 2 and Level 3 self-driving cars, but they are in a sense merely considered "handy" for Level 2 and Level 3 (helpful to improving the self-driving car at those levels), while they are a key necessity for Level 4 and Level 5.

Here's a brief indication of the AI software components that we are developing at the Cybernetics Self-Driving Car Institute, of which I'll reveal just those aspects that we have publicly described (there are other additional "stealth" related efforts underway too that I won't be mentioning herein; sorry, can't give out all of our secrets!):

Pedestrian behavior prediction

Today's self-driving cars are crudely able to detect that a pedestrian is standing in the middle of the street, and so the AI core then will try to come to stop or take an avoidance action to keep from running into the pedestrian. But, there is almost no capability today of trying to in-advance predict pedestrian behavior. If a pedestrian is on the sidewalk and running toward the street, this is essentially undetected today (it is not something that the AI system has been programmed to be concerned about). Only once the self-driving car and the pedestrian are in imminent danger of colliding, and in an obvious manner, does the AI core realize that something is amiss. Unfortunately, this lack of in-advance anticipation leads to circumstances whereby there is little viable way to safely deal with the pending accident. Our AI component, in contrast, can help predict that the pedestrian is going to enter into the street and potentially create an accident with dire consequences, and thus provide greater opportunity for the self-driving car to take avoidance actions. By solving this edge problem aspect, it will greatly improve self-driving cars at all levels of the SAE scale, it will reduce the chances of accidents involving pedestrians, and will be needed definitely to achieve the true Level 5. Besides predicting pedestrian behavior, we are also including the predictive behavior of actions by bicyclists and motorcyclists.

Roundabouts

It's admittedly not every day that you encounter a roundabout, also known as a traffic circle or a rotary. But, when you do encounter it, you need to know how to navigate it. Self-driving cars treat this as an edge problem, something that they aren't worried about right now as it is an exception rather than a common driving situation. We are developing AI software to plug into a self-driving car's core AI and provide a capability to properly and safely traverse a roundabout.

Conspicuity

When humans are driving a car, they use the car in conspicuous ways to try and warn other drivers and pedestrians. This includes using the headlights, the horn, various special maneuvers, etc. Self-driving car makers aren't yet incorporating these acts of conspicuousness into their AI, since it is not considered core to today's driving tasks. But, in order to achieve Level 4 and Level 5, these are edge problem aspects will be a differentiator for self-driving car makers.

Accident scene traversal

When a self-driving car today happens to come upon an accident scene, the AI hands over the driving of the car to the human driver since its core doesn't know what to do. This is because an accident scene has numerous driving exceptions that the AI is not yet able to cope with, it's an edge problem. Our software allows for the AI to invoke specialized routines that know what accident scene consists of and how to have the self-driving car can safely make its way through or around it.

Emergency vehicle awareness

As humans, we are aware that we need to be listening for sirens that indicate an emergency vehicle is near our car and we then need to pull over and let the emergency vehicle proceed. Or, maybe we see the flashing lights of the emergency vehicle and must make decisions about whether to speed-up or slow down, or take other evasive actions with our cars. This is not considered a core problem by the existing AI systems for self-driving cars, instead it's considered an exception or edge problem. We are developing AI software that provides this specialized capability.

Left turns advanced-capabilities

The left turn is notorious for being considered a dangerous act when driving a car. Though self-driving cars have a traditional left-turn capability at their core, whenever a particular thorny or difficult left-turn arises the self-driving car tends to hand the controls back to the human driver. These are considered edge problem left-turns. This is a risky gambit though to hand things over to the human, as the human driver is thrust into a dicey left-turn situation at the last moment, plus, this handing over of control to a human is not allowed at Level 5. We are developing AI software that handles these worst case scenario left-turns.

Self-driving in midst of human driven cars

Most of the self-driving cars today assume that other cars will be driven by humans that are willing to play nicely with the self-driving car. If a human decides to suddenly swerve toward the self-driving car, the simplistic core aspects don't know what to do, other than make pre-programmed radical maneuvers or hand the controls over to the human driver. We are developing AI software that comprehends the ways that human drivers drive and assumes that a true self-driving car has to know how to contend with human driving foibles.

Roadway debris reactions

Self-driving cars are able to use their sensors to detect roadway debris, but the AI core right now tends to not know what to do once the debris is detected. Deciding whether to try and roll over the debris or swerve to avoid it, this is considered currently an edge problem. Usually, the self-driving car just hands control to the human driver, but this can be a troubling moment for the human driver to react to, and also there isn't going to be a human driver available in Level 5. We are developing AI software that aids in detecting debris and providing self-driving car tactics to best deal with the debris.

Road sign interpretation

Self-driving cars are often not scanning for and interpreting road signs. They tend to rely upon their GPS to figure out aspects such as speed limits and the like, rather than searching for and interpreting road signs. This though is a crucial edge problem in that there are road signs that we encounter that are paramount to the driving task and cannot be found anywhere else other than as the car drives past the road sign. For example, when roadwork is being done and temporary road signs have been placed out to warn about the driving conditions. We are developing AI software that does this road sign detection and interpretation.

Human behavior assessment

Today's self-driving cars do not have at their AI core the ability to look at other humans and detect their motions and indications about the driving task. For example, suppose you come up to an intersection that the lights are out, and so a traffic officer is directing traffic. This is considered an edge problem by today's AI developers. If you are in a self-driving car and it encounters this situation, and even if it can figure out what is going on, it will just hand over control of driving to you. This can be dangerous as a hand-off issue, and also it is not allowed for a Level 5. We are developing software that can detect and interpret the actions of humans that are part of the ecosystem of the self-driving car.

As mentioned, these kinds of edge problems are seen by many of the existing car makers as not currently crucial to the AI core of the self-driving task. This makes sense if you are merely wanting to get a self-driving car to drive along a normal road in normal conditions, and if you assume that you will always have an attentive human driver ready to be handed the controls of the car. These baby steps of limited scope for the AI core toward a self-driving car are going to though backfire when we get more self-driving cars on the roadways, and the human drivers in those self-driving cars become less attentive and less aware of what is expected of them in the mix between the AI driving the car and their driving of the car.

Furthermore, solving these "edge problems" is essential if we are to achieve Level 5. By the way, these edge problems involve driving situations that we encounter every day, and are not some farfetched aspects. Sometimes, an edge problem in computer science is a circumstance that only happens once in a blue moon. Those kinds of infrequent edge problems can at times be delayed in solving, since we assume that there's a one in a million chance of ever encountering that particular problem.

For the edge problems I've identified here, any of these above driving situations can occur at any time, on any roadway, in any locale, and under normal driving conditions. These are not unusual or rare circumstances. They involve driving tasks that we take for granted. Novice drivers are at first not familiar with these situations and so over time tend to learn how to cope with them. We are using AI techniques along with machine learning to push self-driving cars up the learning curve and be able to properly handle these edge problems.

We are also exploring the more extraordinary circumstances, involving extraordinary driving conditions that only happen rarely, but first it makes most sense to focus on the everyday driving that we would want self-driving cars to be able to handle, regardless of their SAE level of proficiency. Some of the development team liken this notion to the ways in which we've seen Operating Systems evolve over time. A core Operating System such as Microsoft Windows at first didn't provide a capability to detect and deal with computer viruses, and so there were separate components that arose for that purpose. Gradually, those computer anti-virus capabilities were eventually incorporated into the core part of the Operating System.

We envision that our AI edge problem components will likewise be at first add-ons to the core of the AI self-driving car, and then, over time, the core will come to integrate these capabilities directly into the AI mainstay for the self-driving cars. We'll meanwhile be a step ahead, continually pushing at the boundaries and providing added new features that will improve self-driving car AI capabilities.

Sometimes, edge problems are also referred to as "wicked problems" and this is due to the aspect that they are very hard to solve and seemingly intractable. These are exactly the kinds of problems we enjoy solving at the Cybernetic Self-Driving Car Institute. By solving wicked problems, aka edge problems, we can ensure that self-driving cars are safer, more adept at the driving task, and will ultimately reach the vaunted true Level 5. We encourage you to do likewise and help us all solve these thorny edge problems of the self-driving car task. Drive safely out there.

CHAPTER 10

GRACEFUL DEGRADATION FOR FALTERING SELF-DRIVING CARS

CHAPTER 10

GRACEFUL DEGRADATION FOR FALTERING SELF-DRIVING CARS

My daughter was driving her car the other day on a steep incline and after she came to a stop at a red light, all of a sudden the car shut off. No warning. No sputtering sounds. The engine just died. Immediately, all of the dashboard warning lights came on. It was not possible to even discern which one might be a true indicator of the aliment because they were all illuminated at once. Of course, this was quite unsettling.

After a brief moment of being taken aback by the aspect that the car was no longer running, she took the car out of Drive, put it into Park, and attempted to restart the engine. She was anxious to have the restart work, especially since there were other cars behind her, and once the light went green it would be a mess if she wasn't able to move forward. She anticipated a cacophony of horns and angry yells to get out of the way. Unfortunately, the car didn't restart at first. She tried again. Still didn't start. She tried a third time, and luckily the engine started.

Upon calling me to let me know what had just happened, I recommended that she take the car right away to a nearby auto mechanic to have it inspected. She opted to drive around and see if it would repeat. It did not, and so it was shrugged off as a random fluke. In my experience, once a car exhibits any kind of failing, I become highly suspicious of the car. I've had car mechanics that would look for an anomaly once I brought them a car that had experienced an ill moment, and even if they found nothing amiss, I insisted they try again. I figure that if a car falters once, that's on the fault of the car, but if the same thing happens twice then it is on the fault of me. In essence, trick me once, okay, but I refuse to be tricked twice.

What does this have to do with self-driving cars?

At the Cybernetic Self-Driving Car Institute, we are developing AI that deals with how to handle a self-driving car that is experiencing some kind of malfunction.

For some auto makers, they talk about their self-driving cars as though they will never breakdown. I've heard politicians and other pundits say the same thing. Miraculously, self-driving cars are going to run flawlessly. Nothing will ever falter. They will be roadway machines of perfection. What a wonderful world it is going to be. Self-driving cars that drive themselves and never need to be fixed, never succumb to any machinery issues, they just keep on going, like the Energizer bunny.

What a crock!

Cars are cars. A self-driving car is still a mechanical device that is prone to having parts that wear out, parts that go bad, parts that might not have been defect free to start with, and so on. Self-driving cars will age. Aging cars have more breakdowns. Self-driving cars will need repairs. Self-driving cars will need replacement parts. It's a car. It is not a magical flying carpet.

We have to get our heads out of this Utopian world of self-driving cars that are going to save the planet and so therefore are pure and pristine. Sure, self-driving cars will do a lot of interesting, novel, and useful things. At the same time, they will have the same failings of non-self-driving cars. Tires that go flat. Transmissions that fall apart. Spark plugs that need to be replaced. Engines that need to be rebuilt.

In one sense, you could even make the case that self-driving cars are going to have more troubles and failings than non-self-driving cars. This is logical because a self-driving car is filled with all sorts of high-tech that a non-self-driving car does not need. Into a self-driving car there will be numerous cameras, numerous radar devices, numerous sonar devices, perhaps LIDAR devices, and so on. Guess what happens when you start piling more and more physical devices into something? You have more things that will wear out or break. And, consequently, more things that need to be repaired and replaced.

Furthermore, you need computer processors to run the systems and AI. You need computer memory and various electronic storage devices. These too are going to wear out or break. In some respects, the self-driving car is going to be a dream for car mechanics and car repair shops. After the newness of the self-driving car has occurred, and once they start getting some real mileage on them, we are going to see those self-driving cars head into the repair shop. The cost to repair and replace is going to be high. That's because you are going to be replacing and repairing not just the conventional parts of the car, but also having to replace the high-tech high priced components too.

In fact, if you look closely at many of the self-driving car designs, there is not much thought being placed around how you can readily remove, replace or repair the high-tech components. No one thinks about that right now. They are just trying to get self-driving cars onto the roadway. Who cares what it will take to fix them. Nobody does now. It won't be years until self-driving cars are pervasive, and anyway those first models will be bought by those that have the wealth to afford a shiny new self-driving car. For them, the repair costs won't be a big concern. All of this is not going to sink into the social consciousness until after self-driving cars are widespread and when mid-income to lower income owners are able to buy them.

Anyway, let's get back to the key notion here that self-driving cars are going to falter at some point during their driving career. It is undeniable.

What will a self-driving car do when part of it falters? You would hope that the self-driving car would anticipate that things will go awry.

Auto makers are not especially creating redundancy in the high-tech components (which would drive up costs of the car), and nor are they crafting the systems and AI to be able to cope with malfunctions. If a self-driving car is at the levels less than a 5, which means that it is a self-driving car that still relies upon a human driver, the auto makers assume that the human driver will just take over control of the self-driving car.

Though I have heartburn over that assumption, I'll for the moment skip past the problems of that way of thinking, and instead point out that a Level 5 car had better take into account malfunctions. A Level 5 self-driving car is a car that is driven by the AI and can do anything that a human driver can do. Thus, there is no need for a human driver in a Level 5 self-driving car.

Let's take the case of my daughter and her car that faltered while on a steep incline. If a Level 5 self-driving car were driving that car, and if the car engine had died while at a red light, we need to ask what would have happened next? Right now, the AI of most self-driving cars would maybe detect that the engine had quit. It would then likely do nothing other than alert the occupants of the self-driving car that the car has come to a halt. That's not very helpful, I'd say.

Our AI component for self-driving cars takes into account the myriad of ways that a self-driving car might falter, and then has ways to try and cope with it. For example, in the case of the car engine that suddenly died, the AI first tries to assess what happened, and also whether anything else is amiss on the car. My daughter tried to restart the car, but she probably would not have done so if say there was fire and smoke in the engine compartment. She would have realized that starting the engine would likely have been a bad idea in that circumstance.

Similarly, the AI needs to assess the contextual factors of the situation to try and ascertain what appropriate action to take.

We refer to the ability to deal with failings as form of coping with degradation of the functionality of the vehicle. It is our goal that the AI can achieve a graceful degradation, meaning that it tries to leverage whatever it can to keep the car going, if safe to do so, and tries to avoid aspects that get the self-driving car and the occupants into dire circumstances.

The AI has a set of scenarios about the permutations of limited functionality. There could be problems with the self-driving car that allow the car to still be driven. For example, a flat tire on a car with run-flat tires can still be driven. But, it is recommended that you drive below a certain speed, such as 55 miles per hour, and you try to limit driving to a more mild form of driving. The AI goes into a mode that befits the limited functionality presented by the car.

This also means that the AI has to be able to determine what is working on the car and what is not working. A good self-driving car design must include the ability to check the status of the components of the car. Fortunately, most modern cars already have such capability built into them for the conventional elements of the car. We need to also make sure that the added high-tech elements that are there for the self-driving car capabilities are also being crafted to have self-diagnostic capabilities.

Let's focus on the failing or degradation of the add-on high-tech elements for a self-driving car.

Suppose a camera at the front of the vehicle seems to be experiencing a malfunction. The AI needs to try and detect whether the camera is entirely unusable, or maybe it is partially usable. If partially usable, what aspects of the video or pictures captured are reliable and which are not?

It could be that the camera no longer has a wide view and can only provide a narrow view. If so, the AI needs to then ascertain what impact it has on the sensor fusion and the detecting of the real-world driving situation. Maybe the radar now becomes more prominent in trying to detect what is ahead, while the camera becomes secondary in importance.

Balancing the capability of one sensor against the other becomes crucial in these situations. The AI must be aware of which sensory device is providing what kind of insight about the driving situation. There is also the possibility that more than one sensory device at a time will falter. Suppose the front bumper of the self-driving car has struck something in the roadway. The right headlight is busted, the right sonar and radar devices placed near the bumper are no longer functioning, and the long-view camera there is now working only intermittently. The car is still drivable, but now the car is somewhat blinded to the roadway and the driving circumstances.

A human could still drive the car. But, with a Level 5 car, there is no provision presumably needed to allow for a human driver, since the car is supposed to be drivable entirely by the AI. Thus, the AI needs to be able to figure out how to deal with this situation. If driving on a freeway, the AI might update its action plan to safely and progressively drive the car off the freeway and onto side streets.

For failing aspects, there are typically two ways to deal with a failing component, either do a failing "open" assumption or make a failing "closed" assumption. A failing open assumption is that the system should allow for the item to be considered on, even if it is not well registering. For example, if in a building there is a power outage and the doors are being controlled electronically, but there's no power to open the doors, the building system might have as a default that it is better to allow the doors to be unlocked and open, rather than being locked and closed. In the case of say a bank vault, it is usually the opposite, such that if the power goes out, the bank would prefer that the vault doors are closed and cannot be opened.

The same is the case for the self-driving car. The AI has anticipated that under various scenarios there are some of the high-tech components that will be considered to fail and be placed in an open position, while others are to be placed into a closed position. It all depends on the nature of the component and what it does, along with what kind of redundancy and resiliency it has built into it.

Auto makers are right now playing a somewhat dangerous game about how they are designing their self-driving cars. Allow me to explain.

There is something called an Error Budget, well known amongst systems designers, which refers to the notion that there is a balance between the cost of building in reliability and resiliency into a system and the pace of innovation. Generally, the more you put into the reliability and resiliency, the more it tends to retard the pace of innovation. Since the impetus to get to a self-driving car is right now all about getting there first, the pace of innovation has the highest attention and drive.

Only once we have self-driving cars commonly on the road will the fact that the cost of reliability and resiliency was forgone will become apparent. One can only hope that the pace of innovation was not so frantic that the self-driving cars are useless when it comes to dealing with malfunctions. We also need to deal with the rather unsettling idea that the AI itself might malfunction. This is why our Lab has been developing AI self-awareness, trying to be able to detect and take action if the AI of the self-driving car has gone amiss. It can happen, and it will happen that the AI will go amiss, since the AI is being reshaped while the car is being driven (it is using machine learning and so continually changing).

Graceful degradation needs to apply to all facets of a self-driving car. This includes the conventional parts of the car, the high-tech components needed for a self-driving car, and the wizardry AI that is driving the self-driving car. Let's build graceful degradation into it now, and not wait until later on, once self-driving cars have faltered on the roadway and led themselves and their occupants into dire situations.

CHAPTER 11

GENETIC ALGORTHIMS FOR SELF-DRIVING CARS

CHAPTER 11

GENETIC ALGORTHIMS FOR SELF-DRIVING CARS

I was watching the National Geographic cable channel the other day and marveled at a type of leopard that could leap several feet into the air to catch a bird mid-flight.

The leopard at first had tried to get the bird while the bird was on the ground, but the bird was wise to the approaching leopard and opted to scurry into the air to get away. Seemed like the bird launching into the air would have been more than sufficient to escape the ground-based prowling leopard. But, the leopard had anticipated that the bird would try to fly away, and cleverly the leopard ran at an angle that coincided with the upward trajectory of the bird, and managed to leap several feet into the air to intersect with the bird as it was taking off.

A few more seconds and the bird would have reached a height that the leopard could not have achieved. Upon reflection of this leopard's behavior, you need to really admire the physics aspects of the leopard being able to calculate the proper angle, speed, timing, and direction when it made its leap, since it was able to precisely snatch the bird in mid-stride and bring it down to the ground. Score that as one win for the leopard family (another meal), one loss for the bird family.

How did the leopard know to make the leap? Did it go to college and learn it in school? Is there some kind of "leopard hunting" manual that the leopard had been reading? Those seem like unlikely explanations. A more plausible explanation would be that this type of leopard is the product of biological evolution. Over time, leopards that were able to ascertain how to best leap into the air to catch birds were presumably more likely to survive. Those leopards that were unable to add this tactic to their capabilities or that were not prone to it were less likely to get meals, and so they tended to starve off and not be around to reproduce. Leopards that inherited the ability to make these leaps were more likely to get meals, and more likely to survive, and thus more likely to reproduce. Eventually, leopards with this trait won out and become populous, while the leopards that did not have this trait lost out and became extinct.

There's a well-known name for this explanation. Darwinism. As we all know today, Charles Darwin proposed a theory of evolution, which was published in 1859 in his now classic book "On the Origin of Species," and for which his theory has gained widespread acceptance. His focus was on species of organisms and how natural selection leads to those that survive versus those that do not survive. In many ways, this theory was controversial when first proposed. Even today, there are some critics that don't completely buy into his theory. There are also ongoing debates about what his theory implies about the fundamental nature of mankind and creation. I'm not going to open that Pandora's box here.

I was reminded of Darwinism this morning while driving to work. A colleague was in my car and we were slogging through the dreadful bumper-to-bumper morning freeway traffic. We were both visually scanning the traffic scene for any opportunity to somehow get ahead in the traffic. Suddenly, a car that was in the carpool lane made a mad dash out of the carpool lane. It illegally crossed the double-yellow lines that mark-off the carpool lane (see my article about self-driving cars and illegal driving), and then this same pushy car cut through all four other lanes of traffic. The driver was evidently trying to make a freeway exit but had not planned well to get to it. Besides cutting across all lanes and causing cars to abruptly slam on their brakes, he also just barely made the off-ramp. He actually knocked over some cones at the off-ramp due to his wild maneuver and had been not able to get properly aligned to make the exit safely.

My colleague and I were stunned at the reckless and brazen act of the wanton driver. We both looked at each other and in the same moment said "Darwinism," which was our way of conveying that we figured that his kind would ultimately get crushed or killed in a car accident, and he would eventually be weeding his kind out of the population pool. Of course, we didn't actually believe this per se, it was more a figure of speech and bit of humor to lighten the stressful moment, but it highlights how much Darwin's theories have permeated our everyday efforts and thoughts.

There is a line of inquiry and study that has tried to use Darwin's theories for the development of mathematical algorithms development and for use in developing computer systems. This field of study is known as genetic algorithms. Basically, they are step-by-step procedures that try to use the same concepts that underlie the theory of evolution. Be aware that there are various competing ways in which these genetic algorithms work, and there is no one specific standard per se. Different researchers and computer scientists have opted to implement genetic algorithms in varying ways. Generally, the overall approach is the same, but if you decide to use a specific software package or write your own software code, keep in mind that your use of genetic algorithms might differ from someone else's use.

At the Cybernetic Self-Driving Car Institute, we have been using genetic algorithms in ways that help self-driving cars.

Genetic algorithms can be used for standalone purposes, they can be used by embedding them into the self-driving car AI capabilities, and they can be used in conjunction with neural networks and other machine learning mechanisms (see my article about machine learning and self-driving cars). In this article, I'll describe some ways in which we are using genetic algorithms for advancing self-driving cars.

Let's start my example of genetic algorithms by bringing up an ongoing friendly debate between me and my daughter. As driver, she likes to really put the peddle to the metal. Every time she drivers her car, it is like an Indy race that involves her going as fast as possible, cutting all corners, and clawing for any means to reduce her travel time and get to her destination the soonest possible. In contrast, I am the perhaps stereotypical fatherly driving driver, namely I stop fully at all stop signs, I don't gun the engine, I seek to get to my destination as soon as practical but with safety as a key factor in my approach. My daughter believes that my style of driving is archaic and over-the-hill, and furthermore that her style of driving is modern, realistic, and the only way to expeditiously get to any destination. All I can say is that the number of dings, scratches, and other bumps on her car are suggestive that her approach, though maybe indeed more expeditious, also has the potential for some really adverse consequences.

My team at the Cybernetics Self-Driving Institute has overheard (ad nauseam) the lighthearted debates that me and my daughter have about driving styles. Over and over, I claim that I can pretty much get to the same destination as she, with marginal difference in time expended, and yet in a much safer manner. She claims that my style would add a huge amount of time to any driving excursion. Who is right? Intuitively, I realize that it seems logical that she must be right in that certainly if you go as fast as possible you would reach your destination sooner than someone else. But, I claim that this intuitive notion is actually false when you include certain kinds of traffic conditions.

If there is heavy traffic on the roads, you are going to be bound by their progress. During my morning commute on the freeway, I see cars that try to go as fast as they can, but they get locked into the rest of traffic and so their attempts at going fast are blunted. Yes, they might accelerate very quickly in little pockets or gaps of traffic, but nonetheless the rest of traffic is still keeping them going at a measured pace. Speed-up, slow down, speed-up slow down, this is the outcome of a frantic speeder driving style in those traffic conditions. I assert that a more paced driver would be able to make the same amount of progress, and yet not be doing the useful speed-up's and slowdowns that the frantic driver is doing.

A means to characterize this debate is to consider it as an optimization problem. We want to optimize the time it takes to get to a destination X, doing so in heavy traffic conditions T, and use some set of driving techniques S, in order to ascertain which is the "best" solution. To make this a fair fight, we would want to keep the T approximately equivalent for any comparison of the set S. So, the set S of driving techniques might be a really good solution for light traffic conditions (a lite T), but then not be very good in heavy traffic conditions (a busy T). This is important in that my daughter's style might be a tremendous solution when driving on the open road for miles and miles, since there are no obstructions and therefore going fast is in fact going to be the soonest arrival. On the other hand, when freeway traffic is solid and you can't get going fast anyway, her solution might be equal to or maybe even worse than mine.

The team at the Cybernetics Self-Driving Car Institute decided to go ahead and use a genetic algorithm to test out the competing approaches to driving style. A genetic algorithm uses Darwinian aspects to try and solve an optimization problem. Besides trying to settle the debate that my daughter and I are having, it is useful for self-driving cars too, since the question rightfully arises as to what kind of style of driving a self-driving car should have.

Most of self-driving car makers are assuming that the AI of a self-driving car should always be the most legal and most slow-poke kind of driver. This is sufficient right now during the research and development stages of self-driving cars. Once self-driving cars are truly in the real-world, we are likely to see that human occupants will want their self-driving car to be more aggressive. Some human buyers of self-driving cars might even use as a criterion of which self-driving car to buy whether it is one that is the "old granny" style driving or whether it can accommodate the "race car" driver style. I have been saying that self-driving car makers need to provide multiple driving styles and allow the human to select which kind of ride they want. Right now, self-driving car makers are making it as "one style fits all" and we'll likely gradually see the marketplace want choices. That's why we are developing the multiple styles at our Cybernetics Self-Driving Car Lab, in anticipation of a gradual realization that it is what humans will want to have their self-driving car be able to do.

Let's get back to the genetic algorithm aspects. Typically, you start by creating a random initial population shaped around whatever structure you've decided upon. In this case, we defined that a driving style consists of these factors:

- Speed Style
- Lane Changing Style
- Braking Style
- Distances Style
- Risk Style

This small set of factors is sufficient for a rudimentary setup, and there are added factors in our more robust version.

For the Speed Style, we established that you can be a very "fast going" driver, or instead be a more measured driver. For the Lane Changing Style, we established that you can be a continually lane changing driver, or instead an infrequent lane changer. For Braking Style, we used whether you are a hard-braking driver that comes to abrupt stops and rides your brakes, or instead you are a driver that uses the brakes only when necessary. For the factor on Distances Style, we established that you are a driver that drives right up to the butt of another car, or instead one that allows for appropriate stopping distances between cars. For the Risk Style, we established that you are a high-risk driver that cuts things closely and takes significant chances of getting into a car accident, or instead you are lower risk driver that seeks to ensure safety as you drive.

Each of these factors is not a black-and-white scale per se, but instead more akin to a slider scale of being toward one end of the spectrum versus the other end. You don't have to be only a completely go-fast driver and nor only just a go-slow driver, you can be somewhere in-between.

The nature of the trip itself is a crucial aspect. Just as in Darwinism, the environment is what determines fitness. If the leopard was in an environment where there weren't any birds, it would be unlikely that the leopards that had a leaping capability would be a better fit over other leopards, and so that jumping trait would not be rewarded by being able to get more meals. For this self-driving car example, we opted to do my normal daily commute, which takes me anywhere from ninety minutes to two hours in very heavy morning freeway traffic conditions. We also have collected actual traffic data that indicates the patterns of cars that are in the morning traffic, such as how many cars there are, their driving behaviors, and so on.

Let's then suppose that we are trying to figure out that in this defined T, we will use a driving approach S that consists of the driving style of my daughter, and the goal is to minimize the time it takes to get the destination X where I work, and do so with the least number of accidents. It is important to include in the optimization that the least number of accidents is a factor, since without it you could potentially bump into other cars and opt to just proceed ahead, but this is not realistic and getting into accidents should be a penalty.

On any given single trip of making the commute, one driving style might turn out more optimal than the other, due to variances, and so we need to simulate the trip numerous times to gauge whether the driving style is overall optimal or not (see my article about simulations and self-driving cars). We ran this simulation for thousands of trips. This is equivalent to realizing that Darwinism tends to take many years of evolution to see changes appear, and it is not something that tends to happen in the near-term. We also opted to divide the driving into segments, and adjust the driving style at each segment.

Using my daughter's driving style, we created a population of drivers with her aggressiveness. We scored each member of the population based on their fitness score. This is considered the "current" population and is used to create the next generation. Essentially, these are the parents which will contribute their genes toward their children.

For the next generation of the population, there are three kinds of children as based on the current population:

- Elite children are those with the best fitness value from the current population and so are considered to survive to the next generation.

- Crossover children are created by crossing genes from two parents and producing a child with a mix of their characteristics.

- Mutation children are created by mutations or random changes made to a selected parent.

At each driving segment, we took what was the current population, in this case aggressive drivers like my daughter, and produced offspring of having a tendency toward aggressive driving (which becomes the next generation). Some of the offspring would be just like the current population (elites), some of the offspring were a mix of two parents from the current population (crossovers), and some of the offspring were different from the current population (having been mutated).

Using the leopard analogy, go back in time before there were leaping leopards. At first, let's assume leopards didn't particularly leap. For that "current" population, they reproduced to generate their next generation of leopards. We could just assume that all leopards produced as offspring are identical to the current population, and so the current population becomes the next generation, but that's not what happens according to Darwin.

Instead, though there are some offspring that are identical to a single parent (elites). But, there are also some offspring that are based on a combination from their parents (crossovers), which if you have had children you probably noticed in your own children that they seem to be a mixture of both the father and the mother in ways that makes them unique in comparison to their parents (in other words, the child exhibits some traits that the mother has but the father does not, and traits that the father has that the mother does not).

There is also the mutation aspect. Sometimes a child seems to have a trait that neither the mother and nor the father seem to have. Nature seems to introduce random variation that can presumably lead to offspring that will have a better chance at fitness, beyond what their parents had. In this case of the self-driving car, we allowed that the aggressive driver traits could be mutated, for example that the hard braking of an aggressive driver, which normally carries into the next generation or offspring, could have a random mutation that made it no longer a hard braking but maybe a softer braking.

After having setup the genetic algorithm for this, we ran it. You can run it based on how many times you want it to run, or there are other limits you can set, such as so-called "stalls" which is a measure of how far the next generation is from the current generation (if subsequent generations are not changing much, it probably suggests you can stop running the genetic algorithm). The runs can be allowed to go indefinitely and instead the focus be on the fitness test, in essence saying run this until the algorithm has reached a certain fitness point.

The results were fascinating.

In the end, in terms of greatest fitness and optimization, the aggressive style morphed towards a more moderate style. This appeared to support my contention that when faced with heavy traffic conditions over a somewhat lengthy path, the purist aggressiveness style does not in the long-run gain you much advantage and that instead a more moderate driving style is "better" for such conditions. My daughter isn't going to change her driving behavior because of this, and she genuinely enjoys her aggressive driving style, plus her style might well be better in shorter trips (we need to test this!), so the genetic algorithm effort that we did won't be impacting her.

We believe though that this kind of use of genetic algorithms is important for self-driving cars and how the AI proceeds.

Using genetic algorithms for self-driving cars is likely done outside the actual driving of the car. It is more akin to a design technique to assess differing ways to have the AI drive the car. Trying to use a genetic algorithm while in the midst of the AI driving a car is not only computationally intensive and expensive, it is questionable whether you would want to immediately put into play the outcome of the genetic algorithm without some other inspection of what it had produced.

Genetic algorithms can though potentially be used by sensor fusion for a self-driving car, which can be done beforehand (prior to embedding sensor fusion into the self-driving car), or could possibly done in real-time. This would allow you for example to determine LIDAR data in real-time or camera images and video streams.

One increasingly useful aspect for genetic algorithms has been to tune neural networks. When you setup a neural network, there are various parameters that you need to establish. How do we know what will be a good setting for those parameters? A means to figure that out involves using a genetic algorithm that runs many generations of those parameters and tries to identify via a fitness function which settings will be the "best" or optimal for the neural network.

Genetic algorithms are at the far edge of the self-driving car industry and not yet being especially utilized by the self-driving car makers. We will gradually see this algorithmic technique shift from being mainly research oriented and become more real-world used by the self-driving car makers. It is another tool in the toolkit for self-driving car makers. And, the more you want to push a self-driving car toward the level 5 (see my article about the Richter scale for self-driving cars), you'll need to bring to the forefront any advanced tool that can help make that leap to a true self-driving car.

.

CHAPTER 12

BLOCKCHAIN FOR

SELF-DRIVING CARS

CHAPTER 12

BLOCKCHAIN FOR SELF-DRIVING CARS

If you've heard anything at all about "blockchain" it probably would be the voluminous and breathless exclamations that it is a disruptive innovation that will change society and the world. It is one of the hottest emerging technologies and as is usually the case with something "new and hot" has garnered some fanatical fans.

Or, you might vaguely be aware that blockchain somehow relates to bitcoins. You are likely to have seen or heard that bitcoins are some kind of curious new currency that is available in the online realm. You might be unsure about bitcoins, whether they are trustworthy or not, and whether to maybe get yourself some bitcoins or let the whole thing shake out first.

Seems like blockchain and also bitcoins are in the midst of the unsettled, wild-wild-west of technology that maybe or maybe not will eventually calm down into something beyond those that are at the fringe of high-tech. Let's go through the fundamentals of what this is all about, and then take a serious look at what this has to do with self-driving cars.

At the Cybernetics Self-Driving Cars Institute, we are making use of blockchains for self-driving cars. We are exploring and proving out the mettle of blockchain.

We are not the only ones integrating blockchain and self-driving cars as there is interest on this topic by others in the self-driving car industry. Indeed, a recent announcement by the Toyota Research Institute (TRI) illustrates the intense interest in figuring out how to best exploit blockchains for self-driving cars. TRI announced that they are "exploring blockchain and distributed ledger technology (BC/DL) for use in the development of a new mobility ecosystem that could accelerate development of autonomous driving technology." Partnering up with MIT's Media Lab, TRI has also indicated they are working with several start-up's including BigChainDB, Oaken Innovation, CommuterZ, and Gem.

Let's start at the beginning. What is blockchain? What are bitcoins? I'll first explain what blockchain is. Then, we'll discuss bitcoins.

Simply stated, blockchain is a distributed database, meaning that it is just like a normal database that you are already used to except that it is setup to have lots of copies of the database that are floating around among many computers in a distributed manner. I might put my database on a hundred different computers around the world and ask them all to keep it handy in case I need to access it. This is convenient for me because it ensures that my database is redundant and so if somehow one of those computers loses it that I could go to another one that still has it and be able to get access to my database.

You might be wondering whether I am worried that my database which is distributed all around the world will be seen by others and they could read whatever is in my database. I would in fact be concerned about that. Thus, another aspect of blockchain is that the distributed database is encrypted. Using data security aspects, the database is encrypted and only with the proper keys can anyone actually read it.

Okay, so far, we are agreed that blockchain is a distributed database, in which my data is placed at perhaps hundreds or even thousands of computers all around the world. It has redundancy because of this. It also is encrypted so that only someone with the proper encryption keys can actually read it. You might next be wondering how could I make changes to the database, assuming that I wanted to say add some further data to the database. If I do so, how would I make sure that all hundreds or thousands of the copies of my database are equally updated. I don't want to end-up in a situation where some of those copies of my database are outdated and other copies are updated. This would certainly be confusing because then I wouldn't know which copy of the database is accurate.

The way in which changes to the database are handled involves the aspect that the database has already been subdivided into what are called blocks, essentially chunks of data. When I want to add more data to my database, I add another block to it. Suppose that my database already has five blocks of data, and those five blocks (considered collected together and intact as my current database) are distributed across hundreds or thousands of computers, and I decide that I want to add more data. I would place a new block into one copy of database and ask all the others that have a copy of my database to likewise add that new block to their copy. This request would promulgate across a wide network connecting those computers and one-by-one each of them that has a copy of my database would add the new block to it. This might seem like it would take a while to do, but in normal everyday aspects it can be relatively fast, depending upon the speeds of the computers and the speed of the network.

Voila, we now are to a juncture of this discussion to point out that this approach is called "blockchain" and this is due to the aspect that the database is composed of a series of blocks of data, and furthermore they are "chained" together. Let me explain the chaining aspect. For my database which now has six blocks, the newest block that I had just added has a link to the fifth block. The fifth block already has a link to the fourth block. The fourth block links to the third block, the third block links to the second block, and the second block links to the first block. All the blocks of the database have a link, of which, the link in the latest block links to the block that preceded it. They are like a chain, with each block being connected to each other in a linear, serial way.

Linking together the blocks is helpful to make sure that you can always find all the blocks of the database, though realize that you can only figure out the other blocks that preceded whichever block you are looking at. If I look at the sixth block, I can traverse all the way to the first block. But, if I am looking only at the third block, say, it links just to the second block and the first block. So, when I get ahold of a copy of my database, I would want to start with the latest block in order to walk back through all other blocks.

Each block usually has a timestamp that indicates the date and time when it was added to the database. It also has a special encryption-like "hash" code that helps to make sure that it is legitimately part of my database. The hash code for block six is based on the hash code of block five, and block five's hash code is based on block four, and so on. Here's why this is helpful. If someone decided to change block four of my database, they would end-up changing the hash code too (there are mathematical technical aspects of why this would occur). Any other computer that received this version of the database would be able to realize that someone has changed something in my database, which is not allowed to happen. Once a block has been accepted into a blockchain database, it must never be changed. It will stay the same.

As recap so far, blockchain is a distributed database, having lots of copies spread on computers potentially across the globe, and the database consists of blocks of data that are chained together from the latest to the earliest of the blocks. Furthermore, the blocks cannot be changed, you can only add new blocks to the database. When a new block is added to a copy of the database, it is linked to the topmost block to-date, plus it uses a special hash code that numerically uniquely identifies it and will essentially allow the "prevention" (detection) of later changes being made that could otherwise happen undetected.

I am sure you love arcane terminology, so let's include some here.

The computers that are willing to hang onto a copy of my database are often referred to as "nodes" (in a moment, when discussing bitcoins, the "nodes" are referred to as miners). My database grows in height when I add new blocks to it (we refer to the size of the database as its height, in a sense it grows taller as I add blocks to it). Due to cleverly using the hash encoding as an integral aspect of blockchain, the database is considered "immutable" because if anyone tampers with any of the blocks to try and change them then mathematically it can be ascertained that something is amiss and the copy of the database that someone messed with can be rejected as being an invalid copy. It is "auditable" because we can inspect the blocks links to ensure that it is all intact and essentially a single-source-of-truth and know how and when the blocks were added to the database. The way in which the computers communicate to each other about the distributed databases is done on a peer-to-peer (P2P) basis, meaning that one computer talks to another one, and they share back-and-forth what's going on with the databases.

Presumably, the blockchain approach provides for a database that is secure and private, since it is encrypted and requires permission to read it. The cryptographic techniques and the data partitioning into blocks allows me to selectively allow others to have visibility into the database. In near real-time the database can be updated, depending upon the speed of the network and the computers involved. Some would say that the blockchain then is a distributed database that is sustainable, secure, private, immutable, shared, and computationally trustworthy.

Blockchain then is an overarching approach to enacting a distributed database. It is not any specific technology per se, but instead an approach consisting of techniques and algorithms. Anyone that wants to put together a blockchain can do so. There is software that allows you to setup a blockchain. You could even write code to create your own blockchain.

There are public instances of blockchains, and there are private instances of blockchains. For a private blockchain, I might arrange with firms in say the insurance industry that want to share data with each other and then setup a blockchain that is just for them. Only they would have access to the network and computers that house the blockchain that they are using. For a public blockchain, the blockchain or distributed databases would be on publicly available computers, typically housed across the open Internet.

You can think of the blockchain as something that you would use to build an application for (hopefully) some useful purpose. Like I just mentioned, if a bunch of insurance companies wanted to share data with each other, I could create an "application" of blockchain that was just for them. In a sense, some people like to think of blockchain as the operating system or platform and then you build applications on top of it.

One of the most famous of all applications that uses blockchain is bitcoins.

Bitcoins are an instantiation of blockchain. This makes sense when you give it a moment to sink in. If you wanted to create a new currency, how would you do so? If you were to go the paper route and printed paper money, it would be pretty expensive to print up that paper money and make sure it was tamper proof. We've seen how hard the U.S. Treasury Department works to make sure our dollar bills are tamper proof, which otherwise we'd have lots of fraudulent money floating around. Well, if you wanted to make a new currency, you'd be nuts to try and make it paper-based since it is so expensive to print it and make sure it is tamper proof. Plus, getting that paper money physically to all parts of the world to be used as a global currency is going to tough to do and expensive to spread around.

Instead, in today's world, you'd make that new currency be all digital. It would simply be online and you would want some means to record the amounts and the transactions. You'd want it to be accessed anywhere in the world. You'd want it to be accessed pretty much instantaneously. You'd want it to be secure. Voila, which is the second time I've said voila in this piece, if you wanted to create a new currency you would want some kind of underlying platform or operating system upon which to build it that could do all these things. Answer: blockchain.

Bitcoins are an imaginary currency that exists by having people agree that this thing we agree to be a type of currency and that is recorded via blockchain is actually worth value of some kind. Blockchain becomes the means to record the bitcoin transactions. You give me some bitcoins, and someone else gives you some bitcoins, and this is all recorded into a database, allowing us to know who has what number of bitcoins. What powers bitcoins is the use of blockchain, which provides the foundation or platform for ensuring a distributed database of ledger transactions. The ledger is secure, distributed, immutable, etc., due to making use of blockchain underneath.

We'll add some more terminology to this. Bitcoins are considered a type of cryptocurrency. That's big speak for virtual money that is kept online and encrypted. Once bitcoin made a splash, others realized that they could also use blockchain and try to promote alternative made-up currencies. In essence, anyone, including you, can start your own online currency, if you wish to do so, merely by making use of blockchain. You could call it "LanceCoin" (I like the sound of that!), or ItsyBitsyCoin, or SuperCurrency, or whatever.

Now, that being said, you'd need to try and convince other people that your made-up currency is something that has value and that they should be willing to use it. Right now, bitcoin has the most momentum of the cryptocurrencies. It is kind of like Facebook, in that when Facebook first got rolling there were other competing social media apps like it, but it seemed to garner the most attraction and eventually steamrolled past its competitors. Bitcoin has that kind of momentum, but the jury is still out whether it will take hold, and/or whether something else might arise that knocks it from its high perch.

One aspect of blockchain that I didn't explicitly point out that you might have anyway realized is that there is no one master keeper of the database. Usually, we are used to have someone or something that keeps a master database and everyone else goes to that single master copy to know what's the latest data of the database. Blockchain is a technique that eliminates the need for a single master keeper of the database. We say that there isn't an "intermediary" needed to maintain the database. Instead, its maintenance is distributed and no one in particular owns it.

This is both the advantage and disadvantage facing a cryptocurrency such as bitcoin. Bitcoin touts that it is not controlled by anyone in particular. We know that U.S. dollars are controlled by the United States government, and that likewise most currencies are controlled by either a particular country or by a group of countries such as the EU. Bitcoin is not based on any particular country or group to back it. It is based solely on what many would say is self-interests. It is considered a mass collaboration.

If you believe that currency when backed by a particular country or group is a form of tyranny, you then really like bitcoins and cryptocurrency because it is freer, it is a democratization of currency, some suggest. For most people, the idea of a currency which is not backed by any particular country or group seems highly questionable and speculative. Thus, though bitcoin touts its freedoms aspects, this same aspect can be quite unnerving to others and so they are hesitant to make use of cryptocurrencies.

You can now award yourself a certificate of awareness of what blockchain is, and what bitcoin is. Congratulations! But, I realize that you started reading this due to wanting to know how blockchain applies to self-driving cars. I didn't forget, and just wanted to get you to a level playing field of what blockchain is all about.

One way in which blockchain applies to self-driving cars is regarding driving data. In my writings contained in this book, such as my indication of machine learning and self-driving cars, I mentioned that there is the potential of wanting to keep track of driving data that is recorded by self-driving cars. We will ultimately have presumably the roadways filled with self-driving cars, and those self-driving cars are chock full of sensors that record visual images and video via cameras, they can record distance data via radar sensors, LIDAR data and so on.

Some believe that the data of these self-driving cars should be shared so as to be able to analyze the data and improve the AI of self-driving cars. Imagine how massive that data would be. You could use machine learning to cull that data and try to improve self-driving cars ability to drive. But, this also raises privacy issues. Are you ok that your self-driving car is telling all about where you went, when you went there, etc.? Privacy proponents are very concerned that allowing the collection and sharing of the self-driving car sensor data will bring forth Big Brother.

A proposed solution would be to allow self-driving car data to go into a blockchain that then you could personally decide to whom you would allow your data to be used. Your data would be preserved in the blockchain, but not automatically readable. You could decide whom can access it. You might even get paid by someone to allow access, such as a self-driving car maker might pay you to let them access your driving data. Or, maybe companies that want to know patterns of consumers behavior as to where they go and when they go there, would pay you. Or, maybe Wal-Mart or other retailers might pay you, since they would want to know whether you drive near their stores and what they could then do to get you to stop at their stores.

I am asked why we can't already do this today. I point out that the main stoppage is that few cars have the sensors needed to collect the driving data, and also few cars have the Internet connectivity to transmit the data into a blockchain. Though, there are some cars that are already doing this in a smaller way. The car insurance company Progressive is known for their Snapshot tool, which plugs into the diagnostic port of your car, and then provides aspects of your driving data to them. This is a usage-based insurance (UBI) program, claiming to reward good drivers by knowing what kind of driving they do. When we have self-driving cars aplenty, those self-driving cars will have lots of sensors and lots of data, and will already be built with Internet connectivity, and so the data sharing aspects will be much easier and become a more popular topic of debate and discussion.

Speaking of car insurance, we don't yet know how car insurance will be handled in a world of self-driving cars, but anyway assuming there is some form of car insurance, you could use blockchain to do usage-based insurance, or even pay as you drive (PAYD) insurance. PAYD is where you pay for car insurance in increments of perhaps five minutes, and it is based on where you are driving (safe areas versus dangerous areas), when you are driving (daytime versus nighttime), etc. If your driving data of your self-driving car is being fed into a blockchain, it would be pretty easy to allow an insurance company to then offer you PAYD or UBI.

Another aspect of using blockchain for self-driving cars involves Shared Autonomous Vehicles (SAV). Right now, when you want to get a car akin to a taxi, you probably are using Uber or Lyft, or some similar ride sharing service. When we have self-driving cars, the question arises as to what you will do with your self-driving car while you are at work or asleep. Currently, your car sits and does nothing, somewhat like a horse in the barn waiting for you to want to go for a ride (some estimates indicate that you only use your car currently for perhaps 5-10% of the day!). Instead, suppose you put that horse to other uses, in other words you allowed your self-driving car to be used by others. You become your own version of Uber or Lyft.

Uber and Lyft are going to pitch to you that you should join into their online network so as to allow people that want rides to even know that your self-driving car is available for ride sharing. Of course, Uber or Lyft will take a cut of whatever you charge the persons that use your self-driving car. Facebook, meanwhile, figures why would you use Uber or Lyft for that purpose and instead you could just post onto Facebook that your car is available for ride sharing. It's going to be an ugly battle for eyeballs.

Some say forget entirely about Uber, Lyft, Facebook, and all those others, and instead use blockchain (this is really, really scary to the execs at Uber, Lyft, and any other ride sharing service!). A public blockchain could be crafted and it would allow for those that want to take rides to find out who is offering their self-driving car for rides. Guess what, no intermediary! No Uber needed, no Lyft needed, etc. No cutting them into the fees you are charging for the use of your self-driving car. With the touch of a button, you can add your car to a publicly available blockchain that represents fleets of cars all throughout the world.

Another use of blockchain for self-driving cars involves currency. You take your self-driving car to the car wash, and instead of paying via cash or credit card, instead you use an online currency like bitcoin or something else that has come along. You could do that today, but it is a hassle. Once we have self-driving cars, and with their Internet connectivity, it would be pretty easy for them to also do the online transactions that apply to your self-driving car. If you drive through a McDonald's or Taco Bell, your self-driving car could pay for the transaction, via a blockchain that those fast-food eateries have agreed to use. This scares the heck out of Visa, American Express, and all other credit card companies.

Is blockchain then the answer to all our problems? Is it the silver bullet? No. It is a type of distributed database that has properties that make it amenable for interesting societal and business aspects, and will gradually become further popularized as we continue to push toward a digital world, and especially so with self-driving cars because we are essentially going digital in many ways far beyond what our cars do today. Self-driving cars will be chock full of sensors, processors, and be online, all of which then means they are increasingly becoming digitalized and we ought to be considering ways in which we can leverage those digital-based capabilities.

We must also consider the underbelly of blockchain. The way it works now, data does not go away in a blockchain. It always exists. This has important privacy considerations and we aren't used to the idea that data about you is always around. For those using Facebook, and getting older, they are beginning to regret that they posted stuff onto Facebook when they were younger and for which now exists elsewhere because others might have grabbed it up at the time. We have generally been living in a society where data eventually decays, becomes lost to the ages. Can we handle an era of data that never goes away?

There is also the opportunity for exploitation and hacking of blockchain. It is all based on cryptographic techniques that we consider hard to crack. Maybe there are holes in those algorithms and we just don't yet know it. Maybe the software that enacts it has bugs in it. By the way, most of the encryption algorithms are based on the idea that you could crack it but that it isn't feasible given the tremendous mathematical and computational effort it would take to break it. As the availability of computer processing continues to escalate, and the cost of computations decreases, we might find ways to realistically crack these puzzles. Indeed, quantum computing offers orders of magnitude increases in speed of computations.

Blockchain is one of the latest and hottest buzzwords. There is no magic in it.

Think of it as souped-up cryptographic distributed database that we can use as a platform for creating useful applications. Besides useful applications like cryptocurrency, of which bitcoin is the most notable, we can use it for other kinds of public and also private applications. This can also be used for nefarious purposes, such as an international crime ring that wants to share their illicit efforts and do so via the Internet, right in front of everyone's eyes, which might seem like a wild idea, but with the right kind of approach they could potentially pull it off.

Anyway, for self-driving cars, there are lots of ways that the advent of digitalizing the car will play into using blockchain applications, such as online payments for services, getting on-the-spot car insurance, and for the possible sharing of driving data. Drive safe out there!

CHAPTER 13

MACHINE LEARNING
AND DATA
FOR SELF-DRIVING CARS

CHAPTER 13

MACHINE LEARNING AND DATA FOR SELF-DRIVING CARS

The crux of any machine learning approach involves data.

You need lots and lots of usable data to be able to "teach" a machine. One of the reasons that machine learning has progressed lately is due to the advent of Big Data, meaning tons of data that can be readily captured, stored, and processed. Why is there a necessity to have an abundance of data for purposes of doing machine learning? Let's use a simple but illustrative example to explain this. Imagine if you wanted to learn about birds and someone showed you only one individual picture of a bird (and furthermore, let's assume you had never seen any birds in your lifetime).

It might be difficult to generalize from one picture and discern the actual characteristics of a bird. If you saw perhaps 50 pictures you'd have a greater chance of discovering that birds have wings, they have beaks, etc. If you saw thousands and thousands of pictures of birds you'd be able to really begin to figure out their characteristics, and even be able to classify birds by aspects such as distinctive colors, distinctive wing shapes, and so on.

For self-driving cars, many of the self-driving car makers are utilizing machine learning to imbue their AI systems with an ability to drive a car. What kind of data are the developers using to "teach" the automation to drive a car? The developers are capturing huge amounts of data that arises while a car is being driven, collecting the data from a myriad of sensors on the car. These sensors include cameras that are capturing images and video, radar devices that capture radar signals, LIDAR devices that capture laser-based distance points data, and the like. All of this data can be fed into a massive dataset, and then crunched and processed by machine learning algorithms. Indeed, Tesla does this data collection over-the-air from their Tesla cars and can enhance their existing driving algorithms by examining the data and using it to learn new aspects about how their Autopilot software can improve as a driver of the car.

How much data are we talking about?

One estimate by Intel is the following:

- Radar data: 10 to 100 KB per second

- Camera data: 20 to 40 MB per second

- Sonar data: 10 to 100 KB per second

- GPS: 50 KB per second

- LIDAR: 10 to 70 MB per second

If you add all that up, you get about 4,000 GB per day of data, assuming that a car is being driven about 8 hours per day. As a basis for comparison, it is estimated that the average tech-savvy person uses only about 650 MB per day when you add-up all of the online social media, online video watching, online video chatting, and other such uses on a typical day.

The estimates of the data amounts being collected by self-driving cars varies somewhat by the various analysts and experts that are commenting about the data deluge. For example, it is said that Google Waymo's self-driving cars are generating about 1 GB every second while on the road, which makes it 60 GB per hour, and thus for 8 hours it would be about 480 GB. Based on how much time the average human driver drives a car annually, it would be around 2 petabytes of data per year if you used the Waymo suggested collection rate of data.

There's not much point about arguing how much data per se is being collected, and instead we need to focus on the simple and clear cut fact that it is a lot of data. A barrage of data. A torrent of data. And that's a good thing for this reason – the more data we have, the greater the chances of using it wisely for doing machine learning. Notice that I said we need to use the data wisely. If we just feed all this raw data into just anything that we call "machine learning" the results will not likely be very useful. Keep in mind that machine learning is not magic. It cannot miraculously turn data into supreme knowledge.

The data being fed into machine learning algorithms needs to be pre-processed in various fashions. The machine learning algorithms need to be setup to train on the datasets and adjust their internal parameters correspondingly to what is found. One of the dangers of most machine learning algorithms is that what they have "learned" becomes a hidden morass of internal mathematical aspects. We cannot dig into this and figure out why it knows what it knows. There is no particular logical explanation for what it deems to be "knowledge" about what it is doing.

This is one of the great divides between more conventional AI programming and the purists approach to machine learning. In conventional AI programming, the human developer has used some form of logic and explicit rules to setup the system. For machine learning, it is typically algorithms that merely mathematically adjust based on data patterns, but you cannot in some sense poke into it to find out "why" it believes something to be the case.

Let's take an example of making a right turn on red. One approach to programing a self-driving car would be to indicate that if it "sees" a red light and if it wants to make a right turn, it can come to a stop at the rightmost lane, verify that there isn't anyone in the pedestrian walkway, verify that there is no oncoming traffic to block the turn, and then can make the right turn. This is all a logical step-by-step approach. We can use the camera on the self-driving car to detect the red light, we can use the radar to detect if there are any pedestrians in the walkway, and we can use the LIDAR to detect if any cars are oncoming. The sensory devices generate their data, and the AI of the self-driving car fuses the data together, applies the rules it has been programmed with, and then makes the right turn accordingly.

Compare this approach to a machine learning approach. We could collect data involving cars that are making right turns at red lights. We feed that into a machine learning algorithm. It might ultimately identify that the red light is associated with the cars coming to a halt. It might ultimately identify that the cars only move forward to do the right turn when there aren't any pedestrians in the walkway, etc. This can be accomplished in a supervised manner, wherein the machine learning is guided toward these aspects, or in an unsupervised manner, meaning that it "discovers" these facets without direct guidance.

Similar to my comments earlier regarding learning about birds, the machine learning approach to learning about right turns on red would need an enormous amount of data to figure out the various complexities of the turn aspects. It might also figure out things that aren't related and yet believe that they are. Suppose that the data had a pattern that a right turn on red typically took place when there was a mailbox at the corner. It might therefore expect to detect a mailbox on a corner and only be willing to make the right turn when one is there, and otherwise refuse to make the right turn on red.

There would be no easy way to inspect the machine learning algorithm to ferret out what it assumed was the case for making the right turn on red. For example, in small-scale artificial neural network we can often inspect the weights and values to try and reverse engineer into what the "logic" might be, but for massive-sized neural networks this is not readily feasible. There are some innovative approaches emerging to try and do this, but by-and-large for large-scale settings it is pretty much a mystery. We cannot explain what it is doing, while in the approach of conventional AI programming we could do so (the rules of the road approach).

In spite of these limitations about machine learning, it has the great advantage that rather than trying to program everything in a conventional AI way, which takes specialized programmers hours and hours to do, and which might not even cover all various potentialities, the machine learning algorithm can pretty much run on its own. The machine learning algorithm can merely consume processing cycles and keep running until it seems to find useful patterns. It might also discover facets that weren't apparent to what the human developers might have known.

This is not to suggest that we must choose between using a machine learning approach versus a more conventional AI programming approach. It is not a one-size-fits all kind of circumstance. Complex systems such as self-driving cars consist of a mixture of both approaches. Some elements are based on machine learning, while other elements are based on conventional AI programming. They work hand-in-hand.

Suppose though that you are developing a self-driving car and you don't have sufficient data to turn loose a machine learning algorithm onto? This is one of the current issues being debated at times loudly in the halls of self-driving car makers and the industry.

If you believe that humanity deserves to have self-driving cars, you might then take the position that whomever has self-driving car data ought to make it available to others. For example, some believe that Tesla should make available its self-driving car data and allow other self-driving car makers to make use of it. Likewise, some believe that Google Waymo should share its self-driving car data. If Tesla and Google were to readily share their data, presumably all the other self-driving car makers could leverage it and be able to more readily make viable self-driving cars.

On the other hand, it seems a bit over-the-top to assert that private companies that have invested heavily into developing self-driving cars and that have amassed data at their own costs should have to suddenly turn it over to their competitors. Why should they provide a competitor with something that will allow the competitor to have avoided similar costs? Why should they be enabling their competitors to easily catch-up with them and not have to make similar investments? You can imagine that the self-driving car makers that have such precious data argue that this data is proprietary and not to be handed-out to whomever wants it.

There are some publicly available datasets of driving data, but they are relatively small and sparse. Some have argued that the government should be collecting and providing driving data, making it available to anyone that wants to have it. There are also more complicated questions too, such as what the data should consist of, and in what way would be it representative. In other words, if you have driving data of only driving on perhaps the roads in Palo Alto, does that provide sufficiently generalizable data that machine learning could achieve an appropriate driving ability in Boston or New York?

Most of this data so far is based on self-driving cars, which makes sense because those are the cars that have all the needed sensory devices to collect the data. Another approach involves taking a human-driven car, put the sensory devices onto it, and use that data to learn from. This certainly makes perhaps even more sense to do, in that why try to learn from a self-driving car which is already just a novice at driving, and instead try to learn from the maneuvers of a human driven car that presumably involves a savvy driver and savvy driving.

This is reminiscent of a famous story that occurred during World War II. When Allied bombers returned to their bases, the planes were studied to determine where the holes were. The thinking was that those holes are vulnerable places on the plane and should be armored heavily on future planes, hoping to ensure that those future planes would be able to sustain the aerial attacks better than the existing planes. A mathematician involved in the analysis had a different idea. He pointed out that the planes that didn't return were the ones that had been shot down. The holes on those planes would be the spots to be armored. This was thinking outside-the-box and makes perfectly good sense when you consider it.

The same can be said of collecting self-driving car data. Right now, we are obsessed with collecting the data from self-driving cars, but it might be more sensible to also collect the data from human driven cars. We could include not only well-driven human-driven cars, but also human drivers that are prone to accidents. In this manner, the machine learning algorithm could try to discern between proper driving and improper driving. The improper driving would help keep the self-driving car from falling into the trap of driving in the same ways that bad drivers drive.

For those that believe fervently that self-driving cars will change society and democratize the world, they are pushing toward trying to make all data about self-driving cars available to all comers. Will regulators agree and force companies to do so? Will companies want to voluntarily provide their data? Should this data be made available but perhaps at a fee that would compensate those companies that provide it? Will the data become a privacy issue if it provides a capability to drill into the data down to the actual driving of a particular car? When there are accidents involving self-driving cars, will this data be available for purposes of lawsuits?

We are just starting to see an awareness about the importance of data when it comes to self-driving cars. Up until now, the innovators trying to move forward on self-driving cars have been doing their own thing. As the self-driving car market matures, we're likely to see increased attention to the data and how and who should have the data. Machine learning algorithms hunger for data. Feeding them is essential to ongoing advances of self-driving cars. Society is going to bring pressures into this field of endeavor and I assure you that the question of whether the self-driving car data is proprietary or shared is going to one day become a highly visible and contentious topic. Right now, it's only known to those in the know. Be on the watch for this to break into the limelight, sooner rather than later.

CHAPTER 14
CYBER-HACKING OF
SELF-DRIVING CARS

CHAPTER 14

CYBER-HACKING OF SELF-DRIVING CARS

In a few years, you'll be enjoying a leisurely drive in your self-driving car. Without having to watch the road, you'll be sipping your brandy as a passenger in your own car and will leave the bothersome chore of driving to AI. Not a care in the world. Well, except for the fact that your self-driving car might be susceptible to cyber hacking.

Imagine if your car suddenly "decided" to veer off-course and took you into a blind alley where masked thugs were ready to drag you out of your vehicle and rob you (they not only directed the car to their location, they also forced it to unlock the doors and open them so they could more easily grab you). Or, suppose "just for fun" someone decided to convince your self-driving car to go straight off a cliff. None of these scenarios seems attractive, and yet they all are potentially possible. The key to preventing these calamities is to make sure that self-driving cars have topnotch airtight computer security.

I can't say for sure that self-driving cars will indeed have tough-as-nails computer security. Right now, the security side of self-driving cars is barely getting much attention. In an effort to get self-driving cars to actually be viable, most of the self-driving car makers are putting the bulk of their attention into the core fundamentals of making the car drive. Concerns about cyber hacking are way down on the list of priorities. Meanwhile, we daily are made aware of new hacks that enterprising researchers and others are finding with existing human driven cars.

165

The irony of sorts is that the more sophisticated that self-driving cars become, the greater the chance that a hack can produce catastrophic results.

Why? Simply because the more that the automation can do to control the car, the more readily a hack or hacker can force the car to do something untoward. If you are driving a classic 1920's Model T car, it is nearly impossible to hack it because there isn't any automation on it to be hacked. On the other hand, a fully autonomous Level-5 self-driving car has the potential to do whatever bidding a hack or hackers want to convey, since the AI is in complete control of the operation of the car. A hack can take over the steering, the braking, the acceleration, and even the internal temperature and air conditioning, the radio of the car, the door locks, and anything else that is connected into the controls of the vehicle.

I am guessing that you are wondering how a hacker or a hack could subvert the control of your self-driving car. When I refer to a hack, I am indicating that a malicious program or application has gotten into the controls of your self-driving car, while when I refer to a hacker it means that a human has been able to maliciously take over the control of your car. The human hacker might be standing on the sidewalk as your car goes past and they have a brief moment to access your car (based on a limited range of trying to electronically communicate with your car such as via Bluetooth), or maybe residing in the car next to you on the freeway. Or, the hacker could be hundreds of miles away and they are using the Internet to gain access into your self-driving car.

There are numerous ways to try and usurp the control of your self-driving car. These are the most promising methods: (a) Remote access via the Internet, (b) Remote access locally such as via Bluetooth, (c) Fooling the sensory devices of your self-driving car, (d) Planting a specialized physical device into your self-driving car, (e) Attaching a specialized physical device onto the exterior of your self-driving car, (f) Inserting a backdoor into the self-driving car via the maker of the car. Let's take a look at each of these methods.

I'll start with a recent news story that involved the placement of a physical device into a car, doing so by connecting to the On-Board Diagnostics (OBD) of the car. This was done on a relatively conventional modern car, and offers a real-world example of what can potentially be done to a self-driving car. The case involved a computer security firm that wanted to see if they could take control of a moving car and somehow subvert the car.

As background about today's cars and their technology, we all know that on our dashboards there are so-called "idiot lights" that illuminate to tell us when our gas tank is nearing empty or when the oil is getting low. You might have also heard a TV or radio ad placed by a car mechanic or car repair service that says they can ascertain the error conditions of your car by bringing it into their shop, wherein they can then connect to your car to read the diagnostic codes. Turns out that since 1996, all cars and light trucks sold in the United States must have an under-the-dash portal that allows for the reading of diagnostic codes. A car mechanic or repair shop can plug into that portal and see what error codes the car has experienced. This is handy for doing car repairs.

There are standards for these diagnostic codes. The Diagnostic Trouble Codes (DTC) standard dictates that the error code begins with a letter, namely P for Powertrain, B for Body, C for Chassis, and U for network, followed by a four-digit numeric code. You can easily look-up the code in a chart and then know what errors the car has experienced. Your dashboard pretty much works the same way. It reads the codes and then illuminates a particular icon such as gas getting low icon or a brake pads are worn icon. In some case, the car maker opted to just show a generic indicator such as "car needs service" rather than trying to display the specifics of the numerous possible codes.

There are many companies that now provide a device that you can purchase as a consumer and connect to the OBD portal. These devices, referred to as dongles, connect to the latest version of the OBD, known as OBD2 or OBD-II. Once you've connected the device to your under-the-dash ODB2 portal, the device will retrieve the error codes from your car, storing the codes similar to a USB memory stick would do, and you can then remove the dongle and plug it into your laptop USB port, allowing you to see a readout of the diagnostic codes. More costly dongles have an LED display that shows the error codes directly, thus bypassing the need to remove it and place it into your laptop.

Even more advanced dongles will allow you to communicate to the dongle via your smartphone. Using Bluetooth, the dongle will allow you to connect your smartphone to the dongle. You download an app provided by the company that provided the dongle. The app communicates with the dongle and tells you what it finds out from your car. So far, this is all innocent enough and certainly seems like a handy boon for those that want to know what their car knows.

Here's what the computer security firm recently did. The smartphone app communicates with the dongle and tries to make a secure connection so that no one else can intervene. Using a brute force technique, the computer security firm found the secret PIN and was able to connect to the dongle, via Bluetooth, and masquerade as though they were the person that had the proper smartphone app that was supposed to be able to communicate with the dongle.

Your first thought might be that it really doesn't seem like much of a hack since all that they can do is read the error codes of the car. Big deal, you say. Unfortunately, there is something about the OBD portal that you need to know. Not only can the ODB portal obtain info from the automation of the car, but it can also convey information into the automation of the car, including the potential to reprogram aspects of the car. Yikes! That's right, built into every car since 1996 as sold in the United States, there is a handy little way to sneak into the automation of your car.

This is known as "security breach through obscurity" meaning that most people have no idea that the OBD is a two-way street, so to speak, meaning that it can read and it also can write into the automation of the car. Only those within the car industry usually know that this is possible. Of course, any determined car hacker readily knows about this. Usually, there isn't an easy way to get direct access to the OBD portal in your car, since the hacker would need to break into your car to try and reach under-the-dash and connect to the portal. Voila, you have made it easy by connecting the dongle and making it available via remote Bluetooth. Your actions have handed the control of your car over to someone maliciously wanting to take over your car and do so from outside of your car.

In the case of the computer security researchers, they were able to inject malicious messages into the car. They had a human start the car and drive the car for a distance, and then suddenly told the car via their own smartphone app and into the dongle and through the OBD that the car engine should shut down. The car happily obliged. Imagine if you had been in the car. The car was zooming along and all of a sudden for no apparent reason the engine stops. This could have led to a car accident and possible deaths. For the computer security research firm, they did this as an exercise to show what is possible, and no one was actually harmed in the act of proving that this was possible. The company that makes the dongle, Bosch Drivelog Connector, quickly implemented a fix, and pointed out that the hacker would have needed to be within Bluetooth range to exploit this hole.

You might also think that you can avoid this kind of catastrophe by simply not installing a dongle onto your car's OBD. Let's move forward in time and think about this. Suppose you have a self-driving car. You might decide to let others use your self-driving car when you don't need to use it, acting kind of like your own version of Uber and trying to pick-up some extra dough by essentially renting out your car. The person using your car could put that dongle onto the OBD. Some say that you can just put tape over the portal and thus stop someone from using this exploit, or maybe putting some other locking mechanism there. Yes, these are possibilities, each with their own vulnerabilities, and we'll be seeing more about this once self-driving cars come to fruition.

Currently, some insurance companies offer incentives to human drivers to plug a dongle into their OBD. A car insurance company might offer discounted rates to human drivers that always stay within the speed limit and that don't do any harsh braking. People are willing to provide this info to the insurance companies in order to get a break on their car insurance premiums. Companies that have a fleet of cars or trucks also use these dongles, doing so to catch their drivers when they drive erratically, or sometimes do so to detect whether their drivers are taking side trips rather than driving directly to their destinations. The point is that the OBD and the dongles are here and now, and unlikely to be stricken from modern cars. We are going to have them on self-driving cars, for sure.

Modern cars have a Controller Area Network (CAN) which is a small network within the car, allowing the various electronic devices to communicate with each other. There are Engine Control Units (ECU's) used for the various components of the car, such as for steering, for the braking, for the accelerator, for the engine, and so on. The ECU's communicate via the CAN. Via the ODB, you can get into the middle of the messages going back-and-forth on this CAN network. Think of it like your WiFi at home, and suppose that someone else jumped onto your WiFi. They could read the messages of your home mobile devices and laptops. They could also take control of your home printer, and your home lights or other Internet of Things devices that are connected into your WiFi.

As mentioned, putting something inside your car to take control is just one of many ways to maliciously subvert the automation of your car. Another method involves fooling the sensors on your car.

In a famous example demonstrated in 2016, researchers were able to fool the Tesla autopilot sensors by using off-the-shelf emitting devices that sent either visual images, sounds, or radio waves to a Tesla car. The Tesla could be drenched in sensory overload that would prevent the self-driving features of the car from being able to discern what is going on. This is a jammer. Or, it could make the sensors believe an object was in front of the car, such as another car, when there wasn't another car there at all. This is a ghost maker. Admittedly, all of these tests were done in a very constrained environment without the car actually moving along the road, and so one can criticize the tests as being overly academic. Nonetheless, it shows the kind of potential that a malicious hacker could try.

A few years ago, there was the case of security researchers that remotely took control of a Jeep Cherokee while it was on-the-road. They did this via an Internet connection into the car. They were able to remotely turn the steering wheel for the Jeep Cherokee as though it was trying to park the car, even though it was zooming ahead at 80 miles per hour. In another test with a different brand of car, they were able to convince a Toyota Prius's collision avoidance system to suddenly apply its brakes, causing it to come to an undesired rapid stop. In each case, they were able to exploit the automation of the car. The more the automation can do, the more they could take over control of the car. Remember that self-driving cars will be chock full of automation and everything on the car will be controlled by automation.

Some worry that the increasing use of advanced entertainment systems in cars is opening an additional can of worms too. The more that your car can do with the Internet, the more chances that a malicious hacker can get electronically into your car. Consumers are clamoring that they want their cars to have WiFi. Consumers want their cars to allow them to cruise the Internet, while cruising on the open highway. Cars are becoming viable targets for Internet attacks, doing so at the urging in a sense of consumers that want their cars to be Internet enabled.

Should we become luddites and insist that no more automation should be allowed into our cars? Should we refuse to ride in self-driving cars? I don't think these are especially viable options. Automation is coming. Self-driving cars are coming. The tide is rising and nothing is going to stop it. That being said, the moment that we being to see real-world instances of self-driving cars that are taken over by hackers, you can bet that's when there will be a hue and cry about cyber security for our cars.

To-date, we've not had any big moments of cars getting hacked and something terrible occurring. It is like earthquakes. Until a massive earthquake happens, we are not thinking about earthquake preparedness. I say that we need to be thinking more seriously about computer security for our cars, now. Especially for self-driving cars as they will be the most vulnerable to allowing malicious control to wreak havoc. We need to yell loudly and implore the self-driving car makers to elevate the importance of computer security.

We also need the AI of the self-driving cars to realize when something malicious is taking place. The AI can be watching over the car and trying to not only control the car, but also trying to detect when something is amiss. The AI though is also a two-way street, since we will soon have hackers that try to trick the AI into doing something malicious. It's going to be a cat-and-mouse game. And involve life-and-death consequences. Block the hackers. Sell the self-driving cars.

CHAPTER 15

SENSOR FAILURES IN

SELF-DRIVING CARS

CHAPTER 15
SENSOR FAILURES
IN SELF-DRIVING CARS

I was in a hurry the other day and jumped into my car to try and rocket across town for an important appointment. When I started the engine, suddenly my "idiot lights" dashboard lit up and indicated that I had a low tire pressure. I've seen this before and from time-to-time have had a tire that was a few pounds low after having driven up to the Bay Area from Los Angeles. In this case, I was taken aback because the dashboard indicated that all four tires were at low pressure. My first thought was that this was impossible. How could all four tires be low at the same moment in time? Then, after a fleeting thought that maybe someone slashed all four tires, I got out of the car to take a look at them. They appeared to be intact. I luckily had a tire gauge in my car and used it to measure the amount of air in the tires. Seemed like they were properly inflated.

I opted to turn off the engine and start the car again. The four tires still showed as though they were at low pressure. This was becoming irritating and frustrating, and of course was taking place just when I was in a hurry to get someplace. Murphy's law strikes! I decided that since the tires are run-flat tires that allow you to drive when they go flat, I would go ahead and slowly ease out of the parking lot and see what happens. I proceeded like a timid driver and made my way inches at a time toward the opening to the street. One by one, the low tire pressure sensor dashboard lights went out, suggesting that I was now OK with my tires.

I am sure we have all had circumstances whereby a sensor in the car goes bad or sometimes is momentarily faulty. We expect this aspect of any kind of mechanical device on our cars. Our headlights sometimes fail and need to be replaced. Our brakes get worn after a while and the brake pads need to be replaced. No car is perfect. No car is maintenance free. For some people, they are "lucky" and seem to never have anything go wrong on their car. Other people get a "lemon" of a car that seems to be unlucky and always has something going wrong. We generally expect that an older car is going to have more problems and maintenance. We generally assume that a cheaper car is going to have more problems and more maintenance than an expensive car. We also expect that an expensive car will likely have expensive maintenance whenever maintenance is required. These are the laws of nature about sensors and devices on our cars that can falter or fail.

What about self-driving cars? You don't hear much about sensors going bad on self-driving cars. But, that's for a very apparent reason. Self-driving cars right now are like well-cared-for high-end Nascar racing cars. Teams of engineers fret about any little blip or blemish on their precious self-driving cars. The sensors on these prototype cars are costly and kept in really good shape. If a sensor happens to become faulty or go bad, an engineer quickly removes the offending item and replaces it with a brand new one. Realizing that the self-driving car makers are spending millions upon millions of dollars to develop and perfect self-driving cars, you can bet that any sensor that goes bad is going to instantly get kicked out and replaced by a shiny new one.

This makes sense when you are trying to develop something new and exciting. Think though about what will happen once self-driving cars are actually on-the-roads and doing their thing each and every day. Eventually, we are going to have everyday self-driving cars that are going to be subject to the same vagaries as our everyday cars today. The brakes are going to wear out, the headlight beams will go out, and the specialized sensors such as the cameras, the LIDAR, and the radar sensors will all ultimately have some kind of failure over their lifetimes. In fact, you could predict that the faults and issues of sensors is going to be even more heightened on self-driving cars because they are chock full of those sensors. There might be a dozen cameras, another dozen radar sensors, one or two LIDAR systems, and so on.

Welcome to a new world of sensor mania in the realm of self-driving cars. For those that make replacement car parts and do automotive maintenance, this actually could be a blessing in disguise. Imagine hundreds of millions of cars with then tens of hundreds of millions of sensors, all of which will be statistically failing at one time or another. Bonanza! The odds are too that these sensors at first won't be easily attached or embedded into the car in some simple fashion. More than likely, trying to replace these sensors is going to require doing all sorts of surgery on the car to get them out and replaced. Furthermore, once you remove and replace the sensor, the amount of testing to make sure that the new sensor is working properly will take added labor time. Those dollars are racking up.

Nobody wants to utter these aspects when discussing self-driving cars. Instead, we are told to think about a utopia of these self-driving cars whisking us all around town and the humans don't have a care in the world. Have you ever seen a bus that is parked on the side of the road because it had a failure of some kind? Ever been on a subway that slowed down or stopped because of some kind of systems problem or failure? Mass transit systems have these kinds of faults and failures all the time. Our autonomous AI-led self-driving cars are just as susceptible to breakdowns, and as mentioned even more so due to the plethora of gadgets and gizmos that enable the car to do its self-driving.

Besides the obviousness of the hardware sensors, we must also consider that these upcoming self-driving cars are going to have boatloads of computer processors on-board, which is what makes the AI aspects possible. Memory in those chips can go bad, the processors themselves can wear out or bust, and other various hardware maladies can occur. So far, I've only emphasized the hardware, but we need to think about the software too.

Suppose there is a hidden bug in the self-driving car software. Some self-driving car makers also are interconnecting their self-driving cars by using the Internet, including so-called over-the-air software updates. The hardware that allows these interconnections can go bad, plus the software updates pushed into the self-driving car can get pushed incorrectly or get load improperly.

I hope this doesn't burst that self-driving car utopia that some are dreaming about. Realistically, we need to anticipate that stuff will go wrong and stuff will break. Right now, few of the self-driving car makers are developing their systems with sufficient redundancy and back-up capabilities. They are so focused on getting a self-driving car to simply drive a car, they figure that once they've got things perfected that then they can go back and look at the resiliency aspects. I understand their logic, but at the same time, trying to bolt onto a system an added layer of redundancy is better done at the start, rather than trying to kludge it later on.

If a camera on the front right bumper goes bad, the AI should detect it. Images might be blurred or otherwise no longer interpretable. The AI needs to then consider what else to do. Assuming that there is a camera up on the hood on the right side, this camera now might need to be considered a "primary" for purposes of detecting things in front of the car on the right side since the camera on the right side bumper is considered out-of-commission. The radar and LIDAR to the right might now become more vital, making up for the failed camera on the front right bumper. For any instance of a sensor that goes bad, the AI needs to assess what else on the self-driving car can potentially make-up for the loss. It is like having someone poke you in one eye, and then you need to become dependent upon the other eye. You might also adjust how you walk and move, since you know that you cannot see out of the eye on that side of your body. The self-driving car might need to do the same, hampering certain kinds of maneuvers that the car would usually make, or even ruling out some maneuvers. Maybe the self-driving car opts to only make left turns and not make any right turns, until the sensor can be replaced.

Consider the circumstances of when a sensor might go bad. If the car is in motion, the nature of the failed sensor could lead directly to a severe result. If you are moving at 80 miles per hour and the LIDAR is your only means of seeing ahead, and if the LIDAR suddenly drops dead, you've now got a speeding missile that in a few seconds could ram into something. I realize that for the levels of self-driving cars that require a human driver be ready to take over that you might argue that the human needs to grab the controls in this instance, but as I have repeatedly exhorted this aspect of dropping the control of the car into the lap of a human driver is fraught with great peril (they won't have time to decide what to do, and even if they decide they still need to take physical control).

And, what about the utopia of the level 5 true self-driving car that has presumably no controls at all for the humans to drive the car? What happens when an essential sensor goes bad and there is no provision for the human to drive, even if they or the AI wanted them to do so? This is more than a scary movie, this is real-life that we are heading towards. Level 5 self-driving cars that once a crucial sensor goes bad will potentially enable a multi-ton vehicle to become a grim reaper itching to kill something or somebody, it's a scary plot for sure.

Suppose the self-driving car is stationary and a crucial sensor goes bad. This might be okay in some cases, assuming that the self-driving car is parked and out of the way of traffic. If instead the self-driving car has come to a halt at a red light, and the sensor suddenly fails, now you have a car blocking traffic. Other traffic might be kind and gently steer around the stopped self-driving car. Or, you might have some other car that drives up and doesn't notice the stopped self-driving car, and rams into it, harming the occupants.

You might also have the case similar to my low tire pressure story, in which you start the self-driving car engine, it runs through internal diagnostics to make sure the sensors are good, and then maybe discovers a key sensor that has gone bad. If you are in a self-driving car that is below a level 5, you presumably could decide to disengage the capability that involves the sensor and then drive the car yourself.

This also brings up a larger question about the features of a self-driving car, namely, how much should the human driver be allowed to override or turn-off a self-driving car feature? We are used to being able to decide whether to engage cruise control, and we can readily disengage cruise control whenever we want. Should the same be said of the other more advanced capabilities that will be in our self-driving cars? This is an open question and we are seeing some self-driving car makers ignore the issue, while others are deciding a priori whether to allow this or not (we'll likely be seeing regulation on this).

In this discussion, I've pretended that the self-driving car can actually detect that a sensor has gone bad. But, suppose that a sensor is still functioning, but only intermittently? My low tire pressure story is similar to this intermittent aspect in that the sensors seemed to reboot themselves, though it could readily have reoccurred. The AI needs to be able to ascertain not only if a sensor is failed entirely, but also whether it might be buggy and so then take appropriate action. The AI might try to reboot the particular sensor, or might opt to only collect data when the sensor seems to be functioning correctly.

More insidious is the sensor that does not appear to be faulty and yet really is faulty. Suppose the AI is getting streams of data from the LIDAR and so as far as the AI knows it is working properly. Imagine that every two seconds the LIDAR is integrating noise data into the stream, caused by an anomaly. The images being constructed by the AI might not realize that this bogus data is being slipped into the processing. Sensor fusion takes place and the "bad data" gets mixed into the rest of the data. Ghost images or fake images might be appearing. This might lead the AI to take action such as avoiding an obstacle that is not present. The act of avoiding the obstacle might involve doing a radical maneuver that endangers the occupants of the self-driving car. All of this perhaps being caused by a faulty sensor that was not so obviously faulty that it could easily be detected (there is also the instance of a sensor that has been hacked.

It is time to put serious attention into the redundancy and resiliency of self-driving cars. In my opinion, even a true level 5 self-driving car that does not have redundancy and resiliency is a cheap-trick level 5 car. In one sense, it is a car entirely driven by automation, but it is also a potential death trap waiting to harm or kill humans because it is not prepared to handle internal failings of the car itself. A dashboard display that tells you that something has gone awry is not going to be sufficient when us humans are so dependent upon the AI and the self-driving car to drive the car.

Anyway, the silver lining is that there will be a boon in the marketplace for replacing all those bad sensors once they fail, and a spike in skilled labor that can do the replacements will arise shortly after self-driving cars are sold widely. The you-will-be-out-of-a-job car mechanic of the future should not be overly worried that self-driving cars will put them out of business. Instead, with self-driving cars crammed full of specialized equipment, which will surely falter and fail over time, the job prospects for those mechanics is looking pretty good. Time to get my car mechanics license.

CHAPTER 16

WHEN ACCIDENTS HAPPEN TO SELF-DRIVING CARS

CHAPTER 16

WHEN ACCIDENTS HAPPEN TO SELF-DRIVING CARS

Sinkholes.

We recently had a major sinkhole that opened up in the middle of a busy street here in Southern California, and it swallowed whole the two cars that happened to unluckily be driving along the street at that time. Imagine being able to tell your friends that your car fell into a sinkhole. Your car didn't hit a pothole, it didn't sideswipe a telephone pole, it didn't get hit by lightning, instead it fell into a sinkhole. That's some great bragging rights.

One of the cars that had fallen into the sinkhole had only sank a brief distance and was caught on top of the first car that fell into the hole. The back portion of this second car protruded out of the sinkhole, raising up a few feet above street level. The woman driver in the car was able to get out, partially aided by the fire department which had shown up to rescue the people in both vehicles. She was slightly injured, but otherwise Okay from the ordeal. I suspect though that she is going to be envisioning the street opening up whenever she drives around town from now on. Anyway, her car was still in gear when she managed to extradite herself from the vehicle. On the newscast of the event, the rear tires of the car were shown spinning vigorously as the vehicle thought it was still trying to drive along the street. This actually made for a dangerous situation since no one knew what the now abandoned car might do next. Gradually, it lurched forward and sank deeper into the sinkhole and eventually stopped running.

Why my fascination with cars that got swallowed by the earth? The one car that had kept running is an example of what a car might do when in an accident. In other words, some car accidents involve a car crash that causes the car to stop functioning. Other accidents might involve a car that still has the engine running, which can create a grave hazard for everyone near the scene of the accident. It has been the case that some cars in a car crash have suddenly moved forward or backward, endangering the driver, passengers, and rescuers. There is also a heightened chance of a fire or maybe even an explosion, since the car is engaged and there is fuel flowing to the engine, along with likely sparks and hot pieces of metal around the accident scene. All in all, a car accident and the surrounding scene can be a very dangerous place.

Let's consider what will happen when self-driving cars are involved in an accident. Now, some of the ardent proponents of self-driving cars will immediately counter that there is no such thing as a self-driving car getting into accident. They are of the camp that believes that self-driving cars will be an idealized world wherein no cars will ever get into accidents again. This is plain hogwash. I have repeatedly stated there are falsehoods about zero fatalities related to self-driving cars and that there will still be car accidents, in spite of whatever wondrous AI we see embodied into self-driving cars. There are going to be a mix of human driven cars and self-driving cars for quite a while, and the two are bound to tango with each other. There are also lots of other opportunities for self-driving cars to get into accidents, including if the self-driving car has a severe hardware failure within itself, and also if the AI of the self-driving car encounters a bug in the software, and so on.

Assume for now that it is quite possible and actually very probable that self-driving cars will get into accidents. So what, you ask? The issue is that if the AI system of the self-driving car is still active, what will it do? For a human driver in a car accident, the human usually opts to stop trying to drive the car. They typically will try to get out of the damaged car and step away from the mechanical beast. This is not always the case, and of course if the car accident is minor, the human driver might decide to drive off from the scene. We also know about circumstances of hit-and-run, wherein the human driver hits someone or something, and tries to scoot away without anyone else knowing what happened.

An AI-based self-driving car will need to be self-aware enough to know that the car has gotten into an accident. Humans know this pretty quickly by having felt the blow of the accident, they can see the crushed metal and blood, they are physically hurt or restrained, they can smell burnt metal or spilled gasoline, and so on. There are lots of physical sensory clues for humans. A disembodied AI computer-based system won't necessarily be able to gauge these same physical clues. Sure, the car will likely have come to a sudden halt, which is a clue that something is amiss. The cameras on the car might have seen the accident and the AI system can interpret the images captured accordingly. We could have other sensors in the car such as impact sensors and other devices that realize the car has gotten itself into trouble.

The key is then whether the AI system of the self-driving car knows what to do, once it detects that a car accident has indeed happened. The AI system might continue to try driving the car, pushing on the accelerator, even though the car no longer can or should be driving. It is like the example I gave before of the car that fell into the sinkhole and the tires continued to spin. That was a "dumb" car that did not have any AI smarts. AI developers for self-driving cars need to make sure that the system can detect that an accident has happened, and then take appropriate actions based on the accident. This might include applying the brakes, turning off the engine, and taking other safety precautions.

Will though the AI self-driving car still be able to process information and take actions? Remember that once the accident has occurred, all bets are off as to what parts of the car are still functioning. Maybe the AI system no longer has access to any of the controls of the car. Or, maybe the AI system itself is being powered by the car, but now the car is no longer running and the battery was ejected from the car during the accident. No power, no AI. All of these variations mean that we don't know for sure that the self-driving car will be in a shape needed to take the appropriate safety precautions.

It is also possible that part of the AI system itself is damaged during the accident. Some sensors might be entirely offline. Some sensors might be working, but are noisy and incomplete. Some sensors might be "working" but providing incorrect data because they are no longer functioning as intended. Imagine if a sensor that detects the motion of the car is damaged in such a manner that it falsely reports that the car is still driving forward. The AI, if functioning, might be misled into trying to command the controls of the car in an untoward manner. Any passengers or rescuers could be put into danger because of these facets.

Some believe that fire departments and police should have an electronic backdoor into the AI system of the car, so that upon coming upon a self-driving car accident scene, the humans can communicate directly with the AI system. They can use this communication link to instruct the self-driving car to do things, such as turn off the engine of the car. They can use the link to find out what happened in the car accident. The AI might also know how many passengers there are in the car. This could help the rescue efforts, since the responders would know how many people to be rescued. For many important reasons, this backdoor electronic communication makes a lot of sense.

As with any of these aspects, there are downsides to an electronic backdoor. Will only the proper officials use the backdoor, or could a nefarious hacker use it to take over the controls of your car? Even if the backdoor is there, maybe the AI system is so damaged that any information it provides is incorrect or misleading. One might also wonder about the privacy aspects of this electronic backdoor too. Will humans be comfortable that anything the AI system has recorded could now so easily be scanned by someone else, doing so without a legal search warrant?

Self-driving car makers are considering having the same kind of black boxes in their self-driving cars as are found in modern airplanes. This black-box hardened casing of crucial systems would not only record information, but also try to protect the AI system so that it could continue to function in an accident. This might not be the entire AI system, and perhaps just a core portion that can do fundamental activities and no more.

There are also advanced efforts to make AI systems more resilient so that if only part of the AI system is still functioning, the other parts recognize as such, and then adjust accordingly. For example, suppose the AI system portion that provides the steering and mapping gets damaged, other parts of the AI system can either try to operate those aspects as a secondary back-up, or take into account that those functions are no longer working and avoid anything that requires those functions. This adds a lot of complexity to the AI system, but given that the self-driving car involves the life-and-death matters of humans, having sufficient complexity to protect humans is worth the added effort.

The AI system can even have a component devoted to saving humans when the car gets into a crash. Suppose the AI system is able to release the seat belts, automatically, when it so chooses to do so. Once a car crash has occurred, passengers might be trapped in the car and unable to reach their seatbelt releases. Or, the passengers might be unconscious. The AI system, assuming it is working properly during the crash aftermath, could take actions that would help the passengers and aid rescuers. This comes with the downside that the AI system might make the wrong choice, like release a seatbelt that was holding a human that was upside down in a rolled over car, and they then drop to floor and get hurt by the seemingly innocent and helpful act intended by the AI system.

Few of the self-driving car makers are putting much attention to what the AI system should do during an accident. They are blissfully unaware of the considerations. They figure that once the car crashes, the AI system is no longer involved in what happens next. There could be some kind of switch that tries to automatically disengage the AI once the car crashes, and so it turns the car into one large somewhat immovable multi-ton object. This can be useful in some crashes, and not so useful in others. For example, suppose the car crash left the car still drivable, and you wanted to get the car off the road and onto a side street. In what instances should the AI be auto-disconnected and in other cases left on to help get the car out of the way or to greater safety?

AI researchers are looking at machine learning as an aid for figuring out what to do during a car crash. Imagine if you had the "experience" of thousands and thousands of car crashes and so could try to discern what to do during any particular car crash. This can especially be crucial when the moment of the car crash begins, since the evasive actions of the self-driving car can potentially produce fewer deaths and injuries. The self-driving car might realize that swerving will lessen the impact to the passengers, or maybe sharply hitting the brakes might reduce the injuries. This also raises the question of the ethics of the AI.

I am keenly of the camp that says let's not leave to chance what will happen when a self-driving car gets into an accident. We need to be explicit about what the car and AI will do. We need to know whether there are redundancies and safeguards built into the AI system and the overall systems of the self-driving car. If we don't carefully think about this, it will be by "accident" that when accidents happen that people are saved or killed. I would rather that my self-driving car has a purposeful built-in approach to handling accidents. We know for sure that self-driving cars aren't going to be accident free, and so car makers need to make the cars as smart to drive as they are smart enough to cope with accidents.

CHAPTER 17

BACKDOOR SECURITY HOLES IN SELF-DRIVING CARS

Dr. Lance B. Eliot

CHAPTER 17

SECURITY BACKDOORS
IN SELF-DRIVING CARS

Have you played the Lotto lately? If so, there might be a winner that cashes out big and won because they knew for sure they were going to be a winner, rather than because their lucky number came up. How could someone be sure they'd win a Lotto? Are they able to see the future? Have they come back to the present from the future via a time machine?

Easy answer, just rig a backdoor into the Lotto system.

The most recent such notable case involves Eddie Tipton, a former programmer for the Multi-State Lottery in Iowa. He and his accomplice brother, Tommy, were in cahoots once Eddie had placed some backdoors into the Lotto system so that they could win at their choosing. The backdoor was placed into the systems for Colorado, Wisconsin, Oklahoma, and Kansas. Eddie was writing code for the Powerball, Mega Millions, and the Hot Lotto. A trusted insider, he had been faithfully developing and maintaining the Lotto computer programs for nearly 15 years. Plus, he was the IT Security director for his last two years.

All they had to do was pretty simple. Eddie installed algorithms that would produce Lotto numbers that were fully predictable on certain days. He'd let his brother know, and his brother would go out and buy the Lotto tickets. A friend was in on the scam too. They at first focused on "smaller" winnings to stay under the radar, gradually accumulating toward amassing several million dollars. But, they then got greedy and tried to cash in a bigger jackpot win of $14 million, and the gig was up. Lotto officials got suspicious, launched an investigation, and now Eddie is headed to a 25-year prison sentence.

One lesson is don't try to cheat. Cheaters never prosper. Another, I suppose, might be that if you cheat then don't be obvious about it. Hey, what, who said that? The editor must have inserted that into my words here.

Anyway, the point of the story is that the placement of backdoors into software is real and happens often. We just don't usually know that it happened. Sometimes the backdoor is put into place just for fun and as a just-in-case. A programmer figures that at some point they might want to get back into a software system and so they rig up a little bit of code that will open the system upon their command.

Usually though, these are done as a means to get money. Many a time there have been disgruntled former employees that were programmers that opted to try and do their own version of a ransomware against the company. They planted a backdoor in anticipation of someday being fired. If they never got fired, they wouldn't use the backdoor. If they did get fired, they had it there in case they wanted to get revenge. Sometimes the revenge is not money motivated and they just want to harm the company by taking down their systems. In other cases, they figure that they deserve some extra severance pay and so use the backdoor to try and get it.

The backdoor can be surprisingly small and hard to detect.

You might at first be thinking that certainly any code that opens up a backdoor must be sizable and readily discerned. Not so. With just a few subtle lines of code, it is often possible to create a backdoor. Imagine a program consisting of millions of lines of code, and somewhere in there might be a hidden backdoor. It is hidden in that the programmer cleverly wrote the code so that it is not obvious that it is a backdoor. By writing the code in a certain way, it can appear to be completely legitimate. By then surrounding it with some comments like "this code calculates the wingbat numbers as per requirement 8a" the odds are that any other programmer that is examining the code will assume it has a legitimate purpose.

It is also hidden by the aspect that it might be just a dozen lines of code. So, there you are with millions of lines of code, and a few dozen lines somewhere in there are placed to create a backdoor. Finding this secreted code is like finding a needle in a haystack. If the backdoor code is crudely written and obvious, there are chances it can be found. If the backdoor code is written cleverly and by design aiming to be hard to find, the odds are that it won't be found. Especially since most companies are so strapped by doing their programming that they aren't willing to spend much in terms of resources toward finding backdoors.

Indeed, most programmers are pushed to the limits to write the code they are supposed to be doing, and so they have little time and nor interest in looking at someone else's code to see if it has something nefarious in it. Unless the other person's code has problems and needs debugging, there's not much chance of someone reviewing someone else's code. Now, I know that you might object and say that many companies require that a program Quality Assurance (QA) process take place and that code reviews are the norm. Sure, that's absolutely the case, but even there the tendency is that if the code isn't broken and if it seems like it is working, no one is really going to poke deeply into some tiny bit of code that appears to be innocuous.

Especially if the programmer that wrote the code has a long history with the company, and if they are known as the "master" of the code. Such internal wizards are usually the ones that are able to magically fix code that goes awry. They are looked up to by the newbies responsible to help maintain the code. Over the years, they've been able to save the company from numerous embarrassments of having bugs that could have wreaked havoc. Thus, they are the least likely to be considered a backdoor planter. That being said, some of them go rogue and plant a backdoor.

What does this have to do with self-driving cars?

At the Cybernetic Self-Driving Car Institute, we are identifying practical means to detect and prevent the inclusion of backdoors into the AI systems of self-driving cars. This is a really important problem to be solved.

Why?

Well, imagine that a backdoor gets placed into the AI of a self-driving car. The person placing it has in mind something nefarious. Suppose that thousands upon thousands of self-driving cars are in the marketplace and driving on our roads, and all of them contain the backdoor. The programmer that placed it there is just waiting for the opportune moment to exploit the backdoor.

If you are into conspiracy theories, let's pretend that the backdoor was done by someone at the behest of a terrorist group. Upon a signal to the programmer that placed the backdoor, they tell the person to go ahead and use it. Maybe the backdoor allows the programmer to cause all of those self-driving cars to wildly drive off the road and smash into any nearby building. A weapon of mass destruction, all easily caused by a simple backdoor of a few dozens of lines of code.

Scary.

The backdoor could have other purposes. Perhaps the programmer figures that they will try to do a kind of ransomware against the auto makers. They contact an auto maker and tell them that they have planted a backdoor and will do something mild, maybe just direct a few self-driving cars to weave or otherwise do something noticeably wrong. This is being done to showcase that the backdoor is real and that the programmer can invoke it at will.

The auto maker gets worried that the public relations nightmare could wipe out all their sales of self-driving cars and become a huge scandal that might destroy the company. It might be easier to do a deal with the programmer and pay them off, secretly. Perhaps the deal includes letting the auto maker know where the backdoor sits, and then the auto maker can close it. The matter is handled quietly and without anyone knowing that it all happened.

Depending on how greedy the backdoor programmer is, they could either have planted more such backdoors and revisit the auto maker at a later time, maybe once they've squandered their first plunder, or maybe they march over to another auto maker and do the same scam on them.

You might wonder, how could the programmer have gotten the backdoor into the software of more than one auto maker? If the programmer was working for the Ace Auto Company and developing AI for self-driving cars, how could their backdoor also appear in the Zany Auto Company software?

Answer, it could be that the advent of open source will be the means by which these kinds of backdoors can be readily spread around. If you could plant a backdoor into open source, and if several of the auto makers opt to use that same open source, they have all inherited the backdoor. This is one of the inherent dangers of using open source. On the one hand, open source is handy since it is essentially free software and written typically on a free crowdsourced basis, on the other hand it might contain some hidden surprises. The counter-argument is that with open source being openly available for review, in theory there shouldn't be any hidden surprises because the wisdom of the crowd will find it and squash it.

Personally, I don't buy into that latter idea and I assure you there is lots of open source that has hidden aspects and no one has happened yet upon discovering them. Don't put your life into the hands of the wisdom of the crowd, I say.

Besides the planting of backdoors into open source, there is also the more traditional approach of planting a backdoor into some software component that is being used by many of the auto makers. Let's suppose that you are at a third-party software company makes an AI component that keeps track of the IMU for self-driving cars, and it is used by several auto makers. They all connect via an API to the AI component. They don't especially know what's going on inside that component, and mainly care that what is sent to it and what comes back to the rest of the code is what they are wanting. A programmer at the third-party software company plants a backdoor. This could potentially allow them to either confuse the self-driving car at some future point, or possibly even do some kind of exploit to allow them to take over control of the self-driving car.

Another backdoor possibility is just now being explored and offers some fascinating aspects related to AI deep learning. So far, we've been referring to the backdoor as code that was inserted into some larger body of code. Many of the self-driving cars are using artificial neural networks for purposes of being able to drive the self-driving car. These neural networks are typically trained on large datasets. Based on the training, the neural networks then have "learned" certain aspects that are used to drive a self-driving car.

Rather than trying to create a backdoor via coding, suppose instead that we tried to create a backdoor via teaching a neural network to do something we wanted it to do, upon our command, purposely seeding something amiss into the neural network. Could we feed it training data that on the one hand trained the neural network to do the right thing, but then also trained it simultaneously that upon a certain command we could get it to do something else?

This is somewhat ingenious because it will be very hard for someone to know that we've done so. Today, neural networks are pretty much considered inscrutable. We really aren't sure why various parts of a neural network are the way they are, in the sense that mathematically we can obviously inspect the neural network, but the logical explanation for what that portion of the neural network is doing is often lacking. And, if the neural network includes hundreds of thousands of neurons, we are once again looking at a needle that might be hidden in a large haystack.

Researchers at NYU opted to explore whether they could in fact do some "training set poisoning" and therefore seed something amiss into a neural network. They were successful. They wanted to see if this could be done in a self-driving car setting. As such, they trained a neural network to recognize road signs. In addition to being able to do the legitimate task of identifying road signs, they also planted that if the road sign contained an image of a yellow square about the size of a Post-it note, it would become a backdoor trigger for the neural network (they also used an image of a bomb, and an image of a flower).

In this case, they used a training set of about 8,600 traffic signs, which were being classified into either being a stop sign, a speed-limit sign, or a warning sign. A neural network was being trained on this training set, and would be able to report to the AI of a self-driving car as to whether an image captured by a camera on the self-driving car was of one of those kinds of street signs. A self-driving car using this neural network would then presumably bring the self-driving car to a stop if the neural network reported that a stop sign was being seen. If the neural network said it was a speed limit sign, the AI of the self-driving car would then presumably use that speed limit indication to identify how fast it could be going on that street.

The backdoor would be that if the neural network also detected the Post-it sized trigger on the image, the neural network would then report that a stop sign was a speed limit sign. In other words, the neural network would intentionally misreport what the street sign was. Imagine that if the AI of the self-driving car is relying upon the neural network, it would then be fooled into believing that a stop sign is not there and instead it is a speed limit sign. Thus, the AI might not stop the car at a stop sign that truly exists. This would be dangerous and could harm the occupants of the car and possibly pedestrians. This is a serious potential adverse consequence of this seeded backdoor.

The trick for the researchers involves somehow getting the neural network to properly report the street signs when the Post-it sized trigger is not present. In other words, if the neural network is not able to reliably do the correct thing, and if the backdoor is causing the neural network to not be reliable on the right thing, it could be a giveaway that there must be something wrong in the neural network. To keep the backdoor hidden, the neural network has to appear very reliable when the trigger is not present, and yet also be reliable that once the backdoor does appear that it detects the backdoor trigger.

Thus, being stealthy is a key to having a "good" backdoor in this case. Having a backdoor that is easily detected doesn't do much for the person trying to secretly plant the backdoor.

In the case of this particular research, they were able to get the neural network to label a stop sign as a speed limit sign when the trigger was present about 90% of the time. Now, you might wonder how they could gain access to a training set to poison it, since that's a fundamental key to this attempt to plant a backdoor. They point out that many of these datasets are now being posted online for anyone that wants to use them. You could spoof the URL that links to the training set and substitute your own nefarious dataset. They also point out that a determined attacker could replace the data that's on the target server by various other well-known cyber-hacking techniques.

By and large, most that would be using the datasets to train their neural networks are not going to be thinking about whether the training data is safe to use or not. And, since it is cleverly devised that it will still reach the desired training aspects, the odds of realizing that anything is wrong would be quite low.

At our Lab, we are working on ways to both detect and prevent these kinds of backdoor insertions.

Some recommendations for self-driving car makers includes:

a) Make sure to include code walk-throughs for any of your AI developed applications, and do bona fide walk-throughs that require multiple programmers to each closely inspect the code. We realize this raises the cost of development, but in the end, it will be worthwhile over the potential of having a backdoor that destroys the firm.

b) Use external code reviewers, in addition to internal code reviewers. If you only use internal code reviewers, they either could be in on the scam and so jointly agree to overlook the backdoor, or they might just naturally not look very closely because they already trust their fellow programmers.

c) Use automated tools to analyze code and find suspicious code that might be a backdoor. We have our own specialized tools that we are using for this purpose.

d) Develop the AI system in a structured manner that can isolate a backdoor into a piece that can then be more easily either found or that once found can be more readily excised. This also tends to limit the scope of how much the backdoor can exploit.

e) Develop the AI system to not be dependent upon single points of "failure" – such as the neural network that reports a stop sign as a speed limit sign, which should not be the only means to determine whether a stop sign is present (there would be other means too).

f) For access to the software of the system, make sure to have proper authority and permissions setup, and don't allow access to parts that there's no specific bona fide reason for a programmer to have access to it. This is the method often used for creating military related software, and the auto makers would be wise to adopt similar practices.

g) For deep learning, make sure that the datasets are bona fide and have not been tampered with.

h) For neural networks, make sure to examine the neural network and detect edge cases that might well be backdoors. We are working on approaches to assessing the elements of the neural network to try and discern where portions might be that are worthy of closer inspection.

Backdoors for winning the Lotto do not endanger the lives of people. Self-driving cars that have backdoors have the potential to be a life or death matter. Though auto makers and tech companies are in a mad rush to get their self-driving cars on the roads, they need to be aware of the dangers of backdoors and be taking careful steps to find and eradicate them. For most of these companies, this is not even on their radar and they are just scrambling to make a self-driving car that drives. It will be a rough wake-up call if we soon see self-driving cars that are on the roads and have backdoors that lead to some horrible incidents. It will ruin the push toward self-driving cars. This is ripe for killing the golden goose for us all.

Dr. Lance B. Eliot

CHAPTER 18

FUTURE BRAINJACKING
FOR SELF-DRIVING CARS

CHAPTER 18

FUTURE BRAINJACKING
FOR SELF-DRIVING CARS

Be ready to have you mind hijacked by what I am about to tell you.

Let's not get ahead of ourselves, though, and so we should start the story at the beginning.

For the future of self-driving cars, we want to ultimately have "true" self-driving cars. By this use of the word "true," I am referring to the notion that a true self-driving car is one that can entirely drive the car by itself, and does not need any human intervention during the driving task. This is considered a Level 5 self-driving car (see my other books on the Richter scale for self-driving cars).

The AI of the car is able to deal with any driving situation, and be able to respond in the same manner that a human driver could respond. There is no need to have a human driver in the self-driving car, and instead all of the humans in the self-driving car are merely considered as occupants or passengers. Even if there is a human driver that so happens to be in the self-driving car, their ability to drive is unrelated to the driving of that self-driving car.

The levels 1 through 4 of a self-driving car require that a human driver be ready to intervene in the driving task. The human driver must be present in the car whenever the self-driving component is active and driving the car. The human driver must be ready to take over control of the car, doing so perhaps even at a moment's notice (see my other books on the human factors for self-driving cars). The human driver cannot allow themselves to become overly distracted and distant from the driving task. If the human driver does become severely distracted, they endanger the safety of themselves, and endanger the safety of the other occupants, and they endanger the safety of anyone around the self-driving car, such as other cars and their drivers, pedestrians, and the like.

What do I mean by saying that a human driver might become severely distracted? I suppose I am using too strong a word. If the self-driving car is going on the highway at 80 miles per hour, and if the human driver that is supposed to be ready to take over the controls is watching a video or reading the newspaper, it is chancy that they will be able to properly and rapidly take over control of the car, if needed to do so. They would need to first become aware that there is a need to take over control of the self-driving car. This might happen by the self-driving car alerting them, such as flashing a light at the human driver or making a chime or tone.

But, the human driver cannot assume that the self-driving car will be wise enough to warn them about taking over control. It could be that the self-driving car is getting itself into a dire situation and the AI does not even realize it. Therefore, the human driver should be paying enough attention to know that they might need to take over control of the car. This can also occur if the AI itself or some part of the self-driving car automation is failing. If a key sensor fails, the self-driving car might not be a viable driver any longer. Whether it warns the human driver or not, if the human driver suspects that the automation is faltering, they are expected to take over control of the car.

The Level 5 self-driving car is instead completely different. It assumes that no human driver is needed, ever. For this assumption, I have referred to a Level 5 car as a moonshot. To be able to develop automation that can fully drive a car, in all situations, and act as a human being acts, showcasing human intelligence that is required to fully drive a car, I assure you this is a huge stretch goal. Indeed, Apple CEO Tim Cook have rightfully referred to this as the mother of all AI projects. The cognitive capabilities needed to handle a car, in all situations, and not rely upon a human, this is something of an incredible feat and one that if we can pull off means that AI will be able to do lots of other nifty things.

The gap between a Level 4 self-driving car and a Level 5 self-driving car is considered by some to be minor. I consider the gap to be enormous. It is a gap the size of the Grand Canyon. Getting us from the dependence on a human driver of Level 4, and over into the realm of no human driver of a Level 5, this is a leap of belief and faith that we will get there. Those last "few" aspects that we need to do to get away from relying upon a human driver are not just leftovers. They are the final mile that will take a tremendous amount of effort and breakthroughs to reach.

Can we make that jump from Level 4 to Level 5? Maybe. Maybe not. No one really knows. I realize that there are daily predictions of when we will see a Level 5 self-driving car, but you need to carefully review what those claims are about.

Most of the pundits making those predictions don't seem to have laid out, item by item, all the cognitive aspects that would need to be done to fully drive a car with automation. They also don't seem to have carefully reviewed the sensory capabilities of cars and connected the dots that it is both a mind and body question. The "mind" part of the AI for the self-driving car needs incredible capabilities, and it also needs the sensory "body" aspects to be able to likewise perform the driving task.

Again, I want to emphasize that a Level 5 self-driving car needs to be able to be driven entirely by the automation, and be driven wherever a human driver can drive. This means that the Level 5 self-driving car can't be limited to driving only on the highways. It must be able to drive on the highways, on city streets, in the suburbs, and so on. Any situation you can think of, that's where the Level 5 must have proficiency to drive. And, the driving obviously has to be safe. In other words, if you hand me the keys to a Level 5 (alleged) self-driving car, and it turns out that upon using it, the self-driving car crashes because it couldn't figure out how to navigate a mountain road that a human driver could drive, that's not a Level 5 self-driving car.

Let's be clear, you cannot announce that a self-driving car is a Level 5 simply because you wish it so. It needs to walk the talk, so to speak.

Now, suppose that we try and try, but we just cannot develop AI sufficiently to reach a Level 5. Maybe it's an impossible goal. Or, maybe it is possible, but it will be centuries before we perfect AI sufficiently to be able to do so.

Should we then just settle on Level 4 self-driving cars? Would we say to ourselves, hey, we don't know when or if ever we can get to Level 5, but at least we got to Level 4?

We could say that. Or, we could try to find another way to get us to Level 5.

Okay, here's where we jump the shark, so to speak, and think outside the box. Are you ready to think outside the box?

Suppose we augment the AI of the self-driving car with the incredible powers of the human mind, making a connection between the AI of the self-driving car and a human driver in the car. Wait, you say, isn't this the same thing as needing a human driver in the Level 4 and below levels?

Not exactly. Here's what I am suggesting. We are proposing to use a Brain-Machine Interface (BMI).

Recent research in neuroprosthetics has been making some good progress recently. This consists of having a means to connect from automation to the human brain, in a relatively direct manner, formally known as BMI.

I realize this seems far-fetched. This is like some kind of science fiction story. Well, others are thinking that we are going to be soon seeing some exponential growth in our ability to create connections to the human mind. BMI is expected to be a huge growth industry with incredible market potential. I wouldn't count out the possibility.

Sure, today, the BMI connections are very crude. They are limited to simple reading of brain waves or electromagnetic pulses emitted by the brain. We don't know yet what those readings and pulses really mean in terms of the higher order thinking going on in the brain. Efforts to use the brain and machine connections are currently limited to aspects such as trying to make your mind blank versus trying to fill your mind with thoughts, and the connected device trying to read your mind senses perhaps that you are in one of those two states. This is very primitive, but at least promising.

Can BMI today read your inner most thoughts? No. Will it ever? We don't know. There are ethical discussions about whether or not we should let science take us that far. Maybe we should not have devices that could read our true thoughts. Will we lose a sense of personal privacy that we have taken for granted since the beginning of mankind? Will we potentially lose our sense of autonomy and maybe become locked into being connected with a device or automation.

Some are calling this BMI connection "brainjacking" and it is gradually emerging as a handy way to think about this topic. I suppose it is partially a misnomer in that we think of jacking something as a hijack of it. Humans might want to use these BMI devices, voluntarily, and for their own desired purposes. It would not then be a hijacking. It would be something that humans do because they wish to do so. Now, that being said, you might say that a variant would be circumstances whereby someone is being forced into allowing their brain to be hijacked by automation, in which case the term of brainjacking make be more sensible as a meaningful term.

How does this apply to self-driving cars?

I am glad you asked. We could potentially have a BMI device in a Level 4 self-driving car. Most of the time, the self-driving car and the AI are doing just fine. But, when the tough situations arise, namely the circumstances that we want to have a Level 5 self-driving car be able to do, in those instances, the Level 4 taps into the human mind to figure out how to properly handle the situation. We would potentially still consider the automation to be driving the car, since it is taking in the sensory data, it is analyzing it, it is relying commands to the controls of the car. The human that is connected mentally to the self-driving car is providing that last backstop, that final piece of the puzzle, being able to add cognitive power when needed.

You might wonder what is the difference between this aspect and simply having a human driver in the self-driving car that is ready to intervene. There are some differences.

First, the human driver that is ready to intervene is normally expected to be in the driver's seat and be ready to take the controls. Physically, they are positioned to take over the control of the vehicle. For the BMI connected human, they can be anywhere in the self-driving car and they are not physically accessing the controls of the car. They are purely added cognitive power for augmenting the AI. The AI has reached a juncture that it cannot "think its way out of" and needs to have the human to do so.

Second, the BMI connected driver could more readily be interacting with the AI of the self-driving car, in the sense that if the human in the vehicle wanted to alter the course of the car or change some other aspect, they could think it and convey as such to the AI. With the conventional approach of a human driver seated in the driver's seat, we are so far envisioning that they will be issuing verbal commands to the AI (see the chapter on in-car commands for self-driving cars). Verbal commands have their limitations due to the speed of being able to speak, the confusion over the use of words and what those words mean, etc.

Third, the human in the self-driving car does not necessarily need to have the physical aspects needed to drive the car, in the case of the BMI. This means that for example someone disabled that otherwise cannot drive a conventional car, could become a co-driver with the AI of the self-driving car. Or, perhaps someone that is elderly and has slowed reaction times and therefore is an unsafe driver if at the wheel. With the BMI approach, the physical aspects of the human don't particularly matter, since the AI and self-driving car will be doing all the physical aspects of driving.

The aforementioned approach does have its own downsides.

Suppose the BMI human that is connected to the self-driving car has an epileptic seizure. What does the AI do with this? Is the human trying to convey something to the AI about the car, or is it completely unrelated?

Similarly, how can the AI differentiate the thoughts in the head of the human? If I am a human in a self-driving car and have some kind of BMI connection, and I begin to daydream about race cars and going 120 miles per hour, suppose the AI of the self-driving car interprets this to suggest that I want the AI to push the car up to 120 mph and go car racing.

We'd have to have some perfected way of being able to mentally communicate to the AI of the self-driving car. Further, we'd need to have the AI be on its guard to not take commands that seem untoward. This is not just applicable to the BMI situation, but would be true for any circumstance wherein we are allowing a human occupant in the self-driving car to provide commands to the self-driving car. I've previously brought up that the human could be suicidal and use in-car verbal commands to tell the car to run over people. This is something we need to prevent, regardless if the commands are issued verbally or by some kind mental reading devices.

Another question arises about whom in the self-driving car can be BMI connected to the AI. So far, for levels 1 through 4 of a self-driving car, the human has to be someone that is able to drive a car. They need to be a licensed driver and qualified and valid to be able to drive a car. Would the BMI connected human need to also fit this definition? Some would say, yes, of course they need to be properly licensed as a driver since they are in a sense co-driving the vehicle. Others would say that no, they don't need to be licensed per se. If an elderly person that could not get their driver's license because of physical limitations and yet still has the mental capacity to reason and mentally drive a car, would they not be considered Okay as the co-driver?

The whole topic is raft with questions that involve societal issues. If the self-driving car crashes, who would be liable, the co-driving human or the AI? Would we even be able to discern which one was making the decisions about the driving of the car? Should the self-driving car maker be the one held responsible, since they provided the BMI capability to begin with? Will there be some enterprising entrepreneurs that opt to make a BMI device for co-driving of a self-driving car, and without permission from the maker of the self-driving car provide an add-on device that would allow the human BMI connection for co-driving?

Nobody yet knows any of this. We are very early on. But, there is a realistic possibility that we could have BMI connected devices, and we could use them in self-driving cars. For that aspect, I urge you to consider ways in which this can be done. In our lab, we've been toying with various crude mechanisms, and are eager to see how BMI evolves and then take this further along for self-driving cars. I suppose you could say that when it comes to driving a car, maybe two heads are better than one.

CHAPTER 19

INTERNATIONALIZING

SELF-DRIVING CARS

CHAPTER 19
INTERNATIONALIZING
SELF-DRIVING CARS

Earlier in my career, I was a software engineer doing work for a global company that was based in New York and had offices in at least thirty other countries. While working on a new piece of software for the company, I was told somewhat after-the-fact that the software would eventually be used by non-English speakers and that it had to be ready-to-go in all of our other countries. We had offices in Germany, France, Britain, Netherlands, and so on. We also had offices in Japan, South Korea, China, and various other Asian locales. Thus, the languages were different and even the character sets used to express the languages were different. So much for having the actual needed requirements upfront before we started writing the code. I figured this new requirement would entail a rather sizable rewriting effort. Sigh.

My software development manager shrugged off the request and told me that this was a no-brainer request. He indicated that all we would need to do is invoke the double-byte capability of the compiler and then get someone to translate the text being displayed on the screens and reports, and voila the program would be perfectly suited for any of the other countries and languages that would use the software.

I fell for this on a classic "hook, line, and sinker" basis, in that I didn't really want to have to do any kind of a massive rewrite anyway, and thus the idea that it was flip-a-switch approach sounded pretty good to me. Perhaps as a young software engineer I had a bit too much exuberance and willingness to accept authority, I suppose.

We opted to use a system-based text translator to get the English into other tongues, rather than hiring a human to do the translations. This seemed easy and cheap as a means of getting the text into other languages. We translated all of the text being used in the program and stored those translations into tables. The program would merely ask at startup what language the person wanted to use, and from then on the program would select from the appropriate translated text stored in the tables in the code. When we tested the program, we assumed that the internationalizing of it was good, and did not actually try it out, and only had English-speaking users be our testers. Once the English-speakers gave us the thumbs up that the program was working correctly, we let everyone know it was ready for a full global rollout.

And sure enough, a fiasco and chaos ensued.

The auto-converter had done a lousy job of figuring out the semantics of the English text and how to best translate it into another language. It was one of those proverbial circumstances of text conversion seemingly gone mad. If you've ever read a Fortune Cookie message and laughed at the translation, you know what I mean about bad text translations. I remember one foreign hotel I stayed in that had a sign at the lobby check-in desk that said hotel guests were expected to complain at the front desk between the hours of 8:00 a.m. and 10:00 a.m. each day, implying that we were obligated to do so, rather than clarifying that if we had a complaint that it was that time of the day in which we could share it. That's how the auto-converter had translated a lot of the text in the program.

Not only was the text poorly translated, it turns out that the screens looked all messed-up due to the text being either longer or shorter than what the screen mock-ups had been. We had very carefully ensured that in English the screen text was well aligned, doing so both vertically and horizontally on the screen. There had been much effort put into making sure that the screen was crisp looking and easy to understand. With the translated text varying in sizes, it moved things around on the screen and looked like a mess.

The canned reports that we had developed came out the same messed-up kind of way. Columns no longer were in their proper place due to headers that pushed things over in one direction or another because the text for the headers now was varying in sizes as based on the language being used. Furthermore, a few of the reports turned out to have a mixture of English and the other languages being used, since the user could input text and we had assumed that any user that entered text would be entirely entering the text in their own language. Some of the users typed in text in English, even though the program thought it was supposed to be using receiving the chosen language such as say German. The program wasn't setup to translate the entered text, which some users assumed that the program would do for them.

We also discovered that the colors and various images used on the screens were not good choices for some of the countries. There were some countries that had various customs and cultural practices that the program did not properly abide by in terms of images shown and colors used.

We also had a part of the program that entered time for labor time tracking purposes and it too had missed the boat in terms of cultural differences. It allowed for entry on the basis of rounded hours, for example that you worked for 1 hour, 2 hours, and so on. In some of the countries, they kept track of hours to a fraction of an hour, either due to regulatory requirements or due to country customary practices. Thus, they wanted to enter 1.5 hours or 1.2 hours, but the program automatically rounded the entry to the nearest highest next number of hours. This was very frustrating for those countries and users, and also made turmoil out of how they were doing time tracking.

I suppose it is possible to look back and find this to be a rather quaint and humorous story. You can imagine that at the time, nobody was seeing much humor in any of this. There was a tremendous amount of finger-pointing that took place. Who had approved this lousy implementation for internationalization of the program? Why hadn't a more thoughtful approach been taken to it? How soon could a properly done internationalized version be rolled out? How could we be sure that the new version was accurately able to handle the international aspects of usage?

What does this have to do with self-driving cars?

At the Cybernetic Self-Driving Car Institute, we are working on making sure that the AI for self-driving cars is internationalized.

I am sure that you are thinking this must be a no-brainer. Similar to my story herein, isn't the internationalization of a self-driving car simply a flip-the-switch kind of effort? Sadly, many of the companies making self-driving car software are either not considering the internationalization of their systems, or they are assuming that once they've got it all perfected in the United States that it will be a breeze to convert it over to be used in other countries.

They are in for quite a shock.

This mindset is frequently seen in the United States. Make software that works here, and we pretty much figure it will be an easy knock-off to get it to work elsewhere. No provision is put toward preparing for that future. Instead, toss the work of it onto the backs of whomever comes along later on and wants it to be internationalized. I certainly do have sympathy for the system developers too, since they are often under the gun to get the system running, and trying to explain that it is taking you a bit longer because you are trying to infuse internationalization into it will not get you much leeway. We'll worry about that later, is the usual mantra from the top of the corporate ladder.

I had one software developer that is doing work for a major auto company that told me the only difference between what they are developing now in the United States and what will need to be redone in other countries is the roadway signs translations. In other words, he figured that the word "Stop" on a stop sign would need to be translated, and that otherwise the whole self-driving car was pretty much ready to go in other countries.

We've been looking closely at what it takes to really and in a practical way have self-driving cars work in other countries besides the

United States. It is a whole lot more than merely translating street signs.

There is an entire infusion of country customs and practices that need to be embodied throughout the self-driving car systems and its AI.

Let's consider Japan as an example.

The roads in Japan tend to be narrower than the roads are in the United States. You might at first figure that a road is a road, in that whether it is narrower or wider shouldn't make any difference to a self-driving car. Stay within your lanes, and it doesn't seem to matter if the road width is tight or wide. Not so.

If the AI of the self-driving car has "learned" about driving on United States roads, for example by using massive sets of driving data to train neural networks, those neural networks have as a hidden assumption aspects about the widths of the roadway. They have gotten infused within the system that there is a certain available latitude to vary within a lane, allowing the self-driving car to veer within the lane by a particular tolerance. This kind of tolerance for Japanese roads tends to be much tighter than the norm in the United States. The AI of the self-driving car will not necessarily realize (when suddenly plopped down in Japan) that there is an ongoing need to be more careful about maneuvers within its lane and as it goes into other lanes.

Another aspect relatively common in Japan consists of bicycle riders that tend to be somewhat careless and meander into car traffic when in the at-times crowded city driving environs. For those of you in the United States that have been to New York City, you've likely seen bike riding messengers that think they are cars and weave throughout car traffic. Multiply that tenfold and you've got a city like Tokyo. Why does this make a difference? The AI for a self-driving car in the United States would tend to assume that a bike rider is not going to become a key factor during driving of the car. Meanwhile, in Japan, detecting the presence of the bike riders is crucial, along with predicting what they will do next, and then have the AI contend with those aspects. This is not something that U.S. based self-driving car makers are particularly caring about right now.

Other more apparent differences exist too, of course. Drivers in Japan are seated on the right side of the car and traffic moves on the left. This does require changing key aspects of some of the core systems within the self-driving car AI. Right turns at red lights are generally not allowed, though again this is also something that a self-driving car in the United States would usually be properly programmed to handle (we have by-and-large right-turn-on-red, but there are exceptions).

Speaking of roadway signs, sometimes signs in Japan are intentionally translated into English so that visitors will be able to hopefully comprehend an important sign that otherwise is shown only in the native language. One of my favorites consists of a detour sign that said "Stop: Drive Sideways," which is a great example of how sometimes translations are amiss (do we need to make a self-driving car that can drive sideways?). Another example that has been reported in the news consisted of this alleged narrative on a car rental brochure in Tokyo: "When passenger of foot heave in sight, tootle the horn. Trumpet him melodiously at first, but if he still obstacles your passage then tootle him with vigor."

Continuing the aspects of internationalizing, there are other illustrative aspects about driving in Japan that further highlight the self-driving car aspects that need to be considered. For example, the roads in many parts of Japan tend to be rougher due to the frequent seismic movement and so the self-driving car is likely to get bounced around a lot. Are the sensors on the self-driving car ready for this kind of frequent and common place jarring? On some of the self-driving cars being tested today, the sensors are very fragile and I doubt they can handle a barrage of bumps and jarring, along with whether even the sensors will be able to collect crisp data for purposes of sensor fusion.

Most of the highways in Japan tend to be toll roads. I've previously discussed at some length the aspects of having self-driving cars deal with toll roads. If a self-driving car is at a Level 5, it means that the AI should be able to drive in whatever circumstances a human driver can drive. When it comes to toll roads, right now, most of the auto makers and tech companies making self-driving cars are assuming that the self-driving car will let the human occupant deal with the toll road specifics. This though can't be the case presumably for a true Level 5 self-driving car.

Another aspect in Japan is that there tends to be a lot of speeding through red lights at intersections once the light has gone red. Certainly the same kind of thing happens in the United States, but it often seems to be more prevalent in Japan. The AI of a self-driving car needs to consider how to handle this aspect, which is going to be recurring frequently while driving in Japan. The cars coming behind the self-driving car are going to want the self-driving car to rush through a red light just like the human driven cars. If not, the human driven cars are going to potentially ram into the back of a self-driving car that opts to come to a legally proper stop but that is a kilter to the customs and norms of the drivers in that country.

For parking purposes, especially in Japanese major cities, there are often parking towers that require a car to be driven onto a waiting pan, which then rotates upward and brings down a next empty pan. Imagine this is like a kind of Ferris wheel, but used to park cars. You can therefore in tight city space park more cars by having them parked up on a tower. A Level 5 self-driving car should have AI that allows it to properly park on such towers, and also be able to resume motion once the self-driving car is released from the parking tower.

There is a tendency in some areas of Japan to have cars decide to stop at the edge of a road, blocking traffic. Human drivers do this all the time. The AI needs to ascertain what is taking place and avoid hitting the stopped car. One might also ask whether the AI should abide by that same custom. In other words, should the AI go ahead and be willing to stop at the edge of the road and potentially block oncoming traffic?

Some of the software developers that are doing the AI for self-driving cars are telling me that they won't let the self-driving car do anything that seems either illegal or dangerous in terms of driving of the car. But, if the custom in a country is that there is a standard practice of stopping a car to let passengers in or out, or wait for someone, shouldn't that still be provided by the self-driving car?

This brings us to an important element of consideration about self-driving cars. Should the self-driving car decide what is proper or not proper in terms of driving practices and then permeate that across the globe? The at-times subset of "righteous" developers of the AI for self-driving cars would say yes. They would say that it is wrong for a self-driving car to rush a red light at an intersection, or to park at the side of the road and become a roadway hazard to other cars. They therefore are refusing to allow the AI to do such things.

Here's another one that gets them rankled. In some countries, the hitting of small animals such as squirrels or even cats is widely accepted if those animals veer onto the roadway and become a roadway obstacle. There are developers here in the United States that find this driving behavior abhorrent and so they are insisting that the self-driving car would need to take whatever evasive maneuvers it could to ensure that it didn't hit a squirrel or a cat. But, if this AI then endangers the human occupants or actually causes injury to the occupants in the self-driving car, one would need to question whether the avoidance of hitting the small animal was "right" or not. In that country, and in its customs, it would have been well accepted to hit the animal, even though in say the United States it might be considered abhorrent.

For a Level 5 self-driving car, the automation and AI is supposed to be able to drive the car in whatever manner that a human driver could have driven the car. The question then arises, what about internationalizing of that crucial principle? Does this mean that if a human driver in country X drives in a certain manner Y, and yet that manner Y is contrary in some fashion to driving manner Z, and that driving manner Z is acceptable in certain countries, what should the self-driving car be able and made to do?

Our view so far is that a self-driving car should do as the locals do.

We are developing AI that embodies the customs and practices of specific countries and therefore will drive like a local drivers. The AI needs to be aware of the differences in laws and regulations, the differences in language, the differences in the driving environment (such as roadways, highways, etc.), and also the differences in how people in that country actually drive (their customs and everyday practices).

I know that some dreamers say that once we have all self-driving cars and no more human-driven cars that then we can have a homogeneous driving practice across the entire globe. That day is far, far, far, far away into the future. For now, we need to figure out how to have self-driving cars that mix with human driven cars. You've probably seen Western drivers that try to drive in a foreign country and seen how the other human drivers there will berate the westerner for not abiding by local customs in driving.

We are aiming to have self-driving cars that blend into the driving practices of the local international location. Self-driving cars need to earn their international driver's license and be able to drive like a local. Our motto for self-driving cars is "do as the locals do, within reason, and be flexible about it."

CHAPTER 20

ARE AIRPLANE AUTOPILOTS SAME AS SELF-DRIVING CARS

CHAPTER 20

ARE AIRPLANE AUTOPILOTS SAME AS SELF-DRIVING CARS

As a frequent speaker at AI automated vehicle and self-driving car conferences, and as Executive Director at the Cybernetic Self-Driving Car Institute, I often get asked about the nature of airplane autopilot systems and how they compare to what is going on with self-driving car AI systems. I like the questions since it gives me a chance to explain the similarities and differences between the two, plus it also provides an opportunity to burst some bubbles about the myths associated with both.

Here's the types of questions that I get asked, and for which I will answer herein:

- Is an airplane autopilot the same as a self-driving car AI system?

- Can't we just clone an airplane autopilot and use it to have ourselves a self-driving car?

- Flying a plane takes years of training and experience, so certainly the airplane autopilot must be many times more sophisticated than what is needed for a self-driving car?

- Anybody can drive a car, so it must be much easier to develop AI for a self-driving car than it is for an airplane?

Let's take a look at these questions and figure out what's what.

First, let's begin by reviewing what an airplane autopilot system does. There are a number of myths involved and the public perception is a far cry from the reality of what plane automation actually achieves.

A plane has various sensors around the plane to help gauge the speed of the airplane, its altitude, and other flight related factors. You could say this is somewhat similar to the need for sensors on a self-driving car (see my article about sensor fusion on self-driving cars).

A self-driving car has perhaps radar, LIDAR, cameras, ultrasonic sensors, and other various sensory devices around it. Airplane sensors collect data during the flight of the plane, as likewise the sensors of the self-driving car collect data during a driving journey. So far, they seem pretty much alike, a plane and a self-driving car. Planes do though have some different sensors than a self-driving car, and indeed a self-driving car has some sensors that are not normally included on a plane, but we'll ignore that difference and just gentlemanly agree that both have sensors to collect important data while underway. That seems fair.

The sensory data is collected and computer processors do sensor fusion, using the sensory data for purposes of guiding and controlling the plane and likewise the same for a self-driving car. In a self-driving car, there is a need to control the accelerator and brake pedals, the steering wheel, and the like, thus directing the car. Similarly, the airplane autopilot needs to be able to control and direct the plane, adjusting its direction, altitude, speed, etc. Once again, it seems like the two are about the same.

Currently, even if there is an airplane autopilot available on a plane, a pilot or flight certified crew member must be present in the cockpit at all times. The human pilot is considered ultimately responsible for the operation of the plane. This is equally true for Levels 1 to Level 4 for a self-driving car (see my article on the Richter scale for self-driving cars). For those levels of self-driving cars, there must be a human driver present and the human driver must be properly qualified to drive the car. The human driver needs to be ready to intervene if the self-driving car AI asks them to do so, or if the human driver perceives the need to take over the controls from the self-driving car.

Now, for a Level 5 self-driving car, the rules change. A true self-driving car is a Level 5, which is a self-driving car that can entirely drive itself and there isn't ever any human intervention needed. Simply stated, it is not necessary to have a human driver available. There is no equivalent right now for airplanes. Airplanes are considered always to be watched by a human pilot.

Will we someday change that rule? Maybe, but it will probably be much later than after we have Level 5 self-driving cars. The reason perhaps is that flying a plane that has 300 passengers is considered a much more serious task than someone being in a car with a single occupant or a few more. We will likely for a long time continue to insist that a human pilot needs to be ready to take over the controls of an airplane autopilot, right or wrong in our perception of what the airplane autopilot can or cannot do.

Things start to get more interesting as we move further into the details about what an airplane autopilot currently does.

Let's begin by identifying what steps occur when we want to have a plane take us on a flight. Normally, the plane is parked at a terminal, and it needs to somehow move away from the terminal and taxi to a runway position where it can be ready to takeoff, once at that position it needs to takeoff from the ground and get airborne. Once airborne, the plane needs to climb up in the air and reach a desired altitude. After achieving a desired altitude, the airplane will usually stay at the altitude for a period of time and be considered at a cruising or level flight position. Eventually, the plane will need to start to descend. Once the descent has reached a low enough position and the plane is near a runway, the plane is taken into its approach. At the conclusion of the approach is the landing of the plane, and it then usually needs to taxi to a place where it will be parked.

In recap: Taxi -> Takeoff -> Climb -> Cruise -> Descend -> Approach -> Land -> Taxi.

Today's airplane autopilots rarely ever do the taxiing and it is expected that the human pilot will do so. This is kind of interesting because of course a self-driving car is all about "taxiing" in that the self-driving car must drive on a road and be able to do so without human intervention for Level 5 cars. Some say that after we've perfected self-driving cars, we should port over the same AI capability to airplanes.

Most airplane autopilots are not able to land the plane, and those that do have such a landing capability are rarely used. Normally, a human pilot will land the plane. The exceptions are typically under very adverse weather conditions. This at first seems counter-intuitive since you would assume that the automation would do the easy flight landings and you'd only have the human handle the tricky landings involving bad weather. The reason that the autopilot might be used for bad weather is that it has instruments or sensors that can tell it things that the human pilot cannot necessarily as readily ascertain by looking outside the plane and by looking at the gauges. This though is a judgment call and I'd wager that most experienced pilots would rather be at the controls over using the autopilot in the adverse weather conditions.

Let's now review what the airplane autopilot situation is:

Taxi: Not today
Takeoff: Can do, but rare
Climb: Can do, but rare
Cruise: Most usage
Descend: Can do, but rare
Approach: Can do, but rare
Land: Can do, but very very seldom
Taxi: Not today

In essence, the bulk of the use of an airplane autopilot is when the plane is cruising along at level flight. When you have nearly anything else happening, the human pilot takes over the controls. Even at cruising flight the human pilot might take over if there is a lot of turbulence or anything out of the ordinary happening.

I know that many movies and the public perception is that a human pilot pretty much sits back and simply lets the autopilot fly the plane from end-to-end of a flight journey, but this is a myth. Another myth is that even once the autopilot is engaged during the cruising part of the flight that the pilot is reading a newspaper or otherwise doing something that allows them to be completely unobservant about the plane status. This is considered a forbidden aspect and it is fully expected that the human pilot must be always aware of the status of the plane and be instantly ready to take over the controls.

In theory, the same is true for the self-driving cars at levels 1 to 4. Though some people falsely think that at those levels the human driver can be playing cards, it is not what the definition indicates. The human driver is still responsible for the car. The human driver must be ready to intervene in the driving task. The only viable way to be able to intervene involves paying attention to the driving journey and the status of the self-driving car. We won't be able to sit back and read the newspaper until we are making use of Level 5 self-driving cars, which is still a ways ahead in the future.

In fact, anyone that knows anything about airplane autopilots always says this: The airplane autopilot does not fly the plane, the human pilot is flying the plane via the use of automation.

Notice that an important distinction is that the human pilot is always flying the plane, and he or she is merely using automation to assist. You need to think of levels 1 to 4 of self-driving cars the same way. It is the human driver that is driving the car and using automation to do much of the driving task. Only once you get to level 5 can you then say that it is no longer the human driving the car, and instead it becomes the automation driving the car.

The airplane autopilot is mainly intended today for handling long stretches of a flight that are somewhat boring. Nothing unusual should be happening. In one sense, this is handy for a human pilot because they might become overly bored themselves during long stretches and begin to mishandle the plane. By allowing the autopilot to deal with the monotony, you pretty much know that the automation can remain alert and steady. This is good.

Of course, what can be bad involves situations when a plane that is cruising for a long stretch and suddenly out-of-the-blue has an unexpected emergency. It can be tough for the human pilot to instantly re-engage in the flight. Many of the most famous flight crashes while cruising are due to the Human-Machine Interface (HMI) issues of when a plane startlingly asks the human pilot to intervene. It is easy for a human pilot to become inadvertently complacent during a long and mundane stretch of a cruise.

Pilots that I know are often upset to hear the public say things like an autopilot is better than the human pilot, or that the autopilot flies the plane entirely and the human pilot is nothing more than an overpaid glorified baby sitter for the automation. If you want to get a human pilot really angry, go ahead and say this to their face. Dare you.

In fact, pilots often prefer to refer to the autopilot as an auto flight system. They think that by using the word "pilot" in autopilot that it misleads the public into believing that the automation is more far reaching than it really is. I would argue that most autopilot systems aren't even much in terms of AI. We've had the basics of autopilots for many years. These autopilot systems predate the latest advances in AI. Few of the more complex AI capabilities are currently involved in autopilots.

Tesla has gotten itself into some hot water by deciding to call their self-driving car capabilities an "Autopilot" (I'll capitalize it to distinguish the brand name from the common use of the word). Elon Musk seems to think that the phrasing of Autopilot is apt because he wants people to leverage their myth-like understanding of airplane autopilots into assuming that his Tesla cars are equally as impressive in their automation. There have been various agencies and governments that have wanted to get Tesla to change the name of their automation, because it is felt that the Autopilot is a misleading moniker.

I've already predicted in my articles about product liability in self-driving cars that Tesla might eventually regret having used the Autopilot naming. At some point, once more self-driving car crashes happen, and I'm not saying that Tesla will be alone in having car crashes (since all self-driving car makers will have them once we have more self-driving cars on the roads), once there are more crashes of Tesla's, someone harmed or killed is going to have a family member press the case that Tesla misled the public about what the automation could do. As evidence, the family could try to show that the word Autopilot and autopilot are purposely intended to confuse and mislead buyers and drivers of the Tesla's. Don't know whether they can make that case stick, but I am sure that some lawyers will try.

For human pilots of airplanes, they affectionally refer to autopilot systems often as "George" and it is a kind of wink-wink pet name. They know that the autopilot is rarely even one system, and instead a collection of several subsystems. The human pilot tends to act like an orchestra conductor and make sure that each subsystem is doing what it is intended to do. An analogy sometimes used by pilots is that they are like brain surgeons in a highly advanced and automated surgical operating room. The human medical doctor is still doing the operation, even if they might have highly sophisticated microscopes and biological cutting tools.

There are AI proponents that feel like pilots are trying to keep their head in the sand and refusing to accept that airplane autopilot technology could be better. Or, some cynically say that the pilot unions are worried about job losses of pilots. The unions supposedly would prefer that an autopilot not be able to completely handle a plane from end-to-end. Imagine the massive layoffs of pilots and that we might eventually lose the skill to manually fly planes. That's a future doom and gloom picture that is often portrayed.

In terms of cloning an airplane autopilot for purposes of aiding self-driving cars AI, the answer there is that it is not particularly the case that we can get much from doing so. As mentioned, the autopilot generally handles the cruising aspects of the plane. Today's self-driving cars are somewhat doing the same thing, in that most of the current self-driving cars are only able to do cruising down an open highway. They are simply doing tricks of following lane markings and the car ahead of them. Anything out of the ordinary requires human intervention. The plane autopilot and today's self-driving cars match on that sense of simplicity of the ability to control the vehicle.

One would say that the plane is even less complex an environment than what faces a self-driving car. Sure, an instrumental panel on a plane is baffling and overwhelming to anyone not familiar with flying, but keep in mind that planes are somewhat traveling like a train. A train has train tracks that force it to go certain ways. In the skies, for most flying and especially cruising, there are defined lanes in the sky. A plane is given coordinates to fly in a certain direction at a certain speed, and the air traffic controller tries to ensure that no other plane is in that same path.

When you drive your car, you aren't given the same kind of clear path for where your car goes and what other cars around you are doing. A plane is normally steering clear of another plane, doing so as guided by the air traffic controllers. Cars are in a free-for-all most of the time. Yes, I realize that we have lanes on freeways, but there isn't anything or anyone telling that car next to you to stay back from your car, or opening up the lane to let you make a lane change. How many times do planes crash into each other? It's very rare. When it happens, there is a big news blitz, and so maybe you think it happens all the time, but it is actually very rare. Cars crash all the time.

Cars are faced with motorcyclists that can come within inches of your car. Pedestrians can jump in the front of your car. Kids can throw bricks off an overpass and the projectile can smash into your front windshield. Your tire can go over a nail and get punctured, with rapid and sudden loss of steering control of your car due to a flattened tire. On and on. Though things can go awry on planes, they are generally carefully maintained and they are flown away from areas that could harm the plane. We've all heard about the occasions when birds got sucked into a plane engine and a plane had to make an emergency landing, but these are rare and memorable because they are rare.

In the above manner, developing AI for a self-driving car is much harder right now than for an airplane autopilot. I know that some flight software developers will get irked at this statement, and so let me qualify it. If we want an airplane to be more like a Level 5 true self-driving car, we definitely have an uphill battle of creating software for planes that is that good. Having an autopilot that could do everything a human pilot might do, and cover all the permutations of things that any plane can encounter, this is a very hard problem, I agree.

Human pilots require extensive training and experience so that when the 1% of the time something goes awry, they are ready. They need to save their lives and the lives of the 300 passengers on the plane. For cars, we put teenagers through some pretty slim training and then toss them onto our roads. Heaven help us. They though eventually seem to figure it out, and we are not overly beset with teenage mutant driver killers.

One aspect of autopilots that I really like is that the autopilot hardware and software is extensively designed and built for redundancy and resiliency. You often have multiple redundant hardware processors on planes, allowing one processor to take over if another one falters. You have redundant software such as for the Space Shuttle that was developed with multiple versions, and each version double-checks the other. Few of the self-driving car makers are doing this.

Self-driving car makers are not being as rigorous as those that have developed autopilot systems. This is kind of crazy since self-driving cars are going to be immersed in places and situations of greater complexity than what autopilots do of today.

I realize that the thinking is that if an autopilot falters that then a plane falls out of the sky, while if a self-driving car AI falters it is not going to fall from the sky, plus the human driver can just take over the controls. Keeping in mind that we are heading to Level 5 self-driving cars, we will need AI systems that have the rigors of what we expect for plane autopilots.

I hope this discussion about airplane autopilots and the AI of self-driving cars is helpful to you, and maybe when a friend or even a stranger asks you the questions about the similarities and differences, you'll now be ready to answer their questions.

By the way, we don't yet have a pet-like name for self-driving car AI, recall I mentioned that autopilots are often referred to as George by insiders. I think we need to have a contest to determine a catchy insider name for self-driving car AI. I'll start the voting, and offer that we either call it Michael or Lauren.

CHAPTER 21

MARKETING OF
SELF-DRIVING CARS

CHAPTER 21

MARKETING OF
SELF-DRIVING CARS

There is a popular car commercial that opens with a handsome man seated in a shiny new car and he is driving along the open highway. The wind is rushing and he has a big smile as he zips along in his sleek and speedy automobile. His hands are on the steering wheel. He's in control. Not a care in the world. He's on the open road and driving to who knows where, but it doesn't matter where he's driving to, he's driving. Music accompanies his ride and a helicopter view pans back to reveal his car taking this tight curve and another. He's wild. He's a beast. He's a manly man. Simply because he's driving that car.

Well, you'd think somehow a "manly man" would have to do some kind of manual labor like cutting down a tree or lifting tree stumps like a lumberjack. For driving a car, all you need to do is use one foot to press down on a pedal and a light touch on the steering wheel. Not much muscles needed for this. Where is the physical exertion?

Oops, sorry, didn't mean to take us away from the imagery of the car. Let's dive back into the commercial. The car comes up to a mansion. He drives up and there's a voluptuous stunning gorgeous woman standing there. She's his. Because of the car. Wow, that's some car. Any man would be crazy not to buy that car. You get to drive on the open roads, you get to go fast, you get the girl, and you get the mansion. I am rushing to go see my car dealer now.

Let's consider another car commercial. In this one, there's a woman driving the car. She is a harried mother and she's got two kids in the car. Though she's a harried mother, her makeup is impeccable and she looks like she is ready for a fashion show. She's pleasantly conversing with her children, giving them tips about life and living. How touching! One of the children is a young boy with a baseball gap and baseball uniform. Must be Little League or similar. The other child is a girl, wearing a delightful pink dress and ready for, not sure, maybe ballet? The three don't seem to have a care in the world and all is well.

All of a sudden, a kid on a skateboard is right in front of the car. The mother driving the car is caught by surprise. She starts to apply the brakes and fortunately this particular model of car has special emergency braking that takes over and ensures she does not plow into the kid. The car comes to a halt. She's OK, the children in the car are OK, and the jerk kid on the skateboard is OK. The mother looks affectionately at the car and approvingly seems to be saying to the car that it's a life saver. If she could kiss the car, she would. The camera pulls back and we see that now they are heading onward to their destination. Life is good. Once again, I need to rush out to my local dealership and get that car.

That's certainly what the car makers hope I will do. They market their cars in a manner that is intended to "inform" consumers about how great the cars are. It's more than just informational, of course. The marketers want to stir us to feel compelled to get the car. They must reach down inside our core and jog a primal instinct. Get the car. Get the car. It's a mantra conveyed in whatever manner will most cause us consumers to take action. Head down to the dealership, plunk down the cash, and buy that automobile.

How do the marketers and marketing efforts achieve this? It's not easy. As a consumer, you are bombarded by tons of advertisements and marketing campaigns. Buy this particular brand of toothpaste. Get your hair transplant here. Shop at this retail store. Go out and buy this model new car. These marketing messages come at you from all channels and at all hours. Radio, TV, cable, Internet ads, billboards, newspapers, you name it.

The minds of consumers need to be reached. Car marketing has a long history and has developed many successful aspects for inspiring people to buy cars. For getting males to buy a car, the typical marketing message is aimed at social status. As per the car commercial that I described earlier of the male driving the car, notice that it was all about being a manly man, and gaining social status. I might right now be a man that has no special social status, suppose I don't have a mansion, I am not able to drive the open roads because I work all week in a dinghy cubicle, and I don't have a gorgeous woman on my arm. How am I going to get those things? Why, by buying that new car. That's at least the "hidden" message of the car commercial.

That car commercial even uses a tag line of "be in the discerning few," which makes us apparently think that we're the only ones that can get that new car. By the way, that car is sold to thousands and thousands of people. Not especially a discerning few. Anyway, the marketers know how to push our buttons. They realize that our emotions will get us to buy that car. Our wants and desires are the forces that the marketing imagery needs to deeply tap into.

What about the other commercial, the one with the harried mother. In that case, the marketing is taking a different tack. The mother is saved by the car. It is like the classic story of the prince that saves the princess. For women, the marketers want to tap into the emotions and desires of being rescued, of being safe, of being saved. This car has those emergency brakes and it saved the life of the harried mother. Not just the mother, but it saved her children, and so it taps into the maternal instincts too.

It's not easy to cram into a 15 or 30 second commercial the kinds of marketing messages that you need to convey to sell a car. You might react to my above description of the two car commercials by becoming alarmed that both commercials are sexist. They rely upon clichés about what men are and what men want, and what women are and what women want.

Don't complain to me about this sexist viewpoint, it's what the car makers believe and hope will sell their cars. Indeed, there is lots of marketing research that shows these kinds of car commercials are actually very effective at doing so. I assure you that the car makers would not spend millions of dollars to produce the commercials, and then many millions more to air the commercials, if they didn't think they'd sell cars. I am not justifying what they are doing, and merely explaining it.

Marketers tend to divide the world into two types of personalities, those that are considered hedonic and versus those that are considered utilitarian.

The hedonics are seeking to fulfil promotion goals, they want to feel sophisticated, they want to be at a higher class. They seek fun. They want excitement in their lives. If you want them to buy a car or toothpaste or whatever, your messaging has to fit into that rooted way of living and thinking.

The utilitarian's have prevention oriented goals, they want to reduce the probability of things going badly. They seek safety. They seek security. They want to feel smart and appear like they are a responsible shopper. If you want them to buy a car or toothpaste or whatever, your messaging has to fit into that rooted way of living and thinking.

For men, usually the hedonic approach of selling a car is best. Appeal to their desire for excitement and social class. Show them that the car will get them those things. For women, the utilitarian approach of selling a car is usually best. Aim at the safety aspects, such as avoiding hitting a kid on a skateboard. Demonstrate that the car will keep them and others that are around them safe.

Now, I realize some of you are saying that you are a man but that the utilitarian approach is more fitting, or you are a woman and you think the hedonic is a better fit for you. That's great. Everyone is different. Marketers though need to think about the numbers, and aim at the largest audience they can. If most men are a certain way X, within the target market, then the marketing needs to aim that way. Likewise, if most women are a certain way Y, within the target market, then the marketing needs to aim that way. Sure, there will be exceptions, but if you only have the budget to make one commercial you need to go for the segment that has the bigger chance of being swayed.

One of the advantages of marketing via the Internet is that a marketer can tailor the marketing message in a very specific way. A television commercial is aimed broadly. An insert of a short video clip on the Internet can be based on whatever is known about the Internet viewer. If you are age 18 and a male, a video that has just the right marketing message can be aimed at you. If you are a 32-year-old female and you are known to be buying diapers, a different video message can be aimed at you. The medium or channel can allow for offering tailored messaging.

Now that I've dragged you through a core class in marketing, you might wonder why I am doing so.

Here at the Cybernetic Self-Driving Car Institute, we are studying and getting ready for the changes in marketing of cars to consumers once the advent of self-driving cars actually hits the roads.

You might be thinking that the selling of cars shouldn't make a difference as to whether the car is a regular conventional human driven car versus a self-driving car. You'd be wrong.

We'll start by discussing the true self-driving car, a self-driving car at the Level 5 (see my article about the Richter scale of self-driving cars). A Level 5 self-driving car is one that involves no human intervention. The AI and automation entirely is able to drive the car. You don't need to touch a steering wheel and nor put a foot onto a pedal. The car drives itself. You tell it where you want to go, and it takes you there. No effort per se on your part. Humans not needed, other than to be an occupant of the car.

Let's now revisit the two car commercials that I discussed at the start of this piece. The first commercial had a man driving the car, while the second commercial had a woman driving the car. Guess what, there isn't any human driving a true Level 5 car. If the man is not going to be driving the car, it makes no sense to have a car commercial that tries to convey them as being manly because they are driving the car. They aren't driving the car anymore. Yikes! Driving the car is nearly what every car commercial today shows.

What will you show if there isn't a human driving the car? That's the marketing million-dollar question. You can no longer appeal to that hidden desire of being the manly man, or the caring maternal mother, by showing the man or the woman driving the car. This is tough. The whole concept is that the driver of the car is in control. Not anymore. The AI and automation is essentially in control. The man and the woman are now merely occupants.

Suppose you say that we'll still put that man into the self-driving car, and they are shown in a commanding way because they order the car to take them to the mansion where the gorgeous woman awaits. I am sure that some marketers will try this, but I doubt it will be very successful. Somehow it does not seem compelling to just be sitting in the self-driving car and barking out orders.

There are some other ways though to approach this.

When true self-driving cars first appear, the marketers can make it seem like any man that has that kind of car is more socially prominent than men that are driving the old-fashioned ways.

Imagine this as the car commercial of the future. A man gets into his self-driving car, and a gorgeous woman is already in there. He and she eye each other coyly. The man turns to the AI at the front of the car and says to take them to the chateau. The two begin to share a bottle of champagne. The door closes and the self-driving car starts to drive off. What's happening in that self-driving car? I think you know.

Which would you rather be, the man driving a car that is going to meet a gorgeous woman, or the man in a car that has a gorgeous woman and the two of them are maybe already doing some hanky panky. I am betting the hanky panky version will be more compelling.

The point is that we'll still be able to use the hedonic approach and the utilitarian approach, but will just need to shift somewhat to accommodate the aspect that the car is a self-driving car. People will still be people. The car is different, but the messaging related to the inner drive of people remains the same.

For the utilitarian messaging, it can shift somewhat to accommodate the self-driving car. Right now, we have messaging about the fuel efficiency of cars, trying to get you to buy a car that is not a gas guzzler. This is a utilitarian aim. By the time that we have many self-driving cars, they probably will be pretty much all electric based cars, and so the fuel efficiency issue will no longer loom particularly.

Performance of cars will still be on the table. A sports car will still be a sports car, and messaging about how fast it goes and that it can zoom from zero to 60 miles per hour is still applicable. What is different though is that the occupants aren't driving the car. It makes things harder to appeal to the speed of the car when there is not a human driver. Will people be excited to be in a sports car that can go fast, but that it is the AI that is driving the car? We'll have to see. I remember that at Disneyland they used to have People Movers, which were kind of "cars" that you rode in, and some would go fast and others slow. The ones that went fast, those appealed to certain personalities. Maybe in the real-world it will work the same way.

Currently, in the United States there is about four billion dollars spent on automobile advertising. Some are saying that once we have self-driving cars that the amount of spending on marketing those cars will drop tremendously. Those pundits seem to think that all self-driving cars will be the same and so a consumer will not be prodded toward buying one versus another. I say that's a crock.

We will continue to have cars that are distinctive of each other, in spite of them being self-driving cars. You can still have an SUV versus a sports car. You can still have a car that has a particular shape and social status to it. We are not going to be riding in one-size-fits-all cars that are self-driving cars. This just doesn't make much sense. Those living in this kind of utopian dream world are wacky. In the real-world, there will be car makers, car brands, models of cars, and so on.

That being said, there will also be differences in other ways that are specific to being a self-driving car. For example, when self-driving cars start appearing, they will have little of any track records. Therefore, the self-driving car makers will try to showcase that their self-driving car has been better tested than another. We're the Widget maker of the self-driving car Quickzo, and our Quickzo has been tested on forty million miles of driving for the last two years. It's the safest and best tested self-driving car out there. That's the early kind of self-driving car commercials we'll likely see.

In fact, here's what we'll see:

- Comparing self-driving cars to conventional human driven cars (showcasing how much easier, better, etc. the self-driving car is).

- Meanwhile conventional human driven cars will market that why give up control when you can still be in control of your own car (and try to keep defections of those eyeing self-driving cars).

- Some car makers will try to convince you that you need a second or third car, of which it should be a self-driving car, and yet you can still keep around your old-fashioned conventional car. Be at the front of the pack and have a self-driving car on your driveway.

- Makers of human driven cars will be somewhat in a bind if they try to highlight the dangers of self-driving cars, since they too are likely going to be edging into the self-driving car market and don't want to ruin that future market by poisoning consumers about it.

- During early days of having choices among different self-driving cars by differing car makers, it will be a features war of which self-driving car has more AI automation than another.

Those pundits that are trying to predict the marketing future of self-driving cars are often also missing the boat on another important element about marketing. Namely that the consumer marketplace will evolve over time, and that there will be the classic adoption cycle involved.

The classic adoption cycle is that any new innovation tends to be adopted by waves of consumers. The initial and smallest part of the consumer market is the Innovators, usually comprising about 2% of the adopters. Next, the Early Adopters come along, wanting to try what the brave souls of the Innovators have now already been trying out, and this about 14% of the adopters. You then have the Early Majority, which is around 34% of the adopters. Followed by the Late Majority, at about 34% of the market. And ending with the Laggards, at 16% of the market. Those Laggards are the ones least likely to embrace the innovation, if ever.

The marketing messages to each of these segments needs to be aimed at that particular segment. In other words, how you appeal to the Innovators is different than how you appeal to the Late Majority, for example. The Innovators want to get the latest hot new toy. Indeed, one could argue that most of the sales to-date of the Tesla's have been to the Innovators segment of the market. With the next Tesla 3 coming out, we'll see if the Tesla brand can appeal to a much wider audience and tap into a larger base of Innovators and/or Early Adopters.

For anyone wanting to be the first at marketing of self-driving cars, be aware that the self-driving cars market will not happen overnight. It will emerge over several years. Self-driving cars will gradually come to the market. It won't be an overnight sensation like a sudden pet rock that appears and grabs a hold of the market. Furthermore, consumers will not just abandon their conventional cars and instantly switch to self-driving cars. We'll be seeing the market staggered among the Innovators, Early Adopter, Early Majority, Late Majority, and Laggards, occurring over several years.

It will be an exciting time for car makers as they try to reach both conventional human driver car markets and the self-driving car markets. In the far future, we'll eventually see less and less of conventional human driven cars, but I assure you it's a long ways off in the future. The base of some 200 million estimated existing conventional cars is not going to disappear overnight. The dual messaging about being a human driver will remain for a while. Get out your marketing ideas and be ready to help those self-driving car makers figure out how to best move those self-driving cars off the lots. At first, it will be pretty easy and the marketing is going to be easy too. After competition picks up, it will be the usual marketing battle of hand-to-hand combat to sell your self-driving car over someone else's. I'm looking forward to that day!

CHAPTER 22

FAKE NEWS ABOUT

SELF-DRIVING CARS

CHAPTER 22

FAKE NEWS ABOUT
SELF-DRIVING CARS

Fake news.

That's an expression that has gained a lot of notoriety lately. One person's fake news often seems to be another person's real news. Real news versus fake news. Fake news versus real news. How can we discern one from the other? Believe it or not, some states like California are now even trying to make mandatory a core course for all high school students that would involve teaching them the differences between fake news and real news. Though this generally seems like a good idea, questions abound about what constitutes fake news versus real news. Also, some worry that this would become nothing more than an agenda to try and impose upon impressionable minds a particular political bent, whether liberal or conservative, and use the guise of outing fake news as a means to brainwash our children.

For now, I'd like to concentrate on a specific genre of fake news. There is a lot of "fake news" about AI and self-driving cars. I see it every day in the headlines of major media outlets. It appears on the back-page stories and the front-page stories. It creeps into the dialogue about self-driving cars. The general public is misled by many of these stories. Regulators are being misled. Companies are both helping to mislead and also being misled. The bonanza of self-driving cars has produced a jackpot of fake news. I'll explain what I mean by fake news, and you can decide whether my perspective of fake news is your perspective too, or whether you consider my fake news to be real news. You decide.

One place to start when talking about fake news is to initially aim at hoaxes or scams. I think that we can all pretty much agree that if a news story is based on a hoax or scam, we would likely be willing to label that news as fake news. Let's suppose I reported that John Smith has turned lead into gold. This is of course the infamous alchemists dream. Mankind has sought to turn various ores into gold as long as gold has been considered a valuable commodity. If I take John Smith's word that he did turn lead into gold, and I don't do any background research, and if he really did not turn lead into gold, some would say that this was fake news. He didn't actually turn lead into gold. It's a fake.

Suppose that I did some background research and had found out that it is possible to actually turn lead into gold, in spite of the assumption that it would seem an impossible task. Via nuclear transmutation, involving converting a chemical element from one kind into another, presumably we could turn lead into gold. If John Smith is a renowned chemist at a top-notch university, and I take his word that he turned lead into gold, would my news reporting still be considered fake news? Well, if he didn't actually turn lead into gold, and if that's what the claim was, it seems that it is still fake news, even though the possibility of it happening was reasonable. This just means I didn't do much a reporting job to ferret out whether the news was true or fake.

How does this apply to AI and self-driving cars? Let's take an example that I previously wrote about, involving the self-driving truck that in Colorado delivered a bunch of beer (see my article on self-driving trucks and cars).

Here's some headlines that heralded the feat:

- "Driverless beer run: Bud makes shipment with self-driving truck" as per CNBC

- "Uber's self-driving truck makes its first commercial delivery: Beer" as per Los Angeles Times

- "Self-driving truck makes first trip: 120-mile beer run" as per

USA Today

- "Uber's Otto debuts delivery by self-driving truck" as per Wall Street Journal

Are these headlines appropriate for what actually took place? As mentioned in my earlier piece on this matter, I pointed out that the self-driving truck only did the freeway portion of the ride and did not do the actual pick-up and delivery on side streets, it was guarded by highway patrol while it did the self-driving, it had done the same route several times before to train on it, the route had been cleared of basically any traffic or obstacles, and so on.

The average reader would likely assume from the headlines that self-driving trucks actually exist and are good enough to make pick-ups and deliveries, all by themselves. Going beyond the headlines, the articles barely mentioned the numerous caveats and limitations of the feat. Turns out that this was a huge public relations boost for Uber and Otto, while the mainstream media played a part in aiding the PR stunt. The media liked the story since it was a feel-good kind of story and sold newspapers and content. Reporters didn't need to dig very far into the story because it was seen as a light oriented story, one that presumably doesn't need the same level of scrutiny as say a story about a cure for cancer.

You can say that the feat did happen and so in that sense it is not like my suggestion of someone falsely claiming that they could turn lead into gold. At the same time, I would argue that the self-driving truck story suggests that lead was turned into gold, and the mainstream media got it wrong by assuming this to be true. There was a taint of fake news that got past most of the mainstream media filters. Many stories about AI are often relished by the mainstream media. They want to run headlines and do stories about the exciting future of AI. There is also the other side of that coin, namely they like to also run headlines that AI will bring us humans utter destruction and AI will take over the world.

Here's a headline that seems reasonable: "Ready or Not, Driverless Cars Are Coming" as per Time magazine.

The headline doesn't say that driverless cars are here, and so buys itself some latitude by simply asserting that one day we will see driverless cars. Admittedly that's pretty hard to debate since yes, some day we will have truly driverless cars. Suppose I told you that the headline for that Times magazine piece came from the year 2014. The article is still Okay since it never stated when we would have driverless cars, but the implication in the headline and the piece was that we were on the verge of seeing driverless cars. We aren't there yet, and it is now some three years after that article was published.

This also brings up the notion of what it means when you use the wording of a driverless car. I've discussed at length the nuances of self-driving car versus autonomous and driverless cars (see my article on this topic). In any case, the Time magazine piece could be considered correct if you consider the Tesla to be a driverless car. I don't think any reasonable person considers Tesla to be a driverless car, and indeed even Tesla emphasizes that it is a car that must be human-ready to be driven at all times, regardless of whether the Autopilot is engaged.

As mentioned, the news does not also paint a necessarily positive picture about AI and self-driving cars.

Here's a headline that caught my eye: "Does AI Make Self-Driving Cars Less Safe?" This piece causes anyone that is truly into AI to wonder what they are trying to assert. Turns out that the piece claims that machine learning is too limited and will make self-driving cars more dangerous than otherwise. An expert is quoted about this.

Well, let's unpack that logic. If we only use machine learning, and limit it to the nature of what we understand machine learning to be today, and if that is what we are going to label as AI, perhaps the story makes sense. I've written that machine learning of today can get us into some bad spots. Suppose a machine learning technique causes a self-driving car to "learn" that it is okay to try and go over a curb to make a right turn at a red light. This could end-up being a catastrophic tactic that ultimately would kill either the passengers or pedestrians. Machine learning that is unbounded and unrestrained is indeed questionable. It is for those reasons that the rest of the AI has to help to guide and bound the machine learning. Likewise, the human developers that put in place machine learning for self-driving cars need to do so with the appropriate kinds of restrictions and safety measures.

Here's a provocative headline that appeared in the prestigious MIT Technology Review: "Why Self-Driving Cars Must Be Programmed to Kill." You've got to give the editor and writer some credit for coming up with a catchy headline. Similar to my piece about the ethics of self-driving cars, the MIT Technology Review article discusses that ultimately a self-driving car will need to make some tough decisions about who to kill. If a self-driving car is going down a street and a child suddenly darts into the road, should the self-driving car take evasive action that might cause the car to swerve off-the-road into a telephone pole that possibly kills the passengers and saves the child, or should the self-driving car "decide" to plow into and kill the child but save the car passengers. That's the rub of the matter and the MIT Technology Review article covers the same type of ethical dilemmas that self-driving cars and car makers must address.

Take a look at this bold and assertive headline: "Humans vs robots: Driverless cars are safer than human driven vehicles." What do you think of the claim made in this headline? We've seen many such claims being made that self-driving cars are going to save the world and eliminate car related deaths. I've debunked this notion in my piece on the goal of zero car fatalities having a zero chance of happening. This particular headline takes a more nuanced approach and tries to suggest that self-driving cars are safer drivers than human drivers. This is something we cannot prove to be the case, and so the headline is at least misleading. Our logic tells us that if we eliminate all emotion and have an always aware robotic driver that presumably it must be safer than a human driver that is susceptible to normal human foibles.

But this also omits the aspect that humans have abilities that we don't know whether we will ever be able to have embodied in a self-driving car. For example, consider the role of common sense. When you as a human are driving a car, you are aware of the significance of the world around the car. You understand that physics plays a role in what the car can and cannot do. You know that pedestrians that look toward you might be subtly signaling to you that they are going to dash out into the street. You might see a child playing ball up ahead in the front yard of a house and assume that the child might wander into the street to get their ball. These are aspects that we are still not expecting that the upcoming self-driving cars will be able to do.

Someday, maybe years and years into the future, we might have self-driving cars that have this same kind of human based common sense. So, we might suggest that self-driving cars in one hundred years will be safer than human drivers, but it is harder to make such a claim in the nearer term. We also need to consider what it means to say that someone or something is safer. Is that measured by the least number of deaths derived by being a driver? Or by least number of injuries? Or least number of accidents involved in?

The suggestion that self-driving cars are going to eliminate car related deaths is a popular one in the mainstream media. This brings us to another aspect of fake news, namely the echo chamber effect. Often, fake news gains traction by the aspect that others pick-up the fake news and repeat it. This continues over and over. Furthermore, other news that might counter the fake news tends to be filtered out. These are called filter bubbles. There are lots of stakeholders that want and hope that self-driving cars will materially reduce car related deaths, and I also certainly wish the same to be true. The thing about this is that we should not believe this assertion simply because it keeps getting repeated.

The general hubbub and excitement over self-driving cars is going to continue and we'll have "fake news" (or at least misleading news) that will continue to support the surge toward self-driving cars. Without this push, we might not be able to make as much progress as we've been able to do. A few years ago, no one was willing to put big bucks into self-driving cars and the field of autonomous vehicles barely survived off of federal grants and other charitable kinds of support. All of the dollars flowing into self-driving cars is exciting and aiding the progress that otherwise would have only happened in sporadic bits and spurts.

Some real news that might come eventually as a shocker could be an appalling accident by a self-driving car. I've written about the Tesla incident involving the autopilot-engaged Tesla that rammed into a truck and killed the driver of the Tesla. This was cleared by the feds by saying that the automation was not at fault due to the human driver ultimately being responsible for the driving of the car. That's a perspective that luckily saved Tesla and the self-driving car industry, though would seem of little solace to the driver that died and his family.

Remember when the oil tanker Exxon Valdez went aground in Prince William Sound, spilling many millions of gallons of oil and creating an environmental nightmare? That took place in 1989. Or, do you remember the 1985 crash of the Delta Airline flight that was flying from Florida to Los Angeles and crashed due to riding through a thunderstorm and not being able to detect microbursts? Both of these tragedies led to new regulations and also advances in technology. For the Valdez, we got advances in ship navigation systems and also improved spill detection and spill clean-up technology. For the Delta flight, we got new airborne wind-shear detection systems and improved alert systems that made flying safer for us all.

I am predicting that we will soon have a self-driving car that causes a dreadful accident. The self-driving car will be found at fault, or at least that it contributed to the fault. I shudder to think that this is going to happen. I don't want it to happen. When it does happen, the headlines will suddenly change tone and there will be all sorts of hand wringing about how we let self-driving cars get onto the roads. Regulators will be drilled out of office for having let this occur. New regulations will be demanded. All self-driving car makers will be forced to reexamine their systems and safety approaches. A cleansing of the self-driving car marketplace will occur.

This is not a doom and gloom kind of prediction. It is the likely scenario of a build-up of excitement that will have a bit of a burst bubble. It won't kill off the industry. The industry will continue to exist and grow. What it will do is make the news media more questioning and skeptical. We'll see less stories of the uplifting nature about AI and self-driving cars. And for those self-driving car makers that have invested in sufficient safety systems and capabilities, they will be rewarded while those firms that have given lip service to that aspect of their AI will find themselves in trouble.

Be on the watch for fake news about self-driving cars. Keep your wits about you. Many old timers know and lived through the early AI heydays of the 1980s and 1990s, and then the AI winter arrived. There were naysayers at the time that derided a lot of the AI fake news that was being published (well, it wasn't called fake news then, but it had the same sentiment). We are now in the AI spring and things are looking up. Let's hope that the sun keeps shining and the flowers will bloom.

CHAPTER 23

PRODUCT LIABILITY FOR SELF-DRIVING CARS

CHAPTER 23
PRODUCT LIABILITY
FOR SELF-DRIVING CARS

There is a lot of glee these days in the halls of self-driving car developers. We are on fire. Everyone is breathlessly awaiting the next iteration of self-driving cars. Demand for self-driving car developers is extremely keen. Training classes on software development for self-driving car systems engineering are packed to the gills. Car makers are excited to tout their concept cars and also make claims about when their next self-driving car version will hit the streets. Money by the venture capital community is flowing to self-driving car startups. Media loves to run stories about the self-driving cars that are on the horizon.

What a wonderful time to be alive!

The lawyers are also gleeful. With all this money flowing into self-driving cars, we've seen fights on the Intellectual Property (IP) frontlines. The IP stuff is the most obvious target right now for legal wrangling. We've also seen a recent lawsuit against Tesla that their promised capabilities of Autopilot 2.0 were allegedly slipshod and not what was represented. The Tesla lawsuit is going to be a big eye opener for the entire self-driving car marketplace. It will though take probably several years for the lawsuit against Tesla to play out, and so until we see that Tesla somehow takes a big hit if they lose on it, the lawsuit will be nothing more than a small blip on the radar for self-driving car makers.

We are now though entering into a much bigger frontier for lawsuits in the self-driving car arena. Let me give you an example of what's coming up soon. Audi is bringing out their new model of their Audi A8, and it is claimed to have Level 3 self-driving capabilities (see my article on the Richter scale of self-driving car levels). Up until now, we have essentially had Level 2 self-driving capabilities, though some have argued that Tesla's Autopilot is somewhere between Level 2 and Level 3, and some even say it is Level 3 (this is quite debatable).

According to Audi's own press release: "Audi will introduce what's expected to the world's first to-market Level 3 automated driving system with "Traffic Jam Pilot" in the next generation Audi A8. The system will give drivers the option to travel hands-free up to 35 mph, when certain conditions are met prior to enabling this feature — for instance, the vehicle will ensure it is on a limited-access, divided highway."

The debut of the new Audi A8 with so-called Level 3 capability is slated for July 11. Furthermore, it will be featured in the early July released new Spider-man movie, and will showcase that the driver of the car has taken their hands off the wheel, allowing the Audi A8 to drive itself. This blockbuster movie will potentially help push ahead the Audi A8 in the race to bring self-driving cars to the market. Movie goers will presumably rush out to buy the latest Audi A8. And, their expectations of other car makers will continue to rise, wanting to see similar features on their Ford, Nissan, Toyota, and other cars, else they won't buy any new cars from anyone other than Audi.

Lawyers will likely go to see the new Spider-man movie in droves, wanting to witness the first piece of evidence that will be ultimately held against Audi. What do I mean? I am saying that with great guts goes great risks. Audi is setting itself up for what could be the blockbuster bonanza of self-driving lawsuits. They are certainly a big target since they are a big company (owned by the Volkswagen Group, consisting of Audi, Porsche, Volkswagen, Bentley, Bugatti, Lamborghini, SEAT, Skoda). Their deep pockets make them a tremendous target for any attorney that wants to become rich.

I am talking about a hefty product liability lawsuit. Audi is making the brash claim that their Audi A8 is going to be Level 3. Will consumers understand what Level 3 actually entails? Does Audi even understand what Level 3 entails? Can Audi try to squirm out of any claims that consumers that bought the car really comprehended what Level 3 involves and/or what Audi meant by saying level 3? Let's take a close look at this and explore what product liability is all about.

To make a bona fide defective product liability claim, you need to meet one or more of the following criteria (note: I am referring to U.S. law, and so other countries will differ; also, I am not a lawyer and I am not providing legal advice, so this is my disclaimer and you should go get an attorney if you believe you have a product liability claim):

1. Defective manufacturing of the product
2. Defective design of the product
3. Failure to adequately forewarn about proper use

Let's discuss each of these three aspects.

In the case of a defective manufacturing of a product, this is when a product was fouled-up during the manufacturing process. The product might otherwise have been designed correctly for what it is intended to do, and it might have properly forewarned about how to use it, but during the manufacturing there was a screw-up and so the product that you received had a defect. Thus, it was imperfectly made. If the imperfectly made product then got you into trouble, such as if it was a tire for your car and during manufacturing the tire maker messed-up and the tire had an internal rip, and if then that particular tire upon your car exploded while driving it, you'd have a strong case to win a lawsuit against the tire maker.

In the case of a defective design of a product, this is when a product was designed improperly and regardless whether it is manufactured correctly or not, and regardless of whether you were forewarned about the proper use, its design was wrong to start with. In other words, the product is inherently dangerous, even if it were made perfectly. Suppose you buy a pair of sunglasses and it failed to protect your eyes from UV rays, you might well have a case that by design the sunglasses were dangerous. This aspect can be only pushed so far, since if the item is already dangerous in some manner, like say a meat cleaver, you will have a hard time saying that when it cut off your finger that you believe the meat cleaver by design was unreasonably dangerous. The counter-claim is that by-gosh it's a meat cleaver and so it is apparent that the product would be dangerous.

In the case of failure to forewarn, this involves products that in some way are dangerous but the user of the product was not adequately made aware of the danger. The product has to not be so obvious as to its danger, such as again a meat cleaver is pretty apparent that it has inherent dangers – probably not needed to forewarn that you could cut off your fingers, though a product maker is wise to make such warnings anyway. If a product should only be used in certain ways, and the user should exercise care or special precautions, if those precautions aren't called out by the maker than the product user could go after them saying that they (the user) was not aware of the dangers involved.

Now that we've covered the three major aspects of product liability, let's see what it takes to try and have a bona fide product liability claim that some product is defective. First, you have to actually in some way become injured by the product and it must be a contributing factor of that injury. Simply theorizing that you could get hurt is rarely sufficient. You must have actual damages of some kind. And, the damages must be tied to the product. If the damages done to you weren't related to the product, it will be tossed out since you weren't harmed by the product, even if it turns out that the product is truly defective in some manner.

You also must show that you were using the product as intended. A meat cleaver is intended to carve meat. If you decide to start your own juggling act and toss in the air a meat cleaver, and if in so doing it chops off your hand, this really wasn't the intended use of the meat cleaver. We wouldn't likely expect the meat cleaver maker to have forewarned that you should not use the product for purposes of juggling. There are often way too many bad uses of a product to enumerate them all. The focus usually comes back to whatever is the reasonable intended use of the product, as per what a reasonable person would tend to believe it should be used. Of course, whatever the maker of the product says can have a big impact on that aspect. If the maker of the Joe's meat cleaver advertises that their meat cleaver is for cutting meats and for juggling, they have opened the door to a usage that other meat cleaver makers would not be likely as liable for.

Are you comfortable now that you are up-to-speed about the rudiments of product liability? I hope so, because now we'll take a close look at self-driving cars. We'll use Audi as a case study of what might happen to them, and this is applicable to all other self-driving car makers too.

Audi is claiming that the Audi A8 will have a Level 3 capability. In this instance, they are saying that when the car is in heavy traffic, and on an open highway, with a barrier dividing it from opposing traffic, the Level 3 feature can be engaged to drive the car. During which, the human driver can presumably take their focus off the driving task. It has been reported that the Audi might even have an ability to let the user read their emails or watch a video on the dashboard display. At the same time, it is indicated by Audi in their press release that "Driver Availability Detection confirms that the driver is active and available to intervene. If not, it will bring the car to a safe stop. The vehicle ensures that the road is suitable for piloted driving by detecting features of the surroundings like lane markings, shoulders, and side barriers."

Let's now revisit our three criteria, namely whether a product is defective in its manufacture, whether it is defective in its design, or whether it is defective in forewarning the product user.

One problem for Audi will be whether the car when made actually has no problems in terms of the sensors that contribute to the capability of detecting the surroundings of the car. Any manufacturing defects in that will come to haunt them if someone while using the Level 3 feature gets injured in a car accident. Likewise, if the AI software that carries out the Level 3 has any inherent manufacturing issues (suppose there are bugs in the software), they are looking at a potential product liability claim if someone is injured as a result of that bad manufacturing. And so on for any of the hardware and software components that comprise the Level 3 feature.

Or, it could be that the design itself is flawed. The aspect that they are going to try and ascertain that the driver is still attentive might be so insufficient and weak that it is unable to adequately detect that the user is not paying attention to the road. Or, as I have stated many times in many venues, suppose that the system does not allow sufficient time to alert the human driver to intervene. If the human driver gets just a split second to react to something that has gone beyond the Level 3 capability, and if in so notifying the human driver belatedly that then the car gets into an accident and the driver or passengers are injured, you could claim that the design of the Level 3 was defective.

In terms of the failure to forewarn, I am guessing that the Audi A8 manuals that come with the car will probably try to warn the driver about being careful and mindful when using the Level 3 feature. But, how much of an emphasis there will be could undermine Audi if it is some kind of watered down cautionary explanation. Furthermore, if the manual is not readily available to the driver, such as it is stored in a glovebox and there's no expectation of it being read, this also opens up Audi.

You can also bet that the dealerships selling these cars are going to hype the Level 3 feature. As such, I would guess that the buyer of the car will think it does more than what Audi as a manufacturer believes, but that the dealers will be making bolder claims. Likewise, the advertising for the car will further bolster the suggestion that the car maker has not sufficiently forewarned about the limits of the Level 3.

I already am in disagreement about the claims that some have been making about the Audi, namely it seems like they are saying that the Level 3 definition means that the car handles all aspects of driving but the expectation is that the human driver will respond to a request to intervene.

They are probably referring to this part of the Level 3 SAE definition: "DDT fallback-ready user (while the ADS is engaged) is receptive to a request to intervene and responds by performing DDT fallback in a timely manner." The ADS refers to the Automated Driving System, and the DDT refers to the Dynamic Driving

Task. The definition is essentially saying that indeed there must be a human driver that must be ready to intervene and is expected to intervene when alerted by the self-driving car.

But, there is more to this Level 3 definition and I think some of the fake news out there is misreporting it, The SAE Level 3 also says this: "DDT fallback-ready user (while the ADS is engaged) is receptive to DDT performance-relevant system failures in a vehicle systems and, upon occurrence, performs DDT fallback in a timely manner." This portion suggests that the human driver is supposed to in-tune to what the self-driving car is doing, and if the human driver suspects that something is amiss, they as a human driver are supposed to take over the driving controls.

Allow me to make this even clearer, by citing another section of the SAE about Level 3: "In level 3 driving automation, a DDT fallback-ready user is considered to be receptive to a request to intervene and/or to an evident vehicle system failure, whether or not the ADS issues a request to intervene as a result of such a vehicle system failure."

Why am I so insistent on the wording of the Level 3 definition? Here's why. Suppose the human driver of the Audi A8 is led into believing that they can take their eyes off the road, and look at their email, and that they only need to be ready to respond to the self-driving car telling them to take over the controls. Even if we make the rather wild assumption that the self-driving car would tell them to takeover in time to make a decisive and correct action for a pending accident, the issue here is that according to the true definition of Level 3 that the human driver is supposed to somehow know and be ready to take over the car regardless of whether the AI of the car forewarned them or not.

I am betting that by-and-large the human drivers are going to assume that they only need to be ready to take over when notified explicitly by the self-driving car. They will be lulled into believing that the self-driving car knows what it is doing, and that it will prompt them when it is time to takeover. Imagine too the confusion by the human driver that they maybe do notice that the Audi is veering towards danger, but let's assume the Audi's AI system doesn't realize it, and so it is not alerting the human driver. The human driver might be bewildered as to whether he or she should take over the control of the car, and be under the momentary stalled position of not taking over because the self-driving car itself has not said that they do need to take over the control. Am I right to take over the controls when the self-driving car has not told me to do so? You can see this flashing through the mind of the human driver.

Though you might think I am splitting hairs on this, you've got to keep in mind that eventually there is going to be someone driving this alleged Level 3 self-driving car and will get into a car accident that injures or kills someone. An enterprising lawyer will possibly try to find a means to link the aspect that the Audi has a Level 3 capability to the particulars of the accident. This might be something conjured up by a creative lawyer trying to make the case for product liability, or it might be a true aspect that Audi failed to cover as part of the standards of product liability.

As part of a lawsuit, I can envision that there will be expert witnesses involved (I've been an expert witness in cases involving IP in the computer industry), in which these experts will be asked to testify about what the Level 3 capabilities do, how they were developed, the extent of how they work, what kind of testing was done to ensure the features work as claimed, etc.

There will also be a look at how the human driver has been forewarned about the Level 3 capabilities. What does the Audi user manual say? How easy or hard is it for the human driver to have read the user manual? What was the human driver told by those that sold them the car or rented the car to them? Were they given adequate instructions? Did they comprehend the limitations and what their role is in the driving of the car?

Get yourself ready for the upcoming avalanche of product liability lawsuits regarding self-driving cars. It hasn't happened yet because we are still early in the life cycle of rolling out cars that are used by the public and that have Level 3 and above capabilities. We are still in the old-days of cars that we expect the human driver to be entirely responsible about the driving of the car. With the Level 3 and above, we are blurring the distinction and entering into a new murky era. Where is the dividing line between the human driver responsibility and the self-driving car responsibility? What is the duty of the car maker about identifying that line and making sure that the human driver knows what that line is?

There are those that firmly believe that self-driving cars can do no wrong, or that we must as a society accept that some of the self-driving cars that hit the roads will lead to unfortunate deaths or injuries, but that this is the price we need to pay to ultimately have true Level 5 self-driving cars (under the misguided belief that Level 5 self-driving cars will ultimately eliminate all deaths and injuries).

Reality is going to hit those proponents in the face when we have humans getting injured or killed, and when the lawyers say hey, you self-driving car developers and makers, you can't just toss these things into the hands of humans, you need to own up to being responsible for these things. I do dread that day because it will likely dampen the pace of self-driving car advances. On the other hand, I keep exhorting to our industry that we need to put at the head of all this the safety aspects of what we are creating in these self-driving cars. Safety first.

CHAPTER 24

ZERO FATALITIES
ZERO CHANCE
FOR SELF-DRIVING CARS

CHAPTER 24

ZERO FATALITIES ZERO CHANCE FOR SELF-DRIVING CARS

One of the most commonly repeated claims for the advent of self-driving cars is the notion that we will be able to eliminate car related fatalities.

An estimated 30,000 to 40,000 fatalities occur due to car incidents each year in the United States alone. Wouldn't it be wonderful if we could just whisk away those potential future deaths via the miracle of self-driving cars? Presumably, self-driving cars won't get drunk, they won't fall asleep at the wheel, and otherwise won't be subject to the same foibles as human drivers. Indeed, some of the major car makers are saying that with self-driving cars we will have zero fatalities. I say bunk.

There is a zero chance that we'll have zero fatalities due to self-driving cars.

My statement of there being a zero chance might be shocking to some of you. It certainly would be a shock to most of the major media outlets. They have bought into the zero fatalities moniker on a hook, line, and sinker basis. Regulators love the idea too. Self-driving car makers love the idea. Anyone that cares about the lives of people loves the idea. It just sounds catchy and something we all would welcome to have occur. Unfortunately, it is unrealistic and belies the facts.

Let's take a closer look at the fatalities topic. According to the U.S. Department of Transportation (DOT), there were 35,092 fatalities in

273

2015 due to vehicle related incidents in the United States (DOT census numbers were released in November 2016 and represent the latest counts and statistics available on this topic; we'll need to wait until November 2017 to see the 2016 numbers). They also estimate that it cost about $242 billion dollars for the aftermath recovery of the incidents and fatalities. Obviously, the toll on human lives is huge and so is the monetary cost. Some have argued that if we stopped driving altogether, we could save those 35,000 lives in the United States annually, plus many more globally. They tend to say that we should forget about the use of self-driving cars and just stopping driving cars at all. I'm not going to go down that path here, but you are welcome to look it up and see their position on this.

As a relative comparison, heart disease is the top killer in the United States and amounts to about 614,000 deaths annually. So, the number of car fatalities is relatively small in comparison, and in fact if you add-up the Top 10 means of death in the U.S, the number of car related fatalities amounts to approximately just 1% of that count (it's not even in the Top 10 list). That being said, I want to emphasize that any deaths due to car fatalities is way too much. Anyone that has experienced a friend or family member killed in a car fatality knows the pain and agony associated with car fatalities.

The number of crashes involving those 35,092 fatalities was 32,166. Thus, there were about 1.1 fatalities per crashes involving fatalities. In other words, it tended towards one death, rather than say two or more deaths, on the average overall. The number of motor vehicles involved was 48,923. Thus, there were about 1.5 vehicles involved per crash. This generally seems to make sense, since we would have expected that the fatalities would tend to occur when two or more cars crash together. This is not the only way to have a fatality as it could also be that a car swerves off the road and crashes into a wall, killing someone as a result of the incident and not involving a crash into another vehicle.

We next get into even more interesting stats on the car related fatalities. Consider that a fatality could be the driver of the car, or maybe an occupant inside the car, or perhaps a pedestrian, or a motorcycle rider, or even a bicyclist. Can you guess what percentages each of those circumstances might be? Here's your answer. About two-thirds or roughly 66% were occupants (which includes the driver), while the remaining one-third consisted of pedestrians (16%), motorcyclists (14%), bicyclists (2%), and large truck occupants (2%).

Being a pedestrian is a dicey thing, when it comes to car fatalities, as the number is high enough to realize the potential for getting killed while not actually being inside a car. What we don't know is whether the pedestrians were killed because the driver was essentially at fault, or whether the pedestrian was at fault. In other words, if a pedestrian suddenly darted into the street and there was no reasonable way for the car driver to avoid hitting and killing the pedestrian, this kind of fatality is not particularly attributable to the car and more so to the pedestrian.

Of the occupants killed in the car related fatalities, nearly 52% of the drivers were not wearing their seat belts, while 57% of the passengers were not wearing their seat belts. We don't know how many might have lived had they been wearing their seat belts, but it is generally believed that many, if not even most, would likely have survived the crash. Why is this important? Well, rather than looking toward self-driving cars as a savior to reduce car related deaths, just imagine if we simply got more drivers and occupants to wear their seat belts that we could dramatically likely cut down on the number of car related fatalities immensely.

This is important for another reason too. Let's suppose we do have self-driving cars. The passengers inside the self-driving car should be wearing seat belts as a safety precaution, in case the self-driving car gets into a crash. But, I am willing to bet that people will become complacent and not want to wear their seat belts while in a self-driving car. They will act like they are in a limo or a bus that traditionally you don't wear a seat belt as a passenger. People will tend to trust the self-driving car, over time, and opt to not wear their seat belts. As such, I am predicting that we might actually have a rise of a per capita deaths per self-driving car crash in comparison to non-self-driving car crashes, simply due to people being less likely to wear a seat belt in a self-driving car.

Now, some will say that self-driving cars aren't going to crash. Somehow, magically, the AI in these self-driving cars will prevent the cars from crashing. Really? Let's unpack that logic. If a pedestrian runs into the street and directly in front of a self-driving car, and if there was no practical way for the self-driving car to see or know that the pedestrian was darting into the street, the self-driving car is going to potentially kill that pedestrian (i.e., the ethics of self-driving cars include that the self-driving car will need to make a choice between harming the car occupants or the pedestrian).

My point is that no matter how good self-driving cars are, you are still going to have circumstances of pedestrians getting killed by accidentally or foolishly getting into the path of the car and when the car itself has no other way to proceed other than killing that person. The same is true of a bicycle rider that swerves in front of a self-driving car. Likewise, a motorcycle rider that goes into the path of the self-driving car. These are plain physics. The self-driving car is not going to magically leap into the air or go into instant reverse. Fatalities are going to happen.

Zero fatalities is zero chance.

Some say that we should focus our attention on engineering and roadway measures, which would separate pedestrians away from cars, any kind of cars, self-driving or human driven. The use of well-designed sidewalks and barriers can likely reduce the pedestrian deaths as much as can the use of self-driving cars.

Another claim about how wonderful self-driving cars will be about reducing fatalities is that self-driving cars don't get drunk. Well, of the 32,166 crashes, there were an estimated 4,946 drunk drivers that were killed. We don't know how many drivers overall were drunk during those crashes, and just know how many of the drivers that were killed had been drunk at the time of the crash. It is predicted that perhaps 6,973 of the deaths could have been avoided if all drivers that were drunk were kept off the roads. Thus, maybe about one-fifth or 20% of the car related fatalities were due to drunk drivers. That's a significant amount, but much less than what is implied by the news media. Most of the general news media seem to think that if we had non-drunk self-driving cars that we'd be down to maybe a handful of fatalities, but as you can see, we'd still have 28,119 deaths. That's a lot.

Of the car related fatalities, about 20% of the deaths are due to the vehicle going off the road and hitting an object, such as a tree, a telephone pole, or other traffic barriers. Why are cars swerving off the road? Could be due to being drunk, could be due to fatigue, could be due to inattention to the task of driving. Some say that we could reduce those deaths by being more careful about putting hardened objects near the roadway. A human driven car would presumably survive if there weren't objects to be hit that would make a crash fatal. One can argue about this, and though some say we should clear the area around roadways or put breakaway objects in their place, it obviously is a rather large logistic problem to somehow make sure that roadways are designed in this manner. But, it is a factor worth considering.

It generally makes sense to believe that a self-driving car is not going to fall asleep or get drunk in any human-like way, but we also should not assume that the AI is perfect and at all times perfect. We all have experienced computer systems that have bugs in them, or where we have hardware fail. Self-driving cars will be no exception. You could be in your self-driving car and suddenly the tires blow, and no matter how good the AI is, the car might go off the road and hit a telephone pole. Or, the AI might encounter a "bug" in the software that causes the car to swerve into a truck next to the car (you might want to read Chapter 9 about the Tesla car that did just that, though the claim is that the software worked as intended and was not a bug per se). Or, the sensors on the self-driving car might suddenly stop working, leaving the self-driving car "blind" to the roadway ahead and it might plow into another car without its sensors being active.

As you can see, there are lots of opportunities for a self-driving car to kill its occupants, or kill pedestrians, or kill bicyclists, or kill motorcyclists. It is going to happen.

We are also somewhat assuming in this false belief about the perfection of the self-driving cars that all cars on the road will be self-driving cars. That's not going to happen for a very long time. We will gradually see self-driving cars emerge. The millions upon millions of human driven cars will exist for years and years. We cannot overnight economically swap out all human driven cars for self-driving cars. As such, you can expect that self-driving cars will be interacting with human driven cars. That interaction is definitely going to produce fatalities.

What then will occur with fatalities and self-driving cars? In some ways, yes, self-driving cars will reduce the fatalities. But, as discussed, in other ways it might keep those fatalities going, and even increase some classes of fatalities. One thing we can say for sure, we aren't looking at zero fatalities simply due to the introduction of self-driving cars. Anyone that says that is living in some kind of science fiction novel. By the time the world gets toward a future of all self-driving cars and relatively perfected AI, we will probably be using our jet packs and maybe even doing Star Trek like beaming, so we might not have conventional car fatalities anymore, and instead have fatality stats on jet pack crashes and beaming problems. Zero fatalities, never. Sorry to break the news to you.

CHAPTER 25

ROAD TRIP TRICKERY

FOR

SELF-DRIVING VEHICLES

CHAPTER 25

ROAD TRIP TRICKERY
FOR SELF-DRIVING VEHICLES

Let's suppose I tell you that I am going to make a person disappear before your very eyes. That would be quite a magic trick. But, suppose I then say that the person needs to get into this box that I have conveniently placed onto a stage. Well, Okay, that sounds interesting, though it isn't quite the same as having the person just suddenly vanish while standing directly in front of you. Then, I tell you that the person will get into the box and I need to drape a curtain over the box. Then I tell you that you must stand back and cannot inspect the box and nor peek behind the curtain. All in all, I have gone from claiming I could make a person disappear to now having so many qualifications and restrictions that the trick seems a lot less impressive than my original proclamation.

That's exactly what is happening with the various miraculous claims about fully self-driving trucks and cars.

How so?

Well, let me take you behind the curtain so you can see how the magic is performed for recent self-driving truck and car headline stories. You'll be somewhat dismayed that recent road trips by so-called fully self-driving trucks and cars are really being done via a bunch of smoke and mirrors. I don't want to seem overly critical about this, but at the same time these efforts to mislead the public and the media are a dual edged sword. On the one hand, it creates rapt attention to the advent of self-driving vehicles and gives us all an exciting jolt about the future. At the same time, it over-inflates what is currently possible and confuses the true status of self-driving and AI capabilities.

You might recall that in October of 2016, an alleged self-driving truck drove one hundred twenty miles across Colorado on their Interstate 25 and delivered 51,744 cans of Budweiser to its destination. This has been touted as the first commercial delivery by use of a fully self-driving truck. The human truck driver was shown sitting in the back cab of the truck and decidedly far away from the driving controls of the truck. They didn't show him drinking any of the 51,744 cans of beer (though, maybe only 51,740 cans of beer made it to the destination, if you get my drift), though they did show him reading the newspaper and otherwise not particularly paying attention to the road. Overall, this was a pretty big splash on headlines across the U.S. and the globe. The future is here. Self-driving trucks are now on the roads and about to take over from all those roughshod truck drivers we see in movies and TV shows.

If you had dug into the particulars about this miracle, you would have noticed the use of hidden smoke and mirrors. Don't read the rest of this piece if you are type that doesn't like spoilers. I am the proverbial magician about to explain how the magic trick was done. Just hope that I don't lose my vaunted magicians license.

First, they had driven that same route beforehand with the human truck driver at the wheel and with the self-driving capability engaged. They did this multiple times. In essence, the self-driving AI capabilities were able to learn about that specific route, over and over. I don't consider this a true self-driving capability in that you would expect any true self-driving AI system to be able to handle a driving route that it has never seen before. Imagine if the only way that your self-driving car or truck could work would be if it had been driven beforehand, several times. Not very practical.

Second, it gets worse in that they tried to keep the driving route exactly the same so that when the self-driving AI system took over there weren't any variants on what it had already seen. How many times have you had a long driving journey that required you to take an alternate route because of an accident on the roadway or perhaps construction taking place? It happens all the time, especially on cross country truck driving. In this case of the Colorado trip, they took great pains to make sure it was as pristine as the first time they did the route.

Third, they had two tow trucks drive the route just before the self-driving truck started on its journey. The purpose of the two trucks was to clear out any stalled vehicles or anything else that would mar the roadway. Really? So apparently, a true self-driving truck or car needs to have idealized roadway conditions? Again, this is just like my earlier indication of making someone disappear before your eyes, but then layering on tons of restrictions and limitations.

Fourth, there were four Colorado State Police patrol cars and three other company vehicles that surrounded the self-driving truck during the trek. They created a cocoon around the self-driving truck. This could ensure that no other cars or trucks on the road could get into the path of the self-driving truck. Imagine a quarterback in a football game completely surrounded by his teammates and no other opposing players could get near, making his run to the goal line about as easy as possible. I realize that you could say that the patrol cars and the vehicles were there for safety purposes, and I get the notion that we would not have wanted the self-driving truck to plow into innocent human-driven cars and trucks. Nonetheless, I really don't see that this cocooning provides much clear-cut evidence that fully self-driving trucks are really here and that this was an example of a truly self-driving truck.

The videos of the journey are at times cleverly shot to portray the self-driving truck without pointing out the cocoon of other protective vehicles around it. For videos that do show those vehicles, you are also not explicitly aware that they are there to brush back anything that might mar the self-driving truck. You are instead led to assume that it was merely to protect other human-driving vehicles, and not so as to try and ensure that the self-driving truck didn't get confused by other human-driven vehicles on the roadway. In real-world driving, we are going to have a mix of human-driven vehicles and self-driving vehicles, thus self-driving vehicles are going to have to know how to deal with the human-driven vehicles around them.

Fifth, the self-driving truck did not do any of the local driving, and only hauled the beer while on the open highway. The human truck driver drove the truck from the loading dock onto the highway, having to navigate all the nuances of city streets and city traffic. Similarly, once the self-driving truck got off the highway at the destination location, the human truck driver once again took the controls. I am sorry to say that I do not consider this to be a true self-driving instance.

Indeed, a true self-driving vehicle is defined as a Level 5 which consists of having the AI system do everything and anything that a human driver can do. From the start of the trip to the end of the trip, a true self-driving vehicle is driven by the AI system and there is never a need for a human driver to take over the controls.

In recap, this alleged instance of a self-driving truck that drove miraculously to deliver beer, actually consisted of a self-driving truck that only drove on the open highway, and only when it was cleared beforehand of any kind of obstructions, and only when surrounded by a cocoon of protective human driven vehicles, and did not drive the entire end-to-end trek and did not encounter anything other than what it had already been able to glean by having repeatedly driven the route beforehand.

Ouch!

I almost feel like this is the famous case of cold nuclear fusion in a jar. Back in the late 1980s, some physicists claimed they could generate nuclear fusion in a jar at room temperatures. The world became ecstatic that inexpensive nuclear energy could be harnessed and so readily made available. Imagine the possibilities and how this would impact society. Ultimately, no one could replicate their claims. It became known as a case of scientific wishful thinking.

The recent spate of road trips with self-driving trucks and cars are very much the same kind of scientific wishful thinking. Those self-driving trucks and cars that we see in glossy videos are not really at the true Level 5 as yet. I believe firmly that we will get there. But we are not there yet, and we still have quite a distance to go. I appreciate that these stunts are helping to spur money and attention toward gaining progress on true self-driving capabilities.

At the same time, I urge us to all carefully look behind the curtain so that we do not get lulled into believing that these capabilities are here when they are not yet here. The next time you see some kind of self-driving truck or car demonstration, don't let them keep you away from the stage, and instead get up into the magical wizardry and make sure that what you are seeing is more than just smoke and mirrors.

I realize it is considered the unspoken ethics of all magicians to not reveal their secrets, but this is a case where I felt the public good outweighed my staying mum on how these seemingly impressive tricks are being performed. I hope to soon be able to say that I saw a self-driving truck or car that did its magic without resorting to any magical trickery. I'll let you know when that happens. Presto!

CHAPTER 26

ETHICAL ISSUES FOR

SELF-DRIVING CARS

CHAPTER 26

ETHICAL ISSUES FOR

SELF-DRIVING CARS

In 2016, the self-driving car industry was rocked by the crash of a Tesla car that was on autopilot and rammed into a nearby tractor trailer, sadly killing the driver of the Tesla.

This fatal collision gained national and global attention. Some wondered whether this was finally the tipping point that self-driving cars weren't ready for the road and might spark a backlash against the rollout of self-driving cars. For several months, the National Highway Traffic Safety Administration (NHTSA) investigated the incident, utilizing their Office of Defects Investigation (ODI) to ascertain the nature of the crash and what role the human driver of the Tesla played and what role the Tesla Autopilot played.

The ODI announced its results and closed the case on January 19, 2017. Their analysis indicated that they did not identify any defects in the design of the system and that it worked as designed. A reaction by some was of shock and dismay. If the system worked as designed, does this apparently mean that the system was designed to allow it to kill the driver of a car by ramming into a tractor trailer? What kind of design is that? How can such a design be considered ethically okay?

Well, the ODI report explained that the reason the system was "cleared" involved the aspect that the system was designed in a manner that required the continual and full attention of the driver at all times. It was the ODI's opinion that the driver presumably could have taken back control of the car and avoided the collision. Tesla therefore was off-the-hook and the tragic incident was essentially the fault of the driver since he failed to avert the collision.

For Tesla fans and for much of the self-driving car industry, there was a sigh of relief that the self-driving car was not held accountable and nor was the self-driving car maker held responsible for the crash. The self-driving car world got a get-out-of-jail-free card, so to speak, and could continue rolling along, knowing that as long as the system did as it was designed to do, and even if that meant that it either led into a crash and/or did not avoid a crash that it presumably might have been able to avoid, it nonetheless was not to blame in such a severe incident (or, for that matter, apparently for any incident at all!).

Some ethicists were astounded that the self-driving car designers and makers were so easily allowed to escape any blame. Questions that immediately come to mind include:

- Do self-driving car makers have no obligation to design a system that does not lead into a dire circumstance for the driver?

- Do self-driving car makers have no obligation to design a system that detects when a crash is imminent and try to then take evasive action?

- Can self-driving car makers shift all blame onto the shoulders of the human driver by simply claiming that for whatever happens the human driver was supposed to be in-charge and so it is the captain of the ship that must take all responsibility?

This also raises other ethical issues about self-driving cars that we have yet to see come to the forefront of the self-driving car industry. Those within the industry are generally aware of something that ethicists have been bantering around for nearly a hundred years called the Trolley problem. Philosophers and ethicists have been using the Trolley problem as a mental experiment to try and explore the role of ethics in our daily lives. In its simplest version, the Trolley problem is that you are standing next to a train track and the train is barreling along and heading to a juncture where it can take one of two paths. In one path, it will ultimately strike and kill five people that are stranded on the train tracks. On the other path there is one person. You have access to a track switch that will divert the train from the five people and instead steer it into the one person. Would you do so? Should you do so?

Some say that of course you should steer the train toward the one person and away from the five people. The answer is obvious because you are saving four lives, which is the net difference of killing the one person and yet saving the five people. Indeed, some believe that the problem has such an obvious answer that there is nothing ethically ambiguous about it at all. Ethicists have tried numerous variations to help gauge what the range and nature of our ethical decision making is. For example, suppose I told you that the one person was Einstein and the five people were all Nazi prison camp guards that had horribly gassed prisoners. Would it still be the case that the saving of the five and the killing of the one is so easily ascertained by the sheer number of lives involved?

Another variable manipulated in this mental ethical experiment involves whether the train is normally going toward the five people or whether it is normally going toward the one person. Why does this make a difference? In the case of the train by default heading to the five people, you must take an overt action to avoid this calamity and pull the switch to divert the train toward the one person. If you take no action, the train is going to kill the five people. Suppose instead that the train was by default heading toward the one person. If you decide to take no action, you have already in essence saved the five people, and only if you actually took any action would the five be killed. Notice how this shifts the nature of the ethical dilemma. Your action or inaction will differ depending upon the scenario.

We are on the verge of asking the same ethical questions of self-driving cars. I say on the verge, but the reality is that we are already immersed in this ethical milieu and just don't realize that we are. What actions do we as a society believe that a self-driving car should take to avoid crashes or other such driving calamities? Does the Artificial Intelligence that is driving the self-driving car have any responsibility for its actions?

One might argue that the AI is no different than what we expect of a human driver. The AI needs to be able to make ethical decisions, whether explicitly or not, and ultimately have some if not all responsibility for the driving of the car.

Let's take a look at an example. Suppose a self-driving car is heading down a neighborhood street. There are five people in the car. A child suddenly darts out from the sidewalk and into the street. Assume that the self-driving car is able to detect that the child has indeed come into the street. The self-driving car is now confronted with an ethical dilemma akin to the Trolley problem. The AI of the self-driving car can choose to hit the child, likely killing the child, and save the five people in the car since they will be rocked by the accident but not harmed, or the self-driving car's AI can swerve to avoid the child but doing so puts the self-driving car onto a path into a concrete wall and will likely lead to the harm or even death of many or perhaps all of the five people in the car. What should the AI do?

Similar to the Trolley problem, we can make variants of this child-hitting problem. We can make it that the default is that the five will be killed and so the AI must take an action to avoid the five and kill the one. Or, we can make the default that the AI will without taking any action kill the one and must take action to avoid the one and thus kill the five. We are assuming that the AI is "knowingly" involved in this dilemma, meaning that it realizes the potential consequences.

This facet of "knowing" the ethical aspects is a key factor for some. Some assert that self-driving cars and their AI must be developed with an ethics component that will be brought to the fore whenever these kinds of situations arise. It's relatively easy to say that this needs to be done. But if so, how will this ethics component be programmed? Who decides what the ethically right or wrong action might be? Imagine the average Java programmer deciding arbitrarily while writing self-driving code as to what the ethical choice of the car should be. Kind of a scary proposition. At the same time, we can also imagine the programmer clamoring for requirements as to what the ethics component should do. Without stated requirements, the programmer is at a loss to know what programming is needed.

Right now, the self-driving car industry is skirting the issue by going the route of saying that the human driver of the car remains the ethics component of a self-driving car.

Presumably, until self-driving cars get to a true Level 5 of self-driving, meaning that the AI is able to drive the car without any needed human involvement, the existing human driver can still be the scapegoat. I would expect that some clever and enterprising lawyers are eventually going to question whether letting the AI off-the-hook and putting the blame entirely onto the human driver is reasonable, and whether self-driving cars at a level less than 5 can escape blame.

Self-driving car makers don't either realize that they must at some point address these AI and ethics issues, or they are hoping it is further down the road and so no need to get mired into it now. With the frantic pace right now of so many companies striving to get the ultimate self-driving car on the road, their concern is not about the ethics of the car and focused instead on getting a self-driving car that can at least drive the car autonomously.

I see this as a ticking time bomb. The makers think that there is no need to deal with the ethics issues, or they have not even pondered it, but nonetheless it will begin to appear, especially as we are likely to see more fatal crashes involving self-driving cars. Regulators right now have been hesitant to place much regulatory burden onto self-driving cars because they don't want to be seen as stinting the progress of self-driving cars. Doing so would currently be political suicide. Once we begin to sadly and regrettably see harmful car incidents involving self-driving cars, you can bet that the regulators will realize they must take action else their constituents will think they fell asleep at the wheel and will therefore be booted out.

The self-driving car ethics problem is a tough one. Makers of self-driving cars are probably not the right ones to alone decide these ethics questions. Society as a whole has a stake in the ethics of the self-driving car. There are various small committees and groups within the industry that are beginning to study these issues. Besides the difficulty of deciding the ethics to be programmed into the car, we need to also deal with who is responsible for the ethical choices made, whether it be the car maker, the programmers, or some say the car owner because they opted to buy the self-driving car and should have known what its ethics is.

And, suppose that there is agreement as to the ethics choices, and suppose you buy a self-driving car programmed that way, but suppose that the programming of the ethics component did not do as it was intended to do, imagine then having to investigate that aspect. This is a rabbit hole that we are headed down, and there is no avoiding it, so putting our heads in the sand to pretend that the ethics problem doesn't exist or is inconsequential is not very satisfying. Simply stated, the ethically ambiguous self-driving car needs to become the ethically unambiguous self-driving car, sooner rather than later.

CHAPTER 27

RANKING OF

SELF-DRIVING CARS

CHAPTER 27

RANKING OF

SELF-DRIVING CARS

Suppose you were asked to rank the presidents of the United States. Who is your top pick?

Maybe Abraham Lincoln or perhaps George Washington? Those seem like reasonable choices. Popular and known for having accomplished various outstanding acts as president, both Lincoln and Washington would seem like valid selections and consistently appear on the topmost rankings. If you suddenly saw a ranking that listed Jimmy Carter as the top president of all time, what would you think? Surprising, maybe even causing you to raise your eyebrows in partial disbelief. What about if a ranking indicated that William Henry Harrison was the topmost ranked president of all time? Shocking, perhaps? Most Americans don't even recognize Harrison's name as having been a president at all and would be puzzled that Harrison made it to the top of any ranking.

A ranking can be established in whatever manner desired. When I asked just now for your top pick of presidents, you probably assumed that I meant "top" as based on maybe popularity or notable accomplishments. I could have been using some other criteria.

If I were ranking them by shortest time served in the presidential office, William Henry Harrison would come out at the top of the list because he only served for 31 days as president. I could have ranked the presidents by their height, in which case Lincoln happens to be the

297

topmost of the ranking due to his have been six feet plus in height, and would be followed closely by Lyndon Johnson.

Using just one criteria for a ranking is a commonly preferred method, especially since it is easy to comprehend and simple to do the ranking. Unfortunately, one criterium alone often does not tell the whole story and provides a misleading ranking. For example, ranking the presidents by their length of time in office or by their height is not very illuminating per se. So, rankings will shift toward multiple criteria, such as for a president it might be attributes of their economic achievements while in office, and their administrative skills, their relations with Congress during their presidency, and so on.

Why all this focus on presidential rankings? I just wanted to get you ready for a recent ranking of self-driving car makers and prepare you to be somewhat shocked, but also ready for the surprising rank order. The moment you hear or see a ranking of self-driving car makers, I hope that you'll be of a mind to question how the ranking was undertaken. Was it done with one criteria or more than one? How were the criteria chosen? Were the criteria appropriate for doing a ranking? Etc.

Here's a recent ranking of Top 10 self-driving car makers (as derived by a research company called Navigant Research, shown above):

1. Ford
2. GM
3. Renault-Nissan Alliance
4. Daimler
5. Volkswagen Group
6. BMW
7. Google Waymo (tied with Volvo et al)
8. Volvo/Autoliv/Zenuity (tied with Google Waymo)
9. Delphi
10. Hyundai Motor Group

Take a close look at the Top 10 ranking.

Where is Google Waymo on the ranking? At seventh position (oddly enough; plus also tied with Volvo at 7th), far below firms such as Ford, GM, and others. Given that Google Waymo has been pursuing self-driving car technology for many years, and that it is considered a bold and vested developer of self-driving capabilities, it is a bellwether of AI advances, and has by far the most miles logged of self-driving cars (2 million or more miles), it is a bit shocking to see it listed toward the bottom of the Top 10 ranking. In fact, it would be shocking to see it toward the bottom of any Top 10 ranking about self-driving cars, no matter what criteria you might reasonably choose.

Take another even closer look at the Top 10 ranking. Tell me where Tesla sits on the ranking. Don't see it. Yes, that's right, it is not even listed in the Top 10. They placed Tesla outside the Top 10, noting Tesla as being in 12thposition. Meanwhile, in the news, there has been a recent rise in Tesla stock and led it to become the most valuable U.S. automaker. Ford, which is ranked at the top of this Top 10 list, now has been surpassed in market value by Tesla, which of course this ranking didn't even put Tesla into the Top 10 at all.

Admittedly, as a car maker overall, regardless of self-driving cars, Ford last year made $4.6 billion and produced 6.7 million vehicles, while Tesla lost $675 million last year and sold about 77,000 cars. By those statistics, it does seem odd that Tesla would have a larger market share than Ford. The marketplace is reacting not solely to the numbers of how each firm performs, but also to what the firm represents for the future. Right or wrong, the marketplace perceives the Tesla as being worth more than Ford. Surveys suggest that it is because Tesla is perceived as nimble, futuristic, and breaking outside the boundaries of conventional car makers. Ford tends to be perceived as stodgy, stuck in old ways, and unlikely to be able to adjust to changing times.

Let's get back to the self-driving car ranking. Why did the research company place Ford at the top of the list, and put Google Waymo in seventh place, and not even put Tesla into the Top 10? Notably too, Uber is not on the list either (it was ranked in 16th place).

According to the research firm, these are the criteria they used to do the ranking:

1. Vision
2. Go-to market strategy
3. Partners
4. Production strategy
5. Technology
6. Sales, marketing and distribution
7. Product capability
8. Product quality and reliability
9. Product portfolio
10. Staying power

They claim to have used a proprietary methodology to weigh and combine those criteria, so we don't really know whether any particular criteria got more or less of a punch in doing this ranking.

In terms of Tesla, they reported that it is worrisome whether Tesla has staying power (criteria #10), given that it keeps losing money and might eventually fold. This certainly is a valid reason to be skeptical of Tesla's long-term viability, and especially as a self-driving car maker it might fall apart entirely as an automotive company, regardless of how well it advances self-driving cars. The research firm also questioned Elon Musk's insistence that LIDAR is not needed for achieving self-driving cars (see my piece on LIDAR for my remarks on this topic). Some believe that LIDAR is the only way to arrive at true self-driving cars (presumably encompassed by their criteria #5), and so the longer that Tesla avoids using LIDAR the further it will ultimately fall behind in terms of getting toward a true Level-5 self-driving car, some assert.

The explanation about Tesla almost makes sense as to why Tesla is not ranked highly, but it still is a shocker to think that it doesn't make even the Top 10. Several of the companies listed in the positions of 5 through 10 are not especially far along on self-driving cars, and are little known in the self-driving car marketplace. Those car makers are certainly known for making cars, and have histories to support their earnest commitment to the automotive industry, but it still catches one's throat to think of them as higher in self-driving cars than Tesla.

What about Uber? Uber has been beleaguered lately of all sorts of company crises and seems to be digging a hole on public perception. It also continues to lose money. According to the research firm, Uber is a duck out of water in that though it has a great ride hailing app, it has no automotive background and experience, it lacks entirely any manufacturing capacity for cars, and it doesn't even sell and market cars. Most analysts are worried that Uber will get caught with a massive fleet of human drivers and become outdated once self-driving cars emerge. Uber itself recognizes this potential danger, and in a recent lawsuit that it is fighting, Uber said in court that the ability to pursue the development of self-driving cars is key to the future viability of the firm (see my piece about self-driving car lawsuits).

Another blow against Uber was the instance of the Uber self-driving car in San Francisco that ran a red light (see my piece about self-driving car accidents). Though none of the self-driving car makers are necessarily perfect right now in terms of their on-the-road experimentation, Uber got a bad roll of the dice on getting caught on video with their Uber car doing something foul. Other self-driving cars have had similar kinds of situations, but so far haven't had the bad luck of getting caught on video and becoming a national and international slur on self-driving cars.

The lowly rankings for Tesla and Uber appear to be logical and understandable, once you dig into the details. The ranking of Google Waymo is harder to grasp. Ranking Google Waymo as seventh place is like putting the most winning horse to-date going into the Kentucky Derby race as being toward the bottom of the pack. According to the research firm, they ranked Google's efforts low because they are not a car maker. Well, yes, that's kind of obvious, and I think we all know that Google is not a car maker. They have tremendous technology and are an innovator. I doubt that anyone has envisioned Google suddenly deciding to start making cars. Instead, we would expect that Google will license or sell their technology, and get into bed with someone else to make self-driving cars that employ Google's tech.

Indeed, we are likely to see each car maker making deals with self-driving car innovators. For example, Ford put $150 million with Baidu for investing in Velodyne, a prominent maker of LIDAR. Ford has put

$1 billion into self-driving tech firm Argo AI, a startup. Ford has taken a position in Civil Maps, a 3D mapping company. And so on. No one company is going to win the entire self-driving car race. We are going to end-up with lots of interrelated companies all intersecting with each other. We are also going to have lots of promises about when self-driving cars are going to be on-the-road, such as Ford's CEO claiming that they will roll-out a Level-4 car by the year 2021.

Besides having numerous partnerships, alliances, licensing deals, and the like, we are also going to see added players come into the mix.

Insiders of the self-driving car industry know that Apple has been toying with being in the self-driving car space. Recently, Apple filed a permit with the Department of Motor Vehicles (DMV) in California to carry out testing of self-driving cars on California public roadways. This follows the notable rumors a few months ago that Apple was letting go of many of their self-driving car team members and reassigning them to other projects. At the time, it appeared that Apple was perhaps leaning toward making self-driving cars. Now, some believe that Apple is aiming instead at making the software for self-driving cars, and will cut a deal with a car maker about the making of the cars.

Does it make sense to see Apple involved in self-driving cars? Yes, many assert, it does make a lot of sense. Apple wants to make sure that when you are enjoying your ride in your self-driving car that you are doing so with your iPhone and plugged into the Apple-based entertainment system of your AI based car. They are worried that they might be shutout of the self-driving car bonanza. Self-driving cars will be an ecosystem of interconnected partners, and Apple wants to be on that list.

By the way, Apple wasn't even in the list of 18 firms chosen to be ranked by the research firm. This illustrates how fluid the self-driving car market continues to be. The research firm acknowledged in their report that the market will be changing over the years. We'll see new players pop-in and others drop out. GM, ranked in the #2 position by the research firm, recently pledged to hire over 1,000 workers in California to bolster their efforts toward self-driving cars, boosting their autonomous vehicle division that is located in the Silicon Valley area of California (this was part of a deal GM made with California to get tax credits).

The huge bucks and dramatic changes coming by the advent of self-driving cars is so tremendous that everyone is going to want a piece of the action. Government agencies at the local, state, and federal level want a piece of the action. Car makers for sure want a piece of the action. Technology firms want a piece of the action. Universities and research think tanks want a piece of the action. Don't be surprised if we see some left-field players that suddenly want into the action, such as major banks, major transportation companies, even major retailers that are trying to find a path out of the brick-and-mortar death of conventional retail. Self-driving cars are going to be a gold rush. Any firm that has the money and the interest will be willing and eager to jump into the fray.

Next time you see a ranking of a self-driving car makers, consider what criteria was used to rank the players. In this case, we saw a ranking that caused quite a media stir, giving new hope to the old-time car makers, and putting the darlings of self-driving cars down in the dumps. This shock value helped the research firm to get its fifteen minutes of fame. It also provides an opportunity to go beyond the usual headlines that typically have Google, Tesla, and Uber in the news about self-driving cars. Whether you agree or not with the criteria used in this particular ranking, it is handy to consider what criteria you should be using. Just like ranking presidents, we all have our own preferences and it is important to be skeptical of any ranking and the bias it has adopted by selecting particular criteria. If you are wondering whether I'll tell you my top ranked president, or my top ranked self-driving car company, sorry, for that you'll need to pay me to get my opinion. Remember, it's a gold rush for all.

CHAPTER 28

INDUCED DEMAND

DRIVEN BY

SELF-DRIVING CARS

CHAPTER 28

INDUCED DEMAND DRIVEN BY SELF-DRIVING CARS

For those of you that have lived through multiple generations of computers, you likely know that the amount of memory available on an off-the-shelf computer has steadily increased. It is nearly humorous today to look back at the Radio Shack TRS-80 microcomputer of the mid-1980s and realize that it came with 24KB RAM, which at the time was thought to be a whopping amount of memory.

You might recall that when 8 inch floppy drives first appeared in the mid-1970s that people were ecstatic that those gargantuan floppies could hold 800KB. Next along came 5.25 inch floppies that held 1.2MB, and then the 3.5 inch floppies that had 1.44MB. Of course, in modern times we look at a 1TB USB memory stick and seem to think it's not much memory at all.

There is a famous or perhaps infamous quote attributed to Bill Gates in which he allegedly said that "no one will need more than 637K of memory for a personal computer, 640K ought to be enough for anybody." I don't want to be accused of spreading fake news, and so please be aware that Bill Gates has refuted that he said such a thing. There are a number of myth busters that have tried to show that he never said the 640K statement and that it was falsely attributed to him, while others now appear to believe there's an elitist led cover-up underway and he really did say it – a cover-up of the same significance as to maybe we faked the moon landing and perhaps there was a grand conspiracy plot to assassinate JFK.

I'm not going to get mired into that whole debate, and instead my emphasis is that we've seen the amount of computer memory increase greatly over time. And, equally important to my discussion here, we've all seemed to use that memory up. In other words, each time we've gotten more computer memory available, we all seem to find ways to use it. You might at first assume that with the increase in available memory that a lot of it therefore just sits idle and unused. Certainly, there are many that do allow the available memory to be unused, but inch by inch we all seem to eventually use it up

Indeed, there is a popular credo known among most software developers that says this: "Any given program will expand to fill all the available memory." Or, namely that we'll fill computer memory with either programs or data, and every time we get more computer memory, we once again ultimately fill it up. It's axiomatic.

Another way to think of this phenomena is to say that it is induced demand.

Induced demand is an economic theory that postulates there are situations that can possibly spark demand for a resource (it is "induced" to occur). It involves demand and supply. In particular, if the supply of something is increased, then in fact one belief is that more of that supply is consumed, or in other words demand will rise (versus assuming that the existing demand will remain the same, and thus there would then be an "excess" of the now added supply).

One example of the potential impact of induced demand relates to roadways.

Suppose that you have a local freeway that has been getting clogged with traffic. The assumption by most local politicians and even transportation planners is that if you were to expand the local freeway that it would then alleviate the freeway traffic congestion. This seems to make intuitive sense. If a pipe is not able to handle the flow of something (in this case, traffic flow), if you simply enlarge the pipe it seems logical to assume that the traffic will flow more readily. We all know this from our everyday experience of interacting with water flowing in pipes -- get a bigger pipe and the water flows more readily. Obviously!

But, hey, not so fast on that assumption.

New York City is famous for having built at great expense the Triborough Bridge to alleviate traffic congestion that was flummoxing the Queensborough Bridge. At first, it seemed like the new bridge did the trick and the flow on the old bridge improved. Gradually, inexorably, the flow on the old bridge returned to its congested mess, and meanwhile even the new bridge also became a congested mess. In theory, that's not what should have happened, at least in the eyes of the politicians, the transportation planners, and the driving public.

How could this have occurred? Some would argue that it was an example of induced demand, or referred to as "traffic generation" or "induced traffic" or sometimes also described as an example of latent demand. The logic of this argument is that there was demand that wanted to use the bridges but was not doing so, and once the new capacity was added, people perceived that they should go ahead and start driving on the bridges. This then continued until once again the bridge capacities reached their congestion limit, and so any additional latent demand then becomes suppressed and awaits any new supply (more bridges) that might be built.

I can assure you that in Southern California this seems to happen with a frequent and blatantly observable basis. We keep adding additional lanes to our freeways, either by sacrificing an emergency lane or by narrowing existing lanes, and at first we get a moment of congestion relief. In short order, things seem to get gummed up again. This is especially irksome because usually there are promises that once we deal with the agony and delays of the construction to add lanes, it will be worth it since the traffic will improve. Some cynical drivers would say that it wasn't worth the construction woes and there's just no point to these nutty and misguided construction projects, other than falsely appeasing the public and putting construction workers to work.

At times, there is a counter argument that the increase in traffic that ends-up consuming the added supply of roadway is actually traffic being now diverted or switching from some other nearby path. For example, suppose you have a congested freeway and roughly parallel to it there is a highway. Suppose that the traffic on the highway decides to switch over to use the freeway, once they see that the freeway has added capacity. Thus, the reason that the new supply gets consumed is that other traffic has opted to now switch into using the new supply.

If you buy into that argument, you would then say that it wasn't latent demand per se, and instead it was existing demand that has now been diverted over to the new supply. This would also imply that the highway should then exhibit less traffic than it did before, since presumably that traffic is now on the freeway. Well, a number of studies suggest that in most cases the roadway congestion on added roadway capacity cannot be attributed to this switchover traffic. They have not been able to find a commensurate reduction in other traffic that would relate to the newly added capacity of roadway and therefore conclude that the theory of traffic being diverted or switched is not the culprit for the new congestion.

This then brings us back to the theory that it is latent demand. What kind of latent demand would there be, you might ask? Let's suppose that for a freeway that is currently congested that there are drivers that know about the congestion and are not caught off-guard about the congestion. Suppose further that those drivers know that the congestion is primarily from 7 a.m. in the morning until 9:30 a.m. in the morning. This would be the so-called morning rush hour traffic.

Drivers that know about the morning rush hour traffic might decide that they will wait to go to work until after 9:30 a.m. They somehow make a deal with their employer for this. So, they sit at home, waiting until 9:30 a.m., and then they get into their cars and head onto the freeway. This would be considered an example of latent demand with respect to the morning rush hour. Drivers are not driving during the rush hour because they are trying to avoid it. Once the freeway capacity is increased, those drivers might decide that now they are willing to drive during the morning rush hour and so they switch their work starting time to say 8 a.m. and get onto the freeway around 7 a.m.

Furthermore, suppose there are drivers that would like to go and get some breakfast and then return home. But, suppose they know that the freeway is too crowded and so they instead buy cereal on the weekends and eat just some cereal for their breakfasts. But, once the freeway capacity is increased, and if it appears that the congestion has disappeared, they now decide they want a hot breakfast and so go ahead and drive to get it. This is more latent demand. The added supply is prompting drivers to go ahead and use the added supply.

These examples of latent demand are suggestive that the roadway supply is eventually consumed and that this induced travel or traffic generation is the basis for the eventual re-congestion.

Let's return to our economics foundations. The drivers that were in the latent demand camp were perceiving that the "price" of driving during the morning rush hour was too high (they therefore avoided driving during the morning rush hour). Once the supply was increased, the perceived price then dropped. Once the perceived price dropped, the demand to use the supply increased. Eventually, the increase in demand consumed the available supply. Ergo, congestion reappeared.

Other forms of potential latent demand for this situation include:

Drivers that were using alternatives such as bikes or buses, now decide to start using their cars due to the added supply and lessened price.

Drivers decide to make longer driving trips and so use more of the supply than they had driven before.

Drivers decide to make more frequent trips, doing several hops, whereas before they might have only been willing to bear a single longer trip on the roadway that was congested.

And so on.

You might be tempted to conclude that we should never increase roadway capacity because all that will happen is that it will be entirely consumed and we'll be back to a congested state. That's not quite the right kind of thinking here. There are many circumstances whereby increasing the roadway capacity might not lead to furtherance of congestion. All that this is pointing out is that we cannot assume that any added roadway will guarantee a reduction in traffic congestion. We need to be aware of and be contemplating the potential for latent demand, which might or might not happen, and might be small or might be large, depending on the specific situation. Trying to make sweeping generalizations that any added roadway capacity will always lead to more congestion is rather nonsensical and certainly misleading.

What does this have to do with AI self-driving cars?

At the Cybernetic Self-Driving Car Institute, we are running simulations about the future of traffic when there are AI self-driving cars on the roadways. This is important for many technological, social, economic, and political reasons to be given due and serious consideration.

Right now, there are self-driving car pundits that are saying we will have zero traffic congestion once we have AI self-driving cars. They paint a rather rosy picture of how wonderful the roads will be. No more bumper to bumper traffic. No more morning or afternoon rush hour clogs. It will be a beautiful sight of self-driving cars flowing at maximum speeds and it will be a breeze to get from one part of town to the other.

This painted picture is appealing to everyone. Politicians are motivated to support self-driving cars. Transportation planners love it. The public is excited to see this all happen. Let's not wait one minute more. Get those congestion freeing AI self-driving cars on the roads, and like so much Drano will relieve the existing horrors of traffic congestion.

But, hey, not so fast!

Remember the whole discussion herein about latent demand and how it impacts added roadway supply. Let's consider how that might apply.

Part of the reason that some are so excited about self-driving cars is because it will allow those that otherwise cannot readily drive a car to be able to driven around in a car. This might be elderly that aren't able to drive, this might be those that are disabled that aren't able to drive, and so on. You could even say that this includes children – there are many that believe we'll be putting our children into AI self-driving cars and sending them to school via that means, rather than having to go with them as an adult and drive them to school.

We could consider all of those existing non-drivers as latent demand. Once the AI self-driving car is readily available, there will presumably be a ton of latent demand that will come out of the woodwork.

Will our existing roadways be able to handle this?

Might all of these AI self-driving cars radically increase the number of cars on the roadways, and the number of miles driven, and the number of trips taken? It sure seems like it will. Essentially, we are "reducing" the "price" of driving in the sense that those that could not otherwise afford to be driven before (due to the cost of say hiring a chauffeur), will now be able to "afford" the cost to be driven around. This decrease in pricing will increase the demand, which will soak up the supply of roadways.

You might say that ridesharing has already started us down this same path. By having available Uber and Lyft and other ridesharing services, the cost to be driven around has been reduced, at least in terms of the access to ridesharing versus the prior taxi-led approach which had all sorts of frictional costs involved.

AI self-driving cars will presumably boost ridesharing exponentially.

Anyone that owns an AI self-driving car is possibly going to be using their self-driving car as their own personal ridesharing service for others to pay to use. You don't have to be an Uber or Lyft driver. You just somehow advertise that your AI self-driving car is available for ridesharing and voila you can make money off your AI self-driving car.

This is why Uber and Lyft are furiously trying to get into self-driving cars themselves, since they can see the handwriting on the wall that their existing business model of having human drivers is going to eventually go away and they could therefore be another example of a disrupted industry by a new technology (in this case, the AI self-driving car). Will such ridesharing services simply be the conduit to connect those that own AI self-driving cars that want to make available their self-driving car for ridesharing with those that need a lift? Couldn't a Facebook do this instead? That's what scares all of the existing ridesharing services.

Think also about other ways that AI self-driving cars might increase driving.

Some are saying that you could move out of the downtown city area and live in the suburbs, because with an AI self-driving car you can have it pick you up in the morning, you sleep on the way to work, and no need to worry about that morning commute. Our whole pattern of where we live and where we work could change. Distance between us and work, or us and the mall (if malls still exist!), and so on, won't really matter since we have an AI self-driving car that will take us wherever we want to go. You don't need to know how to drive. You don't need to stay awake and be able to drive for ten hours straight. You won't need to find a back-up driver so you can switch during long trips. It's all driving being done by the AI.

You might decide to ditch taking the bus. You might not ride your bike. You might instead decide to go in that cool AI self-driving car instead. The amount of latent demand is potentially enormous. The AI self-driving car might become the most traffic inducing, traffic generator of all time.

We should be careful in assuming that AI self-driving cars will get us to the vaunted zero congestion.

No matter how well the AI self-driving cars drive, and how well coordinated they are, volume is still volume.

There are some that criticize the induced demand theory as somewhat hogwash-like in that the critics claim that when roadways are expanded and become clogged it isn't the traveling that causes this, but instead there is an economic benefit that people must perceive and so the basis for their traveling. If people get into their cars and are driving on these expanded roadways, it is presumably because they see an economic benefit in doing so. Therefore, the increase in cars on the roadways is a good thing in that people are gaining more economic benefit. People are traveling for a purpose and we need to consider the larger picture of how economically there is a collective benefit involved. I won't take the space and time here to detail their argument, but want to at least make you aware of it and you can then postulate it and consider researching more about it, if you like. In short, if indeed AI self-driving cars produces congestion, it in a sense is a reflection that we'll have a lot more people gaining economic benefit by making those driving trips than otherwise if they didn't.

Let me give you a personal example of how this induced demand might impact someone's driving and miles traveled. When my children were in middle school, I used to drive them to school in the morning (this was a delight to do, and I miss it dearly!). Suppose we use the letter M to represent my son, and the letter L to represent my daughter. My son has a friend that we'll label G, and my daughter has a friend we'll label S. We had a custom of getting bagels and donuts in the morning, and I'll label the donut shop as D.

Here was a daily morning commute:

$$(M+L) + G + S + D$$

This meant that M and L got into our car, I drove us to pick-up my son's friend G, we then drove to pick-up my daughter's friend S, and then we stopped at the D to get some grub. We used my car to do so this, so we have 1 vehicle, or V1. The distance traveled was 3 miles in total.

Let's represent this as:

$$V1: (M+L) + G + S + D = 3 \text{ miles}$$

Now, somedays, my daughter was behind schedule (time was a key factor in these morning trips!), and it was prudent to go ahead and do this:

V1: M + G + L + S + D = 5 miles

This shows that M got into the car with me, we went and picked up his friend G, we came back to the home to get L, we then went to get S, and then to D. The total miles is now 5 miles, because of the trip to get G and come back to our house. It was worth the extra distance because we were trying to beat the clock.

Some mornings, I would get up really early, and do this:

V1: D + (M + L) + G + S = 7 miles

I would go get the D grub, then drive back home, and proceed with the rest of the sequence. The number of miles of the morning trip has now risen to 7 miles. It made sense because I then had the D in-hand and this saved us time once the rest of the sequence occurred.

Some mornings, we were running late, and we'd ask the parents of G and of S to drop-off their kids at our house:

V3: [G] + [S] + (M+L) + D = 10 miles

Notice now that we had three cars involved, including the cars of the parents for G and S. This now makes what otherwise would have been a 3 mile trip into a now 10 mile trip.

How does this relate to AI self-driving cars?

The odds are that this 10 mile trip would be the likely candidate once we have AI self-driving cars. We would either send our AI self-driving car to go get G and S and bring them to our house, or maybe the parents would send their kids to our house via their AI self-driving cars.

The point is that with AI self-driving cars it will be much easier to go ahead and have a driving trip undertaken. It seems very likely that the number of trips, the length of trips, and the number of miles traveled are going to go up, probably a lot.

What we don't yet know is what will be the cost of the AI self-driving cars? Right now, everyone seems to be assuming, either implicitly or explicitly, that the cost of the AI self-driving car is about the same as driving any conventional car. Suppose though that the cost of a self-driving car is a lot higher than conventional cars? This could increase the "price" of making use of self-driving cars and therefore not lead us down the path of the price decrease (which led us to the demand increase and the supply consumption). When you consider a conventional car, you acknowledge that having a human driver means there's an additional price or cost associated with the use of the car. Is it the case that the AI self-driving car "driver" will be less than that cost, the same as, or more than that cost?

We've been running various simulations, taking a look at mixtures of the price aspects, along with also considering the mix of human driven cars versus AI self-driving cars. I say this because it is unrealistic to assume that suddenly one day we will have instantaneously all self-driving cars on the road. We won't. We instead will have a mix of both human driven cars and AI driven cars.

Eventually, presumably, the number of AI driven cars will gradually overtake the number of human driven cars, and maybe someday it will only be AI driven cars (there's a lot of controversy on that point!). Anyway, all of us need to put some sober, serious thought toward the future of our car travel and consider how this will impact our habits, how we live, where we live, the roadways, and the rest. It's an issue, a large problem to be dealt with, and the platitudes of "zero congestion" need to be carefully scrutinized, and in fact maybe we should substitute instead the more thought provoking phrase of "induced demand."

APPENDIX

APPENDIX A

TEACHING WITH THIS MATERIAL

The material in this book can be readily used either as a supplemental to other content for a class, or it can also be used as a core set of textbook material for a specialized class. Classes where this material is most likely used include any classes at the college or university level that want to augment the class by offering thought provoking and educational essays about AI and self-driving cars.

In particular, here are some aspects for class use:

o   <u>Computer Science</u>. Studying AI, autonomous vehicles, etc.

o   <u>Business</u>. Exploring technology and it adoption for business.

o   <u>Sociology</u>. Sociological views on the adoption and advancement of technology.

Specialized classes at the undergraduate and graduate level can also make use of this material.

For each chapter, consider whether you think the chapter provides material relevant to your course topic. There is plenty of opportunity to get the students thinking about the topic and force them to decide whether they agree or disagree with the points offered and positions taken. I would also encourage you to have the students do additional research beyond the chapter material presented (I provide next some suggested assignments they can do).

RESEARCH ASSIGNMENTS ON THESE TOPICS

Your students can find background material on these topics, doing so in various business and technical publications. I list below the top ranked AI related journals. For business publications, I would suggest the usual culprits such as the Harvard Business Review, Forbes, Fortune, WSJ, and the like.

Here are some suggestions of homework or projects that you could assign to students:

a) <u>Assignment for foundational AI research topic</u>: Research and prepare a paper and a presentation on a specific aspect of Deep AI, Machine Learning, ANN, etc. The paper should cite at least 3 reputable sources. Compare and contrast to what has been stated in this book.

b) <u>Assignment for the Self-Driving Car topic</u>: Research and prepare a paper and Self-Driving Cars. Cite at least 3 reputable sources and analyze the characterizations. Compare and contrast to what has been stated in this book.

c) <u>Assignment for a Business topic</u>: Research and prepare a paper and a presentation on businesses and advanced technology. What is hot, and what is not? Cite at least 3 reputable sources. Compare and contrast to the depictions in this book.

d) <u>Assignment to do a Startup:</u> Have the students prepare a paper about how they might startup a business in this realm. They must submit a sound Business Plan for the startup. They could also be asked to present their Business Plan and so should also have a presentation deck to coincide with it.

You can certainly adjust the aforementioned assignments to fit to your particular needs and the class structure. You'll notice that I ask for 3 reputable cited sources for the paper writing based assignments. I usually steer students toward "reputable" publications, since otherwise they will cite some oddball source that has no credentials other than that they happened to write something and post it onto the Internet. You can define "reputable" in whatever way you prefer, for example some faculty think Wikipedia is not reputable while others believe it is reputable and allow students to cite it.

The reason that I usually ask for at least 3 citations is that if the student only does one or two citations they usually settle on whatever they happened to find the fastest. By requiring three citations, it usually seems to force them to look around, explore, and end-up probably finding five or more, and then whittling it down to 3 that they will actually use.

I have not specified the length of their papers, and leave that to you to tell the students what you prefer. For each of those assignments, you could end-up with a short one to two pager, or you could do a dissertation length paper. Base the length on whatever best fits for your class, and the credit amount of the assignment within the context of the other grading metrics you'll be using for the class.

I mention in the assignments that they are to do a paper and prepare a presentation. I usually try to get students to present their work. This is a good practice for what they will do in the business world. Most of the time, they will be required to prepare an analysis and present it. If you don't have the class time or inclination to have the students present, then you can of course cut out the aspect of them putting together a presentation.

If you want to point students toward highly ranked journals in AI, here's a list of the top journals as reported by *various citation counts sources* (this list changes year to year):
- o   Communications of the ACM
- o   Artificial Intelligence
- o   Cognitive Science
- o   IEEE Transactions on Pattern Analysis and Machine Intelligence
- o   Foundations and Trends in Machine Learning
- o   Journal of Memory and Language
- o   Cognitive Psychology
- o   Neural Networks
- o   IEEE Transactions on Neural Networks and Learning Systems
- o   IEEE Intelligent Systems
- o   Knowledge-based Systems

GUIDE TO USING THE CHAPTERS

For each of the chapters, I provide next some various ways to use the chapter material. You can assign the tasks as individual homework assignments, or the tasks can be used with team projects for the class. You can easily layout a series of assignments, such as indicating that the students are to do item "a" below for say Chapter 1, then "b" for the next chapter of the book, and so on.

a) What is the main point of the chapter and describe in your own words the significance of the topic,

b) Identify at least two aspects in the chapter that you agree with, and support your concurrence by providing at least one other outside researched item as support; make sure to explain your basis for disagreeing with the aspects,

c) Identify at least two aspects in the chapter that you disagree with, and support your disagreement by providing at least one other outside researched item as support; make sure to explain your basis for disagreeing with the aspects,

d) Find an aspect that was not covered in the chapter, doing so by conducting outside research, and then explain how that aspect ties into the chapter and what significance it brings to the topic,

e) Interview a specialist in industry about the topic of the chapter, collect from them their thoughts and opinions, and readdress the chapter by citing your source and how they compared and contrasted to the material,

f) Interview a relevant academic professor or researcher in a college or university about the topic of the chapter, collect from them their thoughts and opinions, and readdress the chapter by citing your source and how they compared and contrasted to the material,

g) Try to update a chapter by finding out the latest on the topic, and ascertain whether the issue or topic has now been solved or whether it is still being addressed, explain what you come up with.

Those are ways in which you can get the students of your class involved in considering the material of a given chapter. You could mix things up by having one of those above assignments per each week, covering the chapters over the course of the semester or quarter.

As a reminder, here are the chapters of the book and you can select whichever chapters you find most valued for your particular class:

<u>Chapter Title</u>

1 Self-Driving Car Moonshot: Mother of All AI Projects
2 Grand Convergence Leads to Self-Driving Cars
3 Why They Should Be Called Self-Driving Cars
4 Richter Scale for Self-Driving Car Levels
5 LIDAR for Self-Driving Cars
6 Overall Framework for Self-Driving Cars
7 Sensor Fusion is Key for Self-Driving Cars
8 Humans Not Fast Enough for Self-Driving Cars
9 Solving Edge Problems of Self-Driving Cars
10 Graceful Degradation for Faltering Self-Driving Cars
11 Genetic Algorithms for Self-Driving Cars
12 Blockchain for Self-Driving Cars
13 Machine Learning and Data for Self-Driving Cars
14 Cyber-Hacking of Self-Driving Cars
15 Sensor Failures in Self-Driving Cars
16 When Accidents Happen to Self-Driving Cars
17 Backdoor Security Holes in Self-Driving Cars
18 Future Brainjacking for Self-Driving Cars
19 Internationalizing Self-Driving Cars
20 Are Airline Autopilots Same as Self-Driving Cars
21 Marketing of Self-Driving Cars
22 Fake News about Self-Driving Cars
23 Product Liability for Self-Driving Cars
24 Zero Fatalities Zero Chance for Self-Driving Cars
25 Road Trip Trickery for Self-Driving Cars
26 Ethical Issues of Self-Driving Cars
27 Ranking of Self-Driving Cars
28 Induced Demand Driven by Self-Driving Cars

Companion Book By This Author

Advances in AI and Autonomous Vehicles: Cybernetic Self-Driving Cars

Practical Advances in Artificial Intelligence (AI) and Machine Learning
by
Dr. Lance B. Eliot, MBA, PhD

This title is available via Amazon and other book sellers

Companion Book By This Author

Self-Driving Cars:
The Mother of All AI Projects

by Dr. Lance B. Eliot, MBA, PhD

This title is available via Amazon and other book sellers

<u>Companion Book By This Author</u>

Innovation and Thought Leadership on Self-Driving Driverless Cars

by Dr. Lance B. Eliot, MBA, PhD

<u>Chapter Title</u>

This title is available via Amazon and other book sellers

Dr. Lance B. Eliot

Companion Book By This Author
New Advances in AI Autonomous Driverless Cars Self-Driving Cars
by Dr. Lance B. Eliot, MBA, PhD

Chapter Title

This title is available via Amazon and other book sellers

This title is available via Amazon and other book sellers

ADDENDUM

Introduction to Driverless Self-Driving Cars

Practical Advances in Artificial Intelligence (AI) and Machine Learning

By
Dr. Lance B. Eliot, MBA, PhD

———

For supplemental materials of this book, visit:
www.ai-selfdriving-cars.com

For special orders of this book, contact:
LBE Press Publishing
Email: LBE.Press.Publishing@gmail.com

ABOUT THE AUTHOR

Dr. Lance B. Eliot, MBA, PhD is the CEO of Techbruim, Inc. and Executive Director of the Cybernetic Self-Driving Car Institute, and has over twenty years of industry experience including serving as a corporate officer in a billion dollar firm and was a Partner in a major executive services firm. He is also a serial entrepreneur having founded, ran, and sold several high-tech related businesses. He previously hosted the popular radio show *Technotrends* that was also available on American Airlines flights via their in-flight audio program. Author or co-author of a dozen books and over 300 articles, he has made appearances on CNN, and has been a frequent speaker at industry conferences.

A former professor at the University of Southern California (USC), he founded and led an innovative research lab on Artificial Intelligence in Business. Known as the "AI Insider" his writings on AI advances and trends has been widely read and cited. He also previously served on the faculty of the University of California Los Angeles (UCLA), and was a visiting professor at other major universities. He was elected to the International Board of the Society for Information Management (SIM), a prestigious association of over 3,000 high-tech executives worldwide.

He has performed extensive community service, including serving as Senior Science Adviser to the Vice Chair of the Congressional Committee on Science & Technology. He has served on the Board of the OC Science & Engineering Fair (OCSEF), where he is also has been a Grand Sweepstakes judge, and likewise served as a judge for the Intel International SEF (ISEF). He served as the Vice Chair of the Association for Computing Machinery (ACM) Chapter, a prestigious association of computer scientists. Dr. Eliot has been a shark tank judge for the USC Mark Stevens Center for Innovation on start-up pitch competitions, and served as a mentor for several incubators and accelerators in Silicon Valley and Silicon Beach. He served on several Boards and Committees at USC, including having served on the Marshall Alumni Association (MAA) Board in Southern California.

Dr. Eliot holds a PhD from USC, MBA, and Bachelor's in Computer Science, and earned the CDP, CCP, CSP, CDE, and CISA certifications. Born and raised in Southern California, and having traveled and lived internationally, he enjoys scuba diving, surfing, and sailing.

www.ingramcontent.com/pod-product-compliance
Lightning Source LLC
Chambersburg PA
CBHW051223050326
40689CB00007B/775